Landscape Design and Planning at

The SWA Group

*SWA*グループ: ランドスケープとプランニング

CONTENTS

PROCESS : Architecture

Front Cover : Arizona Center
Back Cover, from top to bottom :
Broward County Convention Center
Nasu Highlands Park
Curtis Center

表紙：アリゾナセンター
裏表紙（上から）：
ブロワードカウンティ・コンベンションセンター
那須ハイランドパーク
カーチスセンター

No.103

Publisher：
Murotani Bunji

Editor-in-Charge：
Kalvin Platt

Co-editors：
Theresa Clark, Hiroyasu Tanaka

Editorial Staff：
Miwako Ito, Yumiko Fujimaki

Editorial Assistants：
Akiko Okada, Naomi Susa,
Kazuto Mizuse, Tomoko Amemiya
Akihiko Nagasawa, Chie Ishikawa,
Kyoko Shibazaki

Translator：
Rei Kuroki

Cover Design：
Takahisa Kamijyo (Kamijyo Studio)

Published by
Process Architecture Co., Ltd., Tokyo Japan

Printed by
Isozaki Printing Co., Ltd., Tokyo Japan

Executive and Editorial Office
1-47-2-418 Sasazuka Shibuya-ku Tokyo Japan
Phone(03)3468-0131, 0132 Fax(03)3468-0133

ISBN 4-89331-103-4

奥付
第103号
発行日：1992年5月1日
発行人：室谷文治
責任編集者：カルビン・プラット
編集協力：テリーサ・クラーク，田中弘靖
編集部：伊藤美和子，藤巻由美子
編集アシスタント：
岡田明子，諏佐直美，水瀬和人，雨宮智子，
永沢明彦，石川智恵，芝崎恭子
翻訳：黒木 玲
表紙デザイン：上條喬久(上條スタジオ)
制作・写植：㈱協和クリエイト，㈲ユニット，大西写植
印刷：磯崎印刷㈱
発行所：株式会社 プロセスアーキテクチュア
〒151 東京都渋谷区笹塚1-47-2-418
電話 03-3468-0131 FAX 03-3468-0133
振替 東京6-57446
取次店：トーハン，日販，大阪屋，栗田出版販売，誠光堂
禁無断転載

Editors' Note

For the design professions, *Process* magazine is an excellent tool of communication. It is difficult to find a serial source of this type featuring the landscape architectural profession anywhere in the world. The publisher Mr. Murotani Bunji has provided a great service to our profession through the magazine, and the SWA Group is extremely pleased to be featured in this issue.

For some readers, who are familiar with the SWA Group, this issue may be a concentrated historical resource. To others this may be an introduction to a new collection of work. And for all readers, we hope this issue may reveal insights about the firm's projects, ideas and thoughts about planning and landscape architecture through text and imagery.

We find the role of our professional participation extending beyond the current definition of landscape architecture with our work in the United States and as our practice extends to all parts of the world. The ideas and works presented within this issue mark this evolution.

It was through our growing involvement with work in Japan that we were able to meet and talk with Mr. Murotani Bunji about this issue. Mr. Hiroyasu Tanaka, a planner and landscape architect with the Taisei corporation in Tokyo helped us in 1991 to contact *Process*. At that time he was in our California offices as part of a program of mutual education in international design practice.

Since that eventful meeting with *Process*, many people within the SWA Group have helped to make this issue possible. First, I would like to thank those who contributed to its text. The articles for each of the projects are written by those who participated in the design. The articles may be considered a personal account of the project's design philosophy and of the physical result. It was my hope that the personalities responsible for the thought behind these selected projects would surface.

I would also like to express my thanks to our in-house photographers (who personally provided and selected the photographic imagery), to those who researched data related to the projects and the firm, and to those who conceptualized the graphic presentation.

A special thanks goes out to Mr. Allan Temko who provided an objective view of the firm's contribution to the profession, to Ms. Melanie Simo for her account of our history, to Mr. Hiroyasu Tanaka for his diligent efforts to assist with the translation of the English text into Japanese and to our patient and enthusiastic editor at *Process*, Ms. Yumiko Fujimaki.

Final thanks to Theresa Clark, our managing editor. Through her efforts, direction and coordination with Ms. Fujimaki at *Process*, the entire preparation of the articles and graphics became a reality.

An exchange of ideas is important to the continued growth of the profession. This exchange can challenge current design views and can encourage landscape architects to take part in the immense opportunities that are available in this ever shrinking world. I hope this selection of works and ideas by the SWA Group meets this challenge.
Kalvin Platt

Kalvin Platt, FAIA
Graduated from University of Florida (BA, 1953)
Graduated from Harvard Graduate School of Design (MCP, 1959)
Director of Land Development Studio, Harvard University Graduate School of Design
Chairman of The SWA Group
Affiliate member ASLA, Fellow AIA, Associate member, APA

Theresa A. Clark
Graduated from The Ohio State University (BSLA degree 1980)
Graduated from Harvard Graduate School of Design (MLA, 1986)
Associate Landscape Architect, Designer with The SWA Group (1986-present)

編集言

デザインの分野においては，そのプロセスを発表する雑誌は，コミュニケーションの優れた手段となる．定期出版物で，ランドスケープアーキテクチュアをこのように正面からとらえて紹介するメディアは，世界中どこを探してもなかなか見つけられない．『プロセスアーキテクチュア』誌の発行人である室谷文治氏は，ランドスケープアーキテクチュアという職業に対して，雑誌を通して大いに貢献してくれている．SWAグループはこの特集号にたいへん感謝している．

SWAと親しい読者にとっては，この特集は凝縮された歴史的資産のように見えるだろう．その他の人たちにとっては，新しい仕事を集めて紹介している特集と映るかもしれない．私たちはすべての読者にとって，この特集号が文章や図面，写真を通して，プランニングやランドスケープアーキテクチュアに関するSWAのプロジェクト，アイデア，考えについての洞察を明らかにするものであることを期待している．

私たちは，アメリカにおける作品を通して得たランドスケープアーキテクチュアの現代的な定義をはるかに超える広い範囲で，その職業の役割と責任を見出し，さらに世界中に活動の足跡を広げていこうとしている．ここに掲載したアイデアや作品は，この発展の軌跡を示している．

日本での仕事が増える中で，室谷氏に会う機会も得

られ，今回の特集につながったのである．大成建設のプランナーでありランドスケープアーキテクトである田中弘靖氏が1991年に『プロセスアーキテクチュア』誌とコンタクトをとる手助けをしてくれた．彼は当時，国際的なデザイン活動のための相互教育プログラムに参加するため，カリフォルニアの私たちのオフィスに滞在していたのである．

『プロセスアーキテクチュア』誌との意義ある会合の後，多くのSWAのメンバーがこの特集号を準備するために働いた．まず第一に，私はさまざまな原稿を書いてくれた人たちに感謝しなければならない．それぞれのプロジェクトの原稿は，実際に設計に携わった人たちが書いている．原稿は，プロジェクトのデザイン・フィロソフィやその結果への個人的な評価であるとも考えられる．パーソナリティが，選び出されたプロジェクトの後ろに存在する考えを引き出してくれることを期待する．

また，写真を通じて，そのイメージをビジュアルに整えてくれた事務所のカメラマンたちに大いに感謝したい．そしてプロジェクトや事務所に関するデータを調べてくれた人たち，グラフィック・プレゼンテーションをまとめてくれた人たちにも感謝を述べたい．

私たちの事務所のこの分野への貢献を客観的な視点で発言してくれたアラン・テムコ氏，そして事務所の沿革をまとめてくれたメラニー・サイモ女史に特に謝意を

表したい．また『プロセスアーキテクチュア』誌の忍耐強く，熱心な編集担当の藤巻由美子さんに感謝したい．

最後に日本語の最終確認をしてくれた田中弘靖氏に，そして特に事務所内で私の片腕として編集を担当してくれたテリーサ・クラークに感謝する．彼らは『プロセスアーキテクチュア』誌と綿密なコンタクトをとり続け，本誌の制作に大いに尽力してくれた．

アイデアの交流は職業の成長発展に欠かせない．こうした交流は，現行のデザイン的視野への挑戦を可能とし，ランドスケープアーキテクトが国際化社会における無限の仕事の機会に参加することを促進する．この号のSWAの作品やアイデアの選択が，以上のような挑戦にふさわしいものであることを期待している．
カルビン・プラット

カルビン・プラット 1953年フロリダ大学建築学科卒．1959年ハーバード大学大学院都市計画学修士．現在ハーバード大学大学院デザインスクール・ランドディベロップメント科長．米国ランドスケープ・アーキテクト協会，米国建築学会，米国プランニング協会会員．SWAグループ会長．

テリーサ・A. クラーク 1980年オハイオ州立大学首席卒業，1986年ハーバード大学院修士修了．SWAグループのアソシエイト・ランドスケープアーキテクトとして現在に至る．

ARTICLES

論文

Introduction

The SWA Group is founded upon the idea that design can shape the environment. The firm is structured to facilitate the role of landscape design and land planning in building places that have meaning as well as function, and in using land with sensitivity to environmental and social purposes.

The projects selected for this publication span three decades and speak to the idea of landscape design and planning in several voices. The group works together toward a common idea but with highly individual points of view. In each project, the key design and planning voices are represented in photography, drawing and text.

Unique to The SWA Group is the strong, continuous connection between planning and design in the landscape. This publication presents first the larger, more comprehensive planning works, then more specific design projects. Our practice is dedicated to dealing with larger social, economic and environmental issues with equal sensitivity to the final outcome as we apply to our project-level work. Our planning (deciding what should occur on the land) and our design (deciding what shape and character that should be) constitute a seamless process.

Our work is to create place and community with inspiration. Some of our most successful works do not seem consciously "designed." However, we are not completely satisfied until our work evokes feelings that transcend the creation of place and community — even though these are significant achievements in themselves. We constantly search for a special place, a unique community, one that reflects the hand of the designer and stimulates a fresh response.

Our practice is a constant search for a better approach, or more interesting and informed response, to the wide array of urban and regional challenges brought to us by our clients who may be developers, corporations, cities or universities. Our collaborative approach extends to our clients with whom we work and to architect colleagues with whom we explore new prototypes and new attitudes toward the man-made world. We appreciate working with people who share our goals and who have equally strong points of view. Our stake lies not only with the intricacy or complexity of designing and building a place, but also in discovering the intrinsic qualities of that place. Everything aims toward that accomplishment.

序文

SWA*は,「デザインが環境を形づくることが可能である」という考えの下に設立された.SWAの業務は,機能的かつ意味のある場をつくり,環境的,社会的な目的にも充分配慮した土地利用を行なうためのランドスケープデザイン及びプランニングの役割を促進していくことである.

本誌のために選んだ作品は,過去30年間にわたるもので,ランドスケープデザインやプランニングのアイデアについてさまざまな角度からとりあげた.SWAグループの作品は,共通のアイデアであると同時に,個人個人の思想も反映したものである.どのプロジェクトにおいても,デザインやプランニングの要点は,ここに紹介する写真,図面,文章が物語っている.

SWAのユニークな特徴は,ランドスケープのプランニングとデザインの間の強い連続性である.ここでは,最初に大規模な,より包括的なプランニングの作品を紹介し,次に,より詳細なデザインの作品を紹介する.私たちの仕事は,より大きな社会的,経済的,環境的な問題を扱うと同時に,実際のプロジェクトのレベルで,最終的に形あるものをつくることまでを含む.その土地がどうなるのかを決めるプランニング,どのような形や性格になるべきかを決めるデザインは,継ぎ目のない連続したプロセスを構成している.

作品は,場やコミュニティをインスピレーションによってつくり出したものである.最も成功した作品の幾つかは,意識的にデザインされたようには見えない.私たちは,作品自体がすでに立派な意味のある業績であったとしても,それらの作品が何年もかかって場やコミュニティの創造を越えたと感じられるまでは,完全に満足できない.私たちは常に,特別な場,ユニークなコミュニティ,デザイナーの腕前を反映するもの,新鮮な反応を呼び起こすものを追求し続けている.

SWAの活動は,ディベロッパー,企業,市,大学といったクライアントによってもちこまれる都市的,あるいは地域的な課題に対するよりよい方法や,一層興味深い見識に富んだ対応を恒常的に探究していくことである.私たちは共に働くクライアントや,人間がつくり出す世界に対する新しいプロトタイプや新しい態度を共に探究する建築家たちと共同して仕事に当たっている.目標を共有でき,同じものの考え方をもつ人々と一緒に仕事をすることに感謝している.私たちの関心は,デザインや,場づくりの複雑さだけにあるのではなく,場に本来的に備わっている本質を見出すことにもある.すべてがその目標の達成に向かって進められていくのである.

＊The SWAグループはサウサリートをはじめ,全米にオフィス(ラグナビーチ,ヒューストン,ダラス,ディアフィールドビーチ)をもつ,その総称です.本誌では以下,特に組織としての意味を強調する場合以外には「SWA」と省略させていただきます.(編集部)

The SWA Group: A Retrospective

by Melanie L. Simo

SWAの沿革 メラニー・L. サイモ

The parent firm of The SWA Group was Sasaki, Walker and Associates, established in 1957, in Watertown, Massachusetts, by Hideo Sasaki (who was soon to become chairman of Harvard's department of landscape architecture) and Peter Walker (who would later chair that department). Like some of the most prominent architectural firms of the day, including Skidmore Owings and Merrill (SOM), The Architects' Collaborative (TAC), and Hellmuth, Obata and Kassabaum (HOK), Sasaki, Walker and Associates evolved into a corporate and multi-disciplinary firm; thus it became structured to assume (and largely control) complex projects of planning and design — campus planning, new communities, office parks, corporate headquarters, and so on.

The late 1950s was an opportune time for landscape architects to begin such a practice. The expanding post-war economy involved large-scale land development, increasing productivity, a rising new professional class, and the growing power of corporate enterprises. But other influences — less worldly, more spiritual and altruistic — lay at the foundations of SWA's parent firm and thus formed part of SWA's philosophy.

While teaching at Harvard, Sasaki became a colleague of Walter Gropius, then chairman of Harvard's department of architecture. As the founder of the Bauhaus in Weimar, Germany, in 1919, Gropius had brought together many of the visual and spatial arts — painting, sculpture, textiles, graphic design and architecture — but not landscape architecture. (At that time in Europe, architects or engineers handled planning and site design, while gardeners or horticulturists carried out planting design.) Arriving in America just before World War II, Gropius came with deep commitments to collaboration between artists and designers, the free flow of ideas, teamwork and anonymity, and the

social purposes of building. He also saw the architect as master-builder, superior to other artists — an assumption that made collaborative studios with Gropius a constant challenge for Sasaki. Nevertheless, Sasaki respected the Bauhaus ideals of collaboration, anonymity and social purpose, while developing among his own students and colleagues the rational thought and intellectual inquiry needed to collaborate as equals, even to lead.

Another influence on the work of Sasaki's firm and The SWA Group was Stanley White, the provocative educator in landscape architecture at the University of Illinois, who had worked for the Olmsted Brothers and inspired such students as Sasaki, Walker, Charles Harris, Stuart Dawson and Richard Haag, before teaching intermittently at Harvard in the 1960s. Two of White's notions have since become part of SWA's philosophy. First, White saw a continuum between the intuitive and the rational. "First the idea, then the proof," he would say. The proof had to be logical, methodical. "But what is the idea? Something between magic and philosophy," White began to explain. And to this day, one of the first questions asked among SWA designers and planners is, "What's the big idea?"

Second, White insisted on the objective, critical stance of the landscape architect. While this little-known, hybrid profession lacked a contemporary body of criticism, White asserted that landscape architecture is criticism, for the field had emerged in late nineteenth-century America as a protest against what engineers, architects, horticulturists and others were doing to the American landscape. To practice landscape architecture was, thus, to improve, to restore, to enrich — and to transcend the status quo.

Imbued with these beliefs, and exposed to collaborative practice

SWAの前身は，1957年にマサチューセッツ州ウォータータウンに設立されたササキ，ウォーカー・アンド・アソシエイツである．設立直後にハーバード大学ランドスケープ・アーキテクチュアの学部長に就任したヒデオ・ササキと，その後，やはり学部長に就任することになるピーター・ウォーカーの2人によって設立された．SOMやTACやHOKといった，その当時の優れた建築事務所同様，ササキ，ウォーカー事務所も組織化し，多様な人材を集めて発展していった．そして，キャンパスプラン，コミュニティ計画，オフィスパーク，企業の本社施設などの，計画や設計を含む，さまざまなプロジェクトを遂行できる組織として成長した．

1950年代後半は，ランドスケープアーキテクトにとっては，さまざまな仕事をして発展するチャンスであった．回復した戦後の景気が，大規模な開発，生産性の向上，新しいプロフェッショナル階級の出現，企業の成長発展を促した．しかし，益利的でない，より精神的かつ利他的な影響が，SWAの元の組織の基盤をつくり，今日のSWAのフィロソフィを形成した．

ハーバードで教鞭をとる傍ら，ヒデオ・ササキはハーバードの建築学部長であったワルター・グロピウスと組んで活動した．1919年，ドイツのワイマールでバウハウスを創立したグロピウスは，絵画，彫刻，テキスタイル，グラフィックデザイン，建築と，多くのビジュアルな空間芸術の分野を一体化したが，ランドスケープだけは別であった（当時のヨーロッパでは，建築家や技術者が土地利用計画や敷地造成計画を担当し，庭師や園芸家が植栽計画を実施した）．第2次世界大戦の直前にアメリカに着いたグロピウスは，アーチストとデザイナーの協働，アイデアの自由な交流，チームワークと匿名性，建物の社会的な存在目的などの必要を強く求めていた．そして建築家を，さまざまなプロの人たちの一段上に立つマスタービルダーと見ていた．したがってグロピウスと協同のスタジオ活動をすることは，ササキにとってはひとつの挑戦であった．にもかかわらず，ササキはバウハウスの協働，匿名性，社会的目的という思想を尊重していた．その一方で彼は，学生や彼自身の仲間には，協働と同時に，合理的で知的な探究も必要であり，ときには，それら

が協働に優先することもあると教えていた．

SWAにとって影響の大きかったもう1人の人物はスタンレー・ホワイトである．ホワイトはイリノイ大学のランドスケープアーキテクチュアの個性的な教師で，オルムステッド兄弟と一緒に仕事をし，ササキやウォーカー，チャールズ・ハリス，スチュアート・ドーソン，リチャード・ハーグといった学生たちに多大の影響を与えた．ホワイトは1960年代になると，ときどきハーバードで教鞭をとった．ホワイトの2つの思想がSWAの重要なフィロソフィになっている．1つは，直観と理論の連続である．「最初にアイデア，そして実証」とホワイトはいっていた．実証は論理的で方法論的である．「しかし，アイデアとはなにか，マジックとフィロソフィの間にあるものだ」とホワイトは説明する．今日，SWAでデザイナーやプランナーの間でまず取り交わされる最初の質問が「ビッグアイデアとはなにか」である．

2つ目は，ホワイトはランドスケープアーキテクトの客観的，批評的な姿勢を強調した．あまり知られていない混成の職業であるため，同時代に批評する母体が欠けていたにもかかわらず，19世紀後半のアメリカにおいて技術者，建築家，園芸家，その他の人々がアメリカのランドスケープに対して行なったことへの抗議として，現われてきた分野であることから，ホワイトは「ランドスケープアーキテクチュアは批判である」と断言した．ランドスケープアーキテクチュアは，改善し，もとに戻し，価値を高め，そして現状を越えるものであると……．

こうした信念を吹き込まれ，ササキが信じる協同の作業という方針の下で活動を続けたカリフォルニア生まれのピーター・ウォーカーは，1959年に西海岸に戻った．そこで，サンフランシスコのノースビーチのはずれにササキ，ウォーカー・アンド・アソシエイツのサンフランシスコ事務所を開設し，建築家のアーネスト・J.カンプやマステン・アンド・ハードと協働して，ロス・アルトスのフットヒルカレッジのマスタープラン作成や敷地計画，ランドスケープデザインを主に遂行した．続く15年間に，ウォーカーと彼の仲間は，協同体制で活動を続け，エネルギッシュでハイペースな雰囲気の中で成長発展し

under Sasaki's subtle direction, the California-born Walker returned to the West Coast in 1959. There, on the fringe of San Francisco's North Beach, he set up a regional office of Sasaki, Walker and Associates initially to complete the master planning and site and landscape design of Foothill College in Los Altos, in collaboration with architects Ernest J. Kump, and Masten and Hurd. For the next 15 years, Walker and his associates of longer or shorter duration — Anthony Guzzardo, Richard Law, Edmond Kagi, Thomas Adams, Gary Karner, George Omi, Gene Rosenberg, Willie Lang, Bill Callaway, Kalvin Platt, Gerald Campbell, Wendy Simon, Loreen Hjort, Raymond Belknap, Michael Gilbert, James Reeves, Danny Powell, Roy Imamura, Michael Sardina, Kevin Shanley, John Wong, Walter Bemis and others — built a collaborative practice that thrived in an atmosphere of high energy and fast pace. In time, this regional practice became distanced from its parent firm as it responded to the unique conditions of the still-developing West Coast.

Among SWA's earliest collaborations were housing projects with Bay Area architects such as Don Knorr, Claude Oakland, Anshen and Allen, and Wurster, Bernardi and Emmons — architects known for their sensitivity to local climate, conditions, and materials, and their independence from the canons of European or International Style modernism. They used pitched roofs and redwood where appropriate; and they also viewed the "object in space" as less critical than a building integrated within a fine, livable landscape.

SWA's repeat clients of the 1960s included not only architects McCue, Boone, Tomsick (MBT) and SOM, but also builders and developers who had previously hired engineers to lay out small residential subdivisions. SWA would revise the engineer's site plan, fitting in the same number of lots (or more) as well as a community park or green space. And, as a rapport developed, SWA brought these clients along, toward larger, more satisfying planned-unit developments (PUDs).

For a while, most of the external conditions in California and the West were favorable for SWA's blend of idealistic and entrepreneurial practice. With a rapidly growing population, relatively low interest rates and mortgage financing, vast tracts of undeveloped land near the few urban centers, and few legal restrictions (until the long-overdue environmental legislation of the 1970s), developers could move quickly and take risks. In any event, before market analyses were generally available, and before vast fortunes were to be made or lost for a consortium of clients, a new idea entailed less financial risk. Thus, on handsome sites, both natural and artfully created, SWA's clients agreed to cluster the houses and rental units and to pay for such amenities as community centers, tree-lined streets, parks and open space preserves.

As the rate of California's population growth began to taper off in the early 1970s, and as more housing stock accumulated, prospective home buyers would shop around, looking for the best combination of price, location and amenities — thus confirming the economic value of a finely built landscape. Moreover, newcomers to the state included those who searched not only for a home in a good neighborhood, but also for a new lifestyle, one perhaps less dependent on the automobile, and more oriented toward active sports, family recreation or the community. Considering the needs of these people, and building on the pioneering work of community planners Clarence Stein and Henry Wright, SWA continued to explore and push the client forward.

Platt recalls the excitement of working on new project types in the late 1960s — new communities, regional parks, urban renewal sites, office parks, ski areas, and mixed-use projects, largely in the West, the

ていった. この頃の仲間は, 期間が長い人も短い人もいるが, 次のようなメンバーであった. アンソニー・ガザード, リチャード・ロウ, エドモンド・ケギ, トーマス・アダムス, ゲーリー・カーナー, ジョージ・オミ, ジーン・ローゼンバーグ, ウィリー・ラング, ウィリアム・キャラウェイ, カルビン・プラット, ジェラルド・キャンベル, ウェンディ・サイモン, ロリーン・ヒュアート, レイモンド・ベルナップ, マイケル・ギルバート, ジェームズ・リーブス, ダニー・パウエル, ロイ・イマムラ, マイケル・サーディナ, ケビン・シャンレー, ジョン・ウォン, ウォルター・ビーメス, その他. 時が経つにつれて, 西海岸がまだ発展期にあるというユニークな状況を反映して, この事務所の活動は, 東海岸の親組織のそれとは方向が少しずつ異なっていった.

ＳＷＡの初期の仕事の分野は, 主としてベイエリアで活躍するドン・ノアー, クロード・オークランド, アンシェン・アンド・アレン, ウースター, バーナーディ・アンド・エモンズなどの, この地方独特の気候や条件, 材質に忠実に設計することでよく知られ, ヨーロッパやインターナショナルスタイルの近代主義とは違った独自の作風をもった建築家たちとの協働による, ハウジングプロジェクトが中心であった. 彼らはその地方にふさわしい勾配屋根とレッドウッドの建物を建てたし, また, 空間の中のオブジェ, すなわち建物それ自身を目立たせるのでなく, すばらしい, 生き生きとしたランドスケープの中に融合させるという考え方を持っていた.

1960年代の主なクライアントは, 建築家のマッキュー, ブーン, トムシック(ＭＢＴ)やＳＯＭだけでなく, それまでは小さな住宅地の敷地計画を技術者を雇って解決していた工事業者やディベロッパーなどが含まれる. ＳＷＡは技術者の作成した敷地計画を見直し, 区画割りを同じ数だけつくりながら, コミュニティの公園や緑のスペースをつくり出した. そして, お互いの信頼関係が築かれるにつれ, ＳＷＡは彼らクライアントをより大規模な, さらに満足のいく計画単位開発(ＰＵＤＳ)へと導いていった.

しばらくの間, カリフォルニアや西部における外的な状況の多くが, ＳＷＡのアイデアにあふれた, かつ事業的な活動に対して好意的に働いていた.

人口の急激な増加, 比較的低金利の融資, 既存のアーバンセンター近くにある未開発の広い地域, わずかな法的規制(1970年代の度を越した環境法ができるまで)などによって, ディベロッパーは計画を素早く実施でき, リスクを背負うこともできたのである. いずれにしても, マーケット調査が一般的に行なわれる以前, また, クライアントが多くの利益を得たり, あるいは損失を被ったりする以前は, 財政的にリスクの少ない開発を目的とした新しいデザイン・アイデアを生み出さなければならなかった. このように, 敷地の条件がいいところでは, 自然で, 精巧な環境がつくられた. ＳＷＡのクライアントは, 戸建住宅や賃貸ユニットをクラスター状に配置し, コミュニティセンターや並木のある通り, 公園やオープンスペースといったアメニティにも充分に注意を払うという計画に同意してくれた.

1970年代に入って, カリフォルニアの人口増加が先細りとなり, ハウジングストックもたまり出したため, 住宅購入予定者はいろいろと物色し始め, 価格, 敷地やアメニティの条件などが最高のものを探し始めた. つまり, すばらしいランドスケープの環境がもつ経済的な価値に気がついたのである. さらに, すぐれた近隣の中の住まいだけでなく, 新しいライフスタイルを求めて新たにアメリカの住民になった人たちは, それまでほど自動車に頼らず, もっと活動的なスポーツやファミリー・レクリエーション, コミュニティといったことを指向していた. こうした人たちのニーズを考慮し, コミュニティプランナーのパイオニア的な存在であったクラレンス・スタインやヘンリー・ライトと一緒になって, ＳＷＡはさまざまな探究を続け, クライアントをさらに新たな挑戦へと導いた.

カルビン・プラットは1960年代後半の新しいプロジェクトのタイプに取り組んだときの興奮をいまも忘れない. それは, 主として西部, 中西部, そしてフロリダにおける, 新たなコミュニティ計画, 地域公園, 都市再開発, オフィスパーク, スキーリゾート, ミクストユース計画などである. 1967年から1968年にかけて, ＳＷＡの事務所のスタッフは15名から35名へと急増した. この急激な成長にもかかわらず, 事務所ではニューヨーク, フロリダ, アイ

Midwest and Florida. Between 1967 and 1968, the office had grown from about 15 to 35 people (all the professionals were male, recalls Wendy Simon, then the book-keeper). But despite rapid growth, the office maintained a spirit of camaraderie among the designers and planners who had grown up in many parts of the country — New York, Florida, Iowa, Montana, California and elsewhere. Many had also worked for Sasaki and/or studied at Harvard, including Kagi, Karner, Law, Platt, Adams, Callaway, and Lang.

Military service and combat in World War II or the Korean War had given some of these men a common experience, maturing and sobering. The highly controversial Vietnam War was accelerating; and the mood of Northern California was a heady blend of defiant, mellow, exuberant and idealistic spirits. San Francisco was then a mecca for America's counterculture — a blend of affinities for conservation and wilderness, community and anti-materialism, and much more. At that time, too, SWA's stance was expressed in the phrase, "We designers against the world," reflecting their desire to push beyond convention toward more socially responsible and visually satisfying solutions.

There was a brief slowdown in the economy in 1969-70, but no external circumstances hindered Walker, the leading designer, from delegating more responsibilities to the principals and conceiving of an expanded firm. SWA would soon add environmental sciences to its disciplines. And in 1972, an in-house summer school would be formed, for a number of reasons, but mainly to supplement the design training of students whose schools were then emphasizing environmentalism and computer literacy. SWA would offer jobs to the most promising students (including Wong, James Lee and Donald Murakami); and those who taught would gain by having to articulate ideas and goals.

Today, sifting through a quarter century of SWA's goals yields some perennial concerns; growth is one. Accustomed to the quality of work and working conditions induced by the congenial, single-office firm, the senior principals have accommodated growth with some caution. In 1968, Platt noted, "The question is not whether we grow, but how to direct growth ... not a production 'machine' vs. a studio, but how to get the machine under control and subordinate it to the people involved ... not whether we are a corporate body or a family, but how does the corporate 'extended family' communicate within itself."

Growth appears inevitable for any reasonably successful firm in an expanding economy. Bright, ambitious young people, once hired, must have a place to go — upward. But SWA was also growing laterally, with the new divisions and new disciplines, partly in response to the surging environmental movement. By the early 1970s, based in larger quarters in Sausalito, California, SWA was engaged in large-scale regional planning, environmental impact reports and a communications effort to prevent development of the Mendocino coast, while the firm was also working with architects, developers, and corporations to develop land elsewhere. Political controversies arose, both in-house and externally, as the landscape architectural profession itself became torn between goals for conservation and development. But it took a severe economic recession to test all corporate, multi-disciplinary enterprises.

By January 1972, economists were predicting a "nosedive" for the California home-building industry — an industry that provided many of SWA's jobs. Nevertheless, with its diversity of project types and its work for the Irvine Company in Southern California, and Arvida in Florida, SWA was still growing. In 1973, SWA merged with the environmental consulting firm of James A. Roberts & Associates

オワ，モンタナ，カリフォルニアといったさまざまな出身地のデザイナーとプランナーが集まっての協働という精神が変わらず維持されていた．スタッフの多くは，ササキと仕事をしたことがあるか，あるいはハーバードの出身であった．ケーギ，カーナー，ロウ，プラット，アダムズ，キャラウェイ，ラングがそうである．

第2次世界大戦や朝鮮戦争の兵役や軍役が，彼らの何人かに共通の経験，成熟，沈着を付与していた．議論沸騰のベトナム戦争はエスカレートし，北カリフォルニアのムードは，挑戦的で，陽気で，元気いっぱいの，理想主義の精神がしっかりと入り交じったものであった．サンフランシスコは当時のアメリカの反文化の中心であった．環境保全と野性，コミュニティと反物質主義などが調和してミックスしていた．この当時のSWAの姿勢は「私たちデザイナーは古い因習をうちやぶる」という言葉に端的に表れている．これは因習を超えて，もっと社会に呼応できる，視覚的に満足のできる解決に向けて突き進みたいという希望を反映した言葉である．

1969年から1970年にかけて，景気は一段と減速したが，当時のSWAのトップデザイナーであったピーター・ウォーカーは，責任を他のプリンシパルに委譲しながら，事務所の拡大を図っていった．そしてすぐに環境科学の分野も専門領域として加えていった．また1972年に，いくつかの理由で，事務所内でサマースクールが開催された．主たる目的は，当時の教育が環境主義とコンピューターに重点を置いていたために，学生たちにデザイン的な訓練をすることであった．SWAは，ここで優秀な学生（ジョン・ウォン，ジェイムズ・リー，ドナルド・ムラカミなど）に実際に仕事をさせた．教える側はアイデアや目標を表現することで何かを得た．

SWAは設立後の25年が経った結果，組織は成長するという，永遠の問題を抱えた．快適な1か所の単一のオフィスが誘発する居心地のよい仕事や職場に慣れてしまうことに対して，シニア・プリンシパルたちは，成長に伴う警告を発していた．カルビン・プラットは，1968年に次のように語っていた．「問題はいかに成長するかでなく，成長をいかに管理するかである．製造機械対

スタジオでなく，機械をいかに人間がコントロールし，使いこなすかである．そして企業組織か，より家族的なまとまりかではなく，いかにして組織化し，拡大した家族内のコミュニケイトを図っていくかということである．」経済の成長に伴い少なからず成功した組織にとって，成長拡大は必然であった．組織の一員となった有望な，勇気のある若者たちは，さらなる向上を目指すべきである．SWAもまた，その当時の環境問題の顕在化に呼応して，新たな事務所や新しい理念の下に成長していった．1970年代の初めまでに，SWAはノースビーチの狭い事務所から，サウサリートの大きなオフィスに引っ越した．そして，建築家やディベロッパーや企業と協力して，いくつもの開発計画に参加する一方，メンドシーノ海岸の開発を阻止するために，大規模な地域計画や環境影響調査，話し合いを誘導する活動などに従事していた．政治的な論争が国内外で活発化し，ランドスケープアーキテクトも保存か開発かで大きく両極端に分かれた．しかし，こうした動きが経済的な後退を引き起こし，すべての組織や事業に試練を与えることになった．

1972年1月までに，それまでSWAに多くの仕事を出していた産業である，カリフォルニアの住宅産業は大暴落するだろうと，経済学者が予測していた．にもかかわらず，仕事の多様性や，サザンカリフォルニアにおけるアーバイン社の仕事やフロリダにおけるアーバイダ社の仕事のような大規模なプロジェクトを展開することによって，SWAは成長を続けた．1973年に，環境コンサルタント事務所であるジェームズA.ロバーツ事務所（JARA）と合併した．この年，事務所のマイケル・ギルバートはSWAの社員持ち株制度（ESOP）をつくり，全社員によって90％の株が所有されることになった．社長はわずかに10％を所有するだけである．これは長期の財政的安定とともに，社員全員が仕事に励むことにつながる革新的な方法であった．しかし残念ながら，これはある種の誤解を招き，ヒデオ・ササキの事務所との絆にひびが入る結果となった（ササキは実質的にSWAの一員でなくなっていたから，株はもはや持てなかったのである．）

ギルバートは地質学者で，SWAの前はサンフランシスコの開発会社であ

(JARA). Also that year, Gilbert set up SWA's Employee Stock Ownership Plan (ESOP), which allowed for ownership of 90% of the firm by all employees. (Principals would then share ownership of the remaining 10%.) The ESOP was an innovative measure to offer incentives for high performance on the job as well as long-term financial security. Sadly, the ESOP also led to some misunderstandings and the severing of formal ties with Sasaki's office. (Since Sasaki was not, technically, an SWA employee, he could no longer hold stock in SWA.)

Gilbert, a geologist and engineer by training, formerly manager of the San Francisco office of the development company, Cabot, Cabot & Forbes, brought a new professionalism to SWA's fiscal management, along with goals that linked fine design with good business. However, the impact of the 1972-74 recession finally hit SWA — hard. Many of the firm's more than 100 employees had to be let go for lack of work. The alliance between SWA and JARA was dismantled in 1975, just as the economy was recovering. And, with expert financial guidance, SWA survived the recession.

The work illustrated in this publication is drawn largely from the post-recession years — a time when the influence of Walker (who left California in 1976 to teach at Harvard) is less evident. Walker formed his own, smaller firm in 1983; and by now, new leading designers at SWA — including Law, Callaway, Reeves and Sardina — have reached maturity. Some new ideals and philosophies have also emerged. In 1981, when SWA encompassed five offices, Platt noted, "We are a different firm, surely, than when we huddled together in Sausalito with bright eyes for a new world. Now our world is different...Many of the philosophies of our founders still ring true, but it is time for us to look at a different world through different eyes, with a different structure to work from."

A survey of SWA's goals over the years (there are now five offices) would reveal moments when SWA's beliefs have been tested or confirmed by reality. As Platt recently observed, downturns tend to make professionals more reflective, focusing more attention on what they do, or ought to do. Survival then depends on better management and better professionalism — that is, more creative use of available resources. Shortly after the 1972-74 recession, Gilbert set up his own management and investment firm in order to advise SWA from the outside and thus leave SWA policy decisions in the hands of SWA's professionals. In the early 1980s, Platt thought of growth in terms of "what we do, not more of the same"; and Kagi emphasized growth in ability, influence and recognition. Now younger principals manage SWA's offices, and their values and goals are setting the tone of the offices.

Agreement among some 40 principals of a multi-office firm is difficult to reach. But, clearly, the stance of "We designers against the world" has given way as new responses to the increasingly complex issues and projects of our time are required. SWA's combined social, environmental and aesthetic concerns (for which no phrase has yet been coined) are expressed by individuals as well as by the group. Some members teach, some participate in local chapters of the American Society of Landscape Architects (ASLA), a few publish their ideas. All remain committed to pursuing planning and design to the end — the built work, finely crafted, maintained and enjoyed.

るカボット, カボット・アンド・フォーブズのマネージャーをしていたが, SWAに入って以来, 良好な経営状態の中からよいデザインが生まれるという考えの下に, SWAの経理に新しいプロフェッショナリズムを導入した. しかし, 1972年から74年にかけての不景気の影響がついにSWAにも襲ってきた. 従業員が100人以上の組織は仕事がなくて右往左往した. SWAとJARAの合併もちょうど景気が回復の兆しを見せ始めた1975年に解体した. そして, 財政のエキスパートの力を得て, SWAはこの苦しい時期を乗りきることができた.

ここに紹介する私たちの作品は, この不景気以降のものがほとんどであり, この時代はまた, ピーター・ウォーカー(1976年にハーバード大学で教鞭をとるためカルフォルニアを去った)の影響がそれほど明らかでなくなったときでもある. ウォーカーは1983年に自分のオフィスをつくった. そして, ロウ, キャラウェイ, リーブズ, サーディナといったSWAの主要なデザイナーが見事に成長した. 新たにいくつかの目標やフィロソフィが出てきた. 1981年には, SWAは5つの事務所という編成になり, プラットは「新しい世界に期待して目を輝かせてサウサリートに身を寄せ合っていたときとは異なり, もう私たちはそれぞれ違う事務所であるということを認識するべきだ. それに世界も違ってきている. 設立当時のフィロソフィの多くはもちろんいまでも真実であるが, いまや違った目で世界を眺め, 違った構造を導き出す必要がある」と指摘した.

永年のSWAの仕事のゴールは, SWAの信念が実際に試され, 実証されたそのときに現れるだろう. プラットが指摘しているように, 景気の下降という大きな流れは, プロフェッショナルをいっそう慎重にさせ, なにをするのか, なにをなすべきかに焦点を絞るようになる. したがって, こうした世の中に生き残るには, 健全な経営とより優れたプロ意識, つまり有効な資源を創造的に使うことが必要である. 1972年から74年の不景気の時期の直後にギルバートは, SWAを外側から応援するために, 政策の決定権を残すSWAの人たちに後を委ねて独立し, 自分の経営管理および投資会社を設立した.

1980年代の初期になるとプラットは, 成長について「同じことの繰り返しでなく, なにをやるべきかを考える」と指摘していた. そしてケーギは能力, 影響力, そして他にみとめられるといった点での成長を強調した. いまや, SWAのオフィスは若いプリンシパルたちによって運営されている. 彼らの価値観や目標がオフィスの新しい気風を形成しつつある.

数か所に分かれたオフィスの約40人のプリンシパルの間で合意を得ることは難しい. しかし, 明らかに「私たちデザイナーは古い因習を打ち破る」という姿勢は, ますます複雑化する問題や, 現代のプロジェクトに求められるランドスケープアーキテクトの新たな対応を見出すことを助けている. SWAの総合的な社会的, 環境的, 美的関心(まだそれを表わす的確な言葉は生み出されていないが)は, 個人によっても, グループによっても表現されている. メンバーの何人かは教鞭をとり, 米国ランドスケープアーキテクト協会(ASLA)の各支部に参加し, その内の何人かは彼らの考えを本にまとめて出版している. 構成員すべての人たちが, 計画, 設計から仕上げにまで関わり, 見事につくり上げ, 維持し, そしてそれを喜びとしている.

Conversation
座談会

On June 16, 1991, **Allan Temko**, Pulitzer prize winning architectural critic for the San Francisco Chronicle, joined a discussion with several SWA principals at the SWA office in Sausalito, California. The conversation centered around the SWA Group's history and the architectural and landscape professions by citing examples of projects, professionals, academics and collaborators. Present from the SWA Group were **Kalvin Platt**, Chairman, **Bill Callaway**, President and **Susan Whitin**, Managing Principal at the Laguna Beach office.

Temko: I'm so old now that I have historical perspective. The good, modern architects of the generation before mine were trained by classical architects, who had learned Beaux-Arts discipline. Typically, they had studied in France. Then they educated a generation of modern architects who had the same classical background but were breaking away. That set up a tension between them, but people like Eero Saarincn could draw you a Beaux-Arts plan, just like that! Then those people, in turn, brought in a new generation of people whom they liked, who were congenial, gifted, cultured. But the generation that's now on top didn't have the same background.

How about the SWA Group? Doesn't SWA run an operation somewhat analogous to SOM? You're both multidisciplinary firms.

Platt: Well, in the early stages of our firm, Pete Walker and I talked about SOM as a role model. But we never reproduced them. We did accept the notion of a multidisciplinary firm, with landscape architects, planners, environmentalists, graphic designers and engineers. But we didn't bring in practicing architects, because we wanted access to all the best architects out there. Actually, we've collaborated with SOM quite a bit. We form a complete team when we work with them.

Callaway: The reason for running a multidisciplinary firm is to control the process. If you can be "on board" at the beginning of the project, working with the raw land at a broad scale, you're able to control more of the outcome, down to the finished design and the built work.

Platt: And that's really where our hearts are. With our focus on professional work, we're trying to have the firm run itself, to some extent. Even our business management is done mainly by outside consultants, although all the principals share some responsibility. And marketing becomes the job of a lot of people, almost in passing. We also rely a lot on architects, on developers, on landowners, and on corporations who are familiar with our work.

Temko: I once gave a talk at one of your SWA principal meetings and brought up the issue of a client base with more spiritual content — working with churches or schools, or...what about that nice little community park in Hercules?

Callaway: Refugio Valley Park. Actually, that was one of the more satisfying jobs I've ever done. It did, I think, put some soul into the community. It was a unique opportunity. Also, the community was so young that there were no politics to get in the way.

Platt: The people in that community were searching for an identity.

Callaway: Right. It was a mixed community, racially, economically.

1991年6月16日，カリフォルニアのSWAサウサリート事務所にて，アラン・テムコ氏を交えてのプリンシパルによる座談会が開かれた．テムコ氏はサンフランシスコ・クロニクル紙への寄稿でピューリッツァ賞を得た建築評論家である．座談会はSWAグループの沿革，職業としての建築・ランドスケープ論を中心に，様々なプロジェクトや専門家，大学教育のあり方，協同設計などの例を挙げながら展開された．

出席者
A. T.：アラン・テムコ（建築評論家）
K. P.：カルビン・プラット（SWA会長）
W. C.：ウィリアム・キャラウェイ（SWA社長）
S. W.：スーザン・ホワイティン（SWAラグナビーチ事務所代表）

A. T. 私もだいぶ歳をとってきたので最近は歴史的な展望を語れるようになってきたよ．私より前の世代のよき近代建築家は，ボザールの原理に基づくクラシックな建築家によって教育されたわけで，だからみんなフランスで勉強した．それから，彼らは同じクラシックな背景をもつ次の世代の近代建築家を教育したけれど，次第にそこから離れていってしまった．その間にはテンションが発生したが，エーロ・サーリネンのような人たちは，彼の作品に見られるようにボザールの伝統にみんなを引き込むことができた．そして，世代が変わって，気風の合った，有能で文化的な人たちによる新たな世代が登場してくる．しかし，いまやトップに立つこうした世代は同じ背景をもっているわけではないよね．

さて，SWAについてはどうだろう．どちらもいろいろな考えが同時に混在できる組織という意味で，SWAの組織はSOMのそれにちょっと似ているように思うんだが．

K. P. そうですね．SWA設立の当初は，ピーター・ウォーカーと私はよくSOMを模範として話し合いました．しかし，私たちは決して彼らの真似をしたわけではありません．ランドスケープアーキテクトやプランナー，環境論者，グラフィックデザイナー，エンジニアといった人たちが集まって，いろいろな考えや思想が混在できる組織という点を参考にしただけです．組織外の優れた建築家すべてと一緒に仕事がしたいので，私たちの組織には建築家はいません．実際，SOMとは数多くのプロジェクトで協働していて，彼らとは完璧なチームを組むことができます．

W. C. いろんな考えの存在し得る組織を維持することは，プロセスをコントロールすることでもあります．何もない裸の広大な土地を前にして計画することを考えればわかるように，そこでは，結果としての最終的なデザインやでき上がったものだけでない，それ以上のものをコントロールすることになるんです．

K. P. 私たちの考えは，まさにそれです．職業的な中心課題をそこに置くことで，私たちは組織を維持し，発展させてきました．組織のビジネス的な運営管理は外部のコンサルタントが主にやってくれますが，役員はすべて責任を持ち合っています．因みに，マーケティングはほとんどすべてのメンバーの仕事になっています．また，私たちはSWAを理解し，仕事を依頼してくれる建築家やディベロッパー，土地所有者，企業などに多くを負っています．

A. T. 私は以前プリンシパル・ミーティングで教会や学校といった，より精神的な内容をもつクライアントについての議論をしたことがある．その時話題にあがったハーキュリーの小さなコミュニティ・パークは何という名前だったかな…．

W. C. ああ，レフュージオバレーパークですね．あれはこれまでのどんな計画にも増して満足のいく仕事でした．コミュニティにある種

You know, that park would never have been designed that way if not for the new tendencies of the seventies.

Temko: You have a classical form in the pavilion by the lake. It's a timeless garden structure; and yet it's rational. It works. You could have ruined it with a little pediment or something. Also, it's white — not postmodern apricot or mulberry.

Callaway: The park was designed back in 1977 — just at the beginning of that movement.

Temko: Oh, I have no objection to color. Look at Legorreta. He uses these panels of color, very daringly. Have you had any jobs where you have been able to use warm color, in this mood, say, in the last 15 years?

Callaway: Riverway, by Jim Reeves, in Houston, Texas. And also Fireman's Fund Headquarters, in Novato, California. I think our designs came out of a release from the modernist or minimalist mode we'd been working in for years. By then Pete Walker, our senior designer, had left, and we naturally looked to other models. Barragan was one. On the Refugio Park project, Susan was here to challenge me. I didn't do it exactly as she would have; but she had an impact.

Temko: That's interesting. I noticed in the history that the firm used to be a male operation. Now women have a sizeable role?

Whitin: Well, in my office — Laguna Beach — we have a strong representation of women. The firm now has two female design principals, Monica Simpson and myself. But SWA's still pretty much a male firm. It's a male profession, generally.

Temko: Some of the greatest landscape designers, like Beatrix Farrand...

Whitin: Actually, the firm is very supportive of women. To keep evolving, moving forward professionally, doing project work, you need to dedicate your life to it...

Temko: All the design professions are that way.

Whitin: ...And some women can do that. But some tend to get to a point, then veer off. I'm very much concerned about that. In our office, we have women who are very intellectual. They're going through

Allan Temko　アラン・テムコ

the patient search for ideas. And we're very supportive of that. In fact, I'm trying to get all my colleagues to articulate their personal vision.

Callaway: One interesting thing I've found, in teaching — even ten years ago — was that, almost without exception, two out of the top three, in terms of talent, interest and general quality, were women.

Temko: Do many of your principals teach?

Platt: Not many. One of our consulting principals, Doug Way, is chairman of the landscape department at Ohio State. Bill Callaway and John Wong have taught at Harvard — and also at Berkeley.

Callaway: Kalvin also taught at Harvard. Gary Karner, David Berkson and Susan have taught at San Luis Obispo (California State Polytechnic University).

の魂を入れることができたように思います. ユニークな機会でしたよ. コミュニティがまだ未成熟で, 計画を阻止するような政策がなかったことも幸いしました.

K. P. そこに住む人々はアイデンティティを探していたんです.

W. C. そうです. あそこは, 人種的にも経済的にも混在のコミュニティでした. ご存知のように, 1970年代の新しい傾向がなければ, あの公園はいまのようには計画され得なかったでしょう.

A. T. 湖の側に古典的なパビリオンが建っているね. あれは時代を超越した庭園の要素だが, 理屈にあっていると思う. それは有効に働いてもいる. ペディメントをつけたり, ポストモダン風に黄色や赤紫にすることもできたと思うけれど, あれは真っ白だね.

W. C. 公園は1977年に設計しました. ポストモダンのごく初期です.

A. T. 私はなにも鮮やかな色彩に反対しているわけじゃないよ. レゴレッタを見てごらん. 彼はいろんな色彩を大胆に使う. SWAでは, この15年ぐらいの間で, たとえば温かい雰囲気の色彩を使った仕事にどんなものがあるのかな.

W. C. ジム・リーブズが担当したヒューストンのリバーウェイがそうです. カリフォルニアのノバトにあるファイアーマンズ・ファンド本社もそうですね. 私たちはここ数年, モダニストないしはミニマリストの様式からの離脱を目指してデザインしてきたように思います. それまでは, ピーター・ウォーカー流だったんですが, 彼が去ってから, なにか別なモデルを探していました. ルイス・バラガンもその1人です. レフュージオバレーパークでは, 担当のスーザンが新しいものをもって挑戦してきた. 私だったらそうはできません. 彼女はそれだけのインパクトをもっていました.

A. T. それは面白い. 私はSWAはてっきり男性社会だと思っていた. いまや女性が重要な役割を担っているんだね.

S. W. 少なくともラグナビーチのオフィスでは女性は強力に参加しています. ここでは私ともう1人モニカ・シンプソンという2人の女性のデザイン担当のプリンシパルがいます. しかし, SWA全体でみると, まだまだ男性社会です. 一般的には男性優位の職業ですね.

A. T. しかしベアトリス・ファランなどの, 偉大な女流のランドスケープデザイナーもいるよ.

S. W. 実際, 会社は女性に対して非常に協力的です. しかし, プロとして発展・向上し, よい仕事をしていくには, 生涯をそれに捧げる必要があります.

A. T. デザインするということは, どんな仕事でもそうだね.

S. W. そして, 何割かの女性にはそれが可能ですが, まだまだ途中で転身してしまう女性も多い. 私はその点にとても注意を払っています. 私たちの事務所には, たいへん才能に富んだ女性が多く, アイデアを忍耐強く探し続けています. 私たちもそれを応援します. 実際, 私は仲間全員がそれぞれのビジョンを発言できるように努力しています.

W. C. 私が教えていたのはもう10年以上も前になりますが, そこで見出した興味深いことは, 才能, 探究心, 仕事の質という点でいえば, トップ3人中の2人までが例外なく女性だということです.

A. T. あなた方プリンシパルの多くは, 教壇に立って教えているのかい?

K. P. そう多くはありません…. コンサルティング・プリンシパルであるダグラス・ウェイはオハイオ州立大学のランドスケープ学部長をしているし, ビル・キャラウェイやジョン・ウォンはハーバードやバークレーで教えていました.

W. C. カルビンもハーバードで教えていたし, ゲーリー・カーナーやデイビッド・バークソン, それからスーザンはカリフォルニア州立工科大学サンルイス・オビスポ校で教えていました.

Kalvin Platt　カルビン・プラット

Whitin: It's important.

Callaway: The dean (at Berkeley's College of Environmental Design) — Roger Montgomery — made an interesting point at our last principals' meeting. His pitch was that we've got to get the professionals together with the academics because the schools are turning out students with broader knowledge and less professional specifics. "And so," he said, "we need you to help us teach them."

Temko: SWA has always been a place to learn. In that sense, it has had its own school, too.

Whitin: It's a continuing education.

Temko: Well, I'm trying to imagine what the firm might look like in ten years — what changes you expect. The world is changing, but it's not clear how. There are some tremendous areas, like the Soviet Union, where land planning of the American order will be needed. My friend, Donald MacDonald, has been trying to get some housing projects going there. Anshen and Allen are doing a conversion of an old school building, turning it into a hospital for children injured by the Chernobyl disaster. Bob Royston's office is working on the gardens. And MacDonald's involved a little — he's also doing a new Soviet headquarters for Green Peace. But it's tough; the Russians tend to put up buildings without doing anything to the land — they just plant grass.

Platt: Right. But it's difficult in Western Europe, too. The Common Market, by making agriculture more universal and more competitive, changes the historic situation, where in all the countries kept large areas of land in agriculture. My concern about Western Europe is that when this surplus land comes out of agriculture, they're going to just suburbanize it all.

Temko: That's a danger.

Platt: Good planning in Europe is really critical, since they will have more room for growth and development than they've ever had. The architects there are relatively new to this area of planning; we've talked with a number of them about that.

Actually, we're working all over the world now. We have people in Turkey, working on urban and resort hotels now — and possibly a new town outside Istanbul. Bill's working on an 70,000m² (18-acre), mixed-use project on the edge of Tokyo.

Whitin: We're also working in Taiwan, doing landscape enhancement of golf courses...

Platt: And our Florida office is working in Portugal, with the Arquitectonica firm. We're also working in Venezuela – and in Mexico, we have a large resort project in the Yucatan area that features nature conservation as well as hotels and resort facilities.

Temko: Are you starting overseas offices?

Platt: Not at the moment. Because we operate extremely well from our offices on the two coasts to the European and Pacific rim.

Temko: And from Texas and Southern California to Mexico?

Platt: Exactly. We also have some affiliated people in Japan and

---

S. W. これは重要なことです.

W. C. バークレー環境デザインカレッジの学部長, ロジャー・モンゴメリー氏が先日, SWAのプリンシパル・ミーティングで面白い指摘をしていました. つまり, 広い知識をもっていても, 専門的には未熟な学生を育てるんだから, 私たちプロは学校と一緒になってやっていかなければいけないというんです. 彼は「だから, 教える場にあなた方の協力が必要なんだ」と言っていました.

A. T. SWAそのものが教育する場になってる. そういう意味では, 事務所に学校があるようなものだね.

S. W. 教育の継承ですね.

A. T. さて, ここで私は, SWAがこの10年の間に, どのように変わってきたかを知りたいな. 世界は変化しているけれど, まだどう変化しているか明確ではない. ソ連のように, アメリカ式の土地利用計画を必要とする広大な国土が, この地球上にはまだまだある. 私の友人のドナルド・マクドナルドは, 目下ソ連でハウジング計画を実施しようとしている. アンシェン・アンド・アレン事務所も, 古い学校の建物を, チェルノブイリ原発事故で傷ついた子供たちのための病院に改造する計画に着手しようとしている. ロバート・ロイストンの事務所は庭園を計画している. そしてマクドナルドはまた, グリーンピース運動のソ連における新しい本部ビルに関与している. しかし, こうした仕事はたいへんむずかしい. ソ連の人たちは, 建物は建てるけれど, その土地に対しては草を植える以外, なにもしないという傾向がある.

K. P. そうですね. しかし, 西欧でも事情は同じです. マーケットの国際化は農業の普遍化, 自由競争化を促し, 広大な農地を保有していたすべての国において歴史的な状況を変化せしめています. 農地に由来する遊休地がすべて郊外地化しつつある点が気になります.

A. T. それは危険だね.

K. P. かつて所有していた以上に成長, 発展のための土地を手に入れるにあたって, 西欧では優れたプランニングが本当に必要とされています. これまで以上に土地を有効に活用して成長していくための, 優れたプランニングが必要です. こうした考えに対して, 西欧の建築家はまだ比較的慣れていませんね. 私たちは多くの建築家とこの点について語り合いました.

実際, いまや私たちは世界中で仕事をしています. トルコには, ホテルやこれから始まるイスタンブール郊外のニュータウンなどを担当しているスタッフがいます. キャラウェイは東京郊外の70,000の複合施設の仕事をしていますし.

S. W. 台湾ではゴルフコースのランドスケープを設計しています.

K. P. フロリダ事務所では, アーキテクトニカと一緒にポルトガルのプロジェクトを. メキシコでは, ユカタン半島で, ホテルやリゾート施設のセンスもさることながら, 自然の保全をも特色とした大規模リゾート・プロジェクトに取り組んでいます.

A. T. 海外事務所の開設予定は?

K. P. いまのところはありません. 西海岸と東海岸の両事務所で充分に太平洋, 大西洋を越えた仕事を掌握できています.

A. T. それでテキサスから南カリフォルニア, そしてメキシコまで含めてやれてるわけだね.

K. P. そうです. 日本には協力者がいるし, 台湾でも子会社をつくりつつあります. ここサウサリートでも, 日本人のプランナーが一緒に働いているし, 今後もっと日本語やスペイン語の話せる人たちを増やそうと考えています.

S. W. 私たちの事務所には中国人の女性や韓国人の男性もいましたが, その後, 別の事務所に勤めた後, いまはアメリカ国内で独立して自分の事務所を開設しています. 今でもこうした人たちと協力し合っ

we're developing affiliations in Thailand. Here in Sausalito, we have a Japanese planner working with us, and we're thinking of getting more Japanese- and Spanish-speaking people into the firm.

Whitin: We had a woman from China and a guy from Korea...eventually they went to work for other firms, and now they're working on their own in the United States. In fact, we're collaborating with them on projects.

Platt: These collaborations help us to understand the cultural and historical differences that are critical to us providing services that are meaningful as well as problem solving.

Callaway: For instance, Japan's greatest works in the landscape were private villas and palaces. The buildings and gardens were wonderfully related to nature — but not necessarily to the community. Then, after the war, our engineers and their engineers did the rebuilding, without a sense of relating to nature *or* the community. Now the Japanese are struggling with environmental issues.

Whitin: Mr. Hiroyasu Tanaka from Taisei Corporation is working in our office for a year to get practical experience in the United States. And of course this sort of one-on-one intercultural experience is invaluable for us because of our work and interest in Asia.

Temko: And do you have local projects for them to work on — to get that sense of continuity, from wilderness, to communities, to...

Platt: Yes, in California, Mr. Tanaka is helping us design a 4000 acre (1,600 ha) new town that transitions between the town itself and the coastal mountains with farmlands surrounding it.

Temko: Are you doing alot of large scale planning that includes environmental issues?

Platt: Yes, for instance on a project for the MacArthur Foundation, in Florida — 40,000 acres (16,000 ha) — we have been trying to develop a practical wetlands strategy. The environmental laws look at every parcel of land equally — whether it's 4 acres or 4,000 acres — and require that you save a certain percentage for wetlands. That, of course, doesn't help the wildlife survive, particularly the species that live in a combination of wetlands and savannah.

Bill Callaway　ビル・キャラウェイ

So, we're proposing that, instead of mandating these tiny patches of wetlands here and there, they should adopt something like Olmsted's "Emerald Necklace" of parks in Boston, or the Chicago forest preserves, on a large scale. Then we could plan places for people to live. We're also promoting the notion of parks as buffers between people and wilderness. We look at wilderness as part of a continuum. We're trying to create a system whereby people can relate to the wilderness — yet still preserve it.

Whitin: We could also talk about the urban wilderness — particularly around Los Angeles.

Temko: There, you're up against a cultural handicap. I was at UCLA 25 years ago for a Sierra Club conference, and they were talking about these tiny little parks in the Santa Monica Mountains. And I said,

ているプロジェクトもあります.

K. P.　こうした協働作業は,アメリカと外国との文化的・歴史的な違いを理解する上でたいへん役立ちます.他国で適切な仕事をし,問題を解決していくには,こうした相互理解が不可欠です.

W. C.　例えば,日本の文化は,自然との関係を誇りにしていました.日本のランドスケープの偉大な作品は,個人の邸宅や社寺,城などに見られます.したがって,建物と庭園はすべて自然に密接に関係し,コミュニティには帰属していなかったわけです.戦後,日米の技術者たちは,そうした環境をつくり直す際に,自然にもコミュニティにも関係させないでつくってしまったんです.日本の人たちはいま環境問題に取り組んでいます.

S. W.　大成建設の田中弘靖氏もアメリカで実践を積むために1年間この事務所で働いています.もちろんこうした文化の交流は,私たちがアジアで仕事をするためにも,なくてはならない経験のひとつです.

A. T.　そうした人たちのために,全くの自然からコミュニティまでつながる,継承という感覚を体得できるような仕事が実際にあるの?

K. P.　はい,彼にはカリフォルニアで街そのものと沿岸の山々,そして周辺を取り巻く農地をうまく調和させるような,4,000エーカー(約1,600ha)からなるニュータウンの仕事を手伝ってもらっています.

A. T.　環境問題を包含するような大規模計画も扱っているのかい.

K. P.　ええ,例えばフロリダの40,000エーカー(約16,000ha)のマッカーサー財団の仕事では,より実践的な湿原保全計画の立案を試みました.環境に関する法規は,それが4エーカーであろうと4,000エーカーであろうと,すべての土地を均一に見ている.そして湿地の何%かを保護することを取り決めています.もちろん,それだけで野生生物が生き残れるわけではありません.特に湿地とサバンナが混在するような環境に生息する生き物はそうです.

そこで,私たちは,あちこちに小さな保護された湿地を残すのでなく,オルムステッドが提案したボストンの公園ネットワークシステム「エメラルドネックレス」や,シカゴの森林保護のような手法の採用を提案しました.そうして初めて人々の住むための場を計画するのです.また私たちは,公園が人々の住む環境と原生の自然との緩衝帯の役割を果たすとの考えを提唱しています.自然環境を保護しつつ,人々の生活との接点を見出すようなシステムをつくり出したいのです.

S. W.　私たちは,都市の自然,特にロサンゼルス周辺についていろいろ議論しました.

A. T.　そこで文化的なハンディキャップに直面するわけだね.25年前のUCLAでのシエラクラブの会議のことを思い出すよ.サンタモニカ山地の小さな公園のことが盛んに議論されていた.「何をいってるんだ,どうして,この山全体を見て考えないのだ」と私はいったよ.

S. W.　その通りですね.私たちは,ディズニーランド近くのアナハイムで大規模な商業／レクリエーション地区の整備計画をしていますが,そこはコンクリート砂漠の中をインターステイトハイウェイI-5が走っているような所です.そんな環境の中になんとか「場」を創出したいと考え,様々なランドスケープを使って,場の個性をつくり出す努力をしています.都市の雑然とした広がりの中に自然を取り戻したい.さもなければ,どうしてそんなところを訪れたいと思うでしょう.今はあまりに非人間的な場所となっています.人々がアミューズメントパークの門を潜っていくのは,ある意味では現実からの逃避なんでしょう.だから,対照的に緑に満ちあふれるディズニーランドはとてもすばらしいんです.

A. T.　ディズニーランドは,ある意味では歴史的に最もすばらしい土地利用計画だと思う.私はかつてチャールズ・イームズと行ったことがある.そこでイームズは数々の魅力的なデザインを私に指摘したよ.

Susan Whitin　スーザン・ホワイティン

"What the hell, why not take the whole mountain!"

Whitin: Exactly. Well, in Anaheim, near Disneyland, we're working in a large commercial/recreation area — where the I-5 (interstate highway) runs through an utter concrete wilderness. We're trying to create a *place* there. We're using landscape, lots of it and in layers, to create a personality for the place. We're trying to bring nature back to the urban wilderness. Otherwise, why would you ever go there? Right now, it's dehumanizing. I think people go through the gate, into the amusement park, to escape. That's why Disneyland is so wonderful: it's so green and lush, in contrast.

Temko: It's one of the most brilliant land plans in history. I went through it with Charles Eames once, and he pointed out many fascinating features of the design. Where else can you be on the Mississippi, and

not be aware that a strikingly different environment — the Amazon, say — is twenty feet away?

Whitin: Well, the site we're working on is tough. Disney's concept is that of an urban destination resort, a garden district in the midst of Anaheim. Because the City of Anaheim is pursuing similar ideas for the entire surrounding district, which includes the Anaheim Convention Center and thousands of hotel rooms, there are real possibilities for success. Everyone recognizes that, because the appearance of the area is so brutal, nothing less than total transformation is needed. A transformation from grey to green. It's about creating a shared vision of the future as a garden paradise!

Temko: Meanwhile, people in Northern California feel they have to be in Yosemite. And, with the new freeways and excellent roads, you can come up from Fresno or Modesto and use it for a day park.

Platt: So, it's important to go back to the original notion of a national park, and ask, "What is of value here? What is unique to this place?"

Callaway: The value of Yosemite to the nation and to the world is one of inspiration. That's its primary value. The way it is now, it's very difficult to have that experience.

Temko: The whole park has to be cleaned up and redone. The Yosemite Fund is raising money. And we're thinking, just as a demonstration of what could be done, that we could start with the approach to Yosemite Falls, the fourth highest waterfall in the world. What's there now is terrible: the road, the signage, everything that's been done for a hundred years has to be re-examined. Should Badger Pass be a ski resort? Why does a national park need a ski resort? You know, by trying to make it produce revenue all year long, the park never rests. It never recovers from this harsh treatment.

Whitin: It's extraordinary, though — if you go up to the High Sierra camps in Yosemite, which I've done for a number of years, immediately there are no people! On a day's hike, you might pass a dozen people. And when you get to a camp, it's very small — holds maybe 60 people a night. Now that natural resource is very hidden. It's wonderful. But to counterbalance this natural, environmental move-

ミシシッピー川のすぐ数メートル先に，全く違う環境のアマゾンがあるところなんて他にあるかい？

S. W. そうですね．私たちが取り組む敷地は厳しいところです．ディズニーのコンセプトは，アナハイムの中心に「ガーデン・ディストリクト」という都市の滞在型リゾートを創出しようとするものです．アナハイム市も，会議場や何千室ものホテル計画も含めて，周辺一帯を同じ考えで整備していきたいと考えているので，この計画が成功する確率は高いでしょう．現在この一帯の景観があまりに殺伐としているため，もはや全面的な転換が必要とされているのです．灰色から緑への転換が．庭園の楽園という共通の将来的なビジョンを達成していこうとしているんです．

A. T. しかし，カリフォルニア北部に住む人たちは，ヨセミテ国立公園に行きたいと考える．そして，新しいフリーウェイや整備のいい道路を走ってフレズノやモデストから上って行って，そこをデイパーク（日帰りのレクリエーションを目的とした公園）として使う．

K. P. だから，ここでいま一度，国立公園の「その価値はなにか，そこはなにがユニークなのか」といった，本来の意味をよく考え直すことが大事なんです．

W. C. アメリカにとっても世界にとっても，ヨセミテがもっている価値はひとつのインスピレーションでしょう．それが本来的な価値だと思います．しかし，現在においてそれを体験することは，たいへん難かしくなっている．

A. T. 公園全体をきれいにしなくてはいけないし，再整備する必要がある．ヨセミテ財団がそのための基金を集めている．何ができるかというデモンストレーションとして，まず世界で4番目に高いヨセミテ滝のアプローチから始めるべきだね．現状はひどいものだよ．100年前に設置された道路やサイン類もすべて再チェックの必要がある．バ

ジャーパスは本当にスキーリゾートにすべきか．国立公園にどうしてスキーリゾートが必要なのか．年間を通じて公園から収益を上げようとすることは，公園に休む間を与えないようなものだ．こうした過酷な扱いをしていれば，自然は決してもと通りに回復できない．

S. W. 何年か前のことですが，ヨセミテのハイシエラキャンプに行ってみるとそこにはまったく誰もいないのです．1日歩き回って，1ダースの人に会うか会わないかです．そしてキャンプ場にたどり着けば，そこはごく小さな，60人ぐらい収容できるところです．現在こうした施設は自然の中にとけこんでいて，たいへんすばらしいものです．しかし，この自然や環境の平衡を保つためには，ランドスケープがよく見えるようにしなければならないという議論もあります．自然は自然です．人がつくり出したものは，それらしく見える必要があります．

W. C. 私は場に応じた処置が必要だと考えています．つまり，時には人が森の中を歩いていてふと立ち止まり，「ちょっと待てよ」と自問するような状況をつくりたい．たとえばそこには岩の角が削られていたり，磨かれていたりといったさりげない仕掛けがあるわけです．また，ある時には，理由は何にせよ風景の中にはっきりした力強い線が描かれてもよいでしょう．

S. W. その通りです．私たちは，ランドスケープは人々の意識にはっきりと映るべきものだと考えています．いつも背景である必要はないのです．人のつくり出したランドスケープは，私たちに新たな物の見方を引き起こさせることが可能です．記憶に残り，私たちを魅きつけ，個性のあるものでなければなりません．

A. T. それに時間の超越も必要だね．

S. W. ダン・カイリーの作品はとても静かですが，同時に緻密です．彼のランドスケープの中にいると，とても安らぎを覚えると同時にどこにいるかという場の意識が鮮明になります．わくわくするような…．

ment, there's the issue of making the landscape visible. What's nature is nature, and everything else created by man should look as if it's created by man.

Callaway: It has to do with appropriate response. I mean, sometimes you want people to be walking through a forest and stop and say, "Wait a minute!" Because it's that subtle that something happened there; maybe it's a rock with an edge cut off and polished. In other cases, it makes sense to draw a big line in the landscape, for whatever reason.

Whitin: Right. We believe that sometimes the landscape should come forward, into your consciousness. It shouldn't always be in the background. Man-made landscape can cause us to see things in a new way; it should be memorable, challenge us, have personality.

Temko: And I think they should be timeless.

Whitin: Dan Kiley's work is very quiet, but very, very intense. You feel good when you're in one of his landscapes, but it also heightens your awareness of where you are. Somehow, it's pulsating...

Temko: I love it.

Whitin: The same is true of the Weyerhaeuser headquarters in the landscape. It's that silence you feel. When that happens, you've left the design world and gone into the world of art.

Callaway: You know, one of the differences between an artist and a designer is, an artist is on his own personal, intuitive or intellectual quest. A designer, typically, must integrate a client's vision with his own work.

Temko: I don't think it's that sharp a division.

Callaway: You're right in the sense that any designer worth his salt should have a personal quest.

Whitin: And some clients will let you do whatever you can dream about.

Platt: Sometimes, though, it's hard for a client to identify with us, personally. Each partner tends to have a clientele; certain architects and developers know us as individuals, even though SWA is a group practice.

Temko: I'm totally in sympathy with that approach — the Bauhaus ideal.

Whitin: Well we do have shared values and a shared culture; but we're doing a lot of quite different things. It's healthy, like a true living organism. One of our partners, Bob Jacob, has a client from Hong Kong — Minoru Chen — who wants to create an elegant new community in Southern California. Bob has done a lot of research on the older planned communities in the area — places like Palos Verdes and Beverly Hills. Now they're publishing Bob's research as a book and Bob is speaking at conferences.

Platt: You know, there's a great diversity in our notion of community-building, which is, I think, an art as well as a science. It's also social. Each of us has his own heroes. One of my mentors was Charles Abrams, the housing expert. I don't know if you remember him.

Temko: Oh, boy, Charlie Abrams! I used to love to go to his favorite delicatessen with him and have a hot pastrami.

Platt: Well, he was not an artist. But his notion was that in order to succeed you have to have both genius and a bias — which is what we've been talking about: a designer's point of view. That notion is part of the culture that's developing in the firm.

Callaway: But working with people, all with strong ideas, calls for a certain tolerance, a willingness to accept a different way of thinking about things. Actually, being in a large group allows us to be more experimental, in a sense, than a smaller firm. We can allow younger people to take a small project and try a different approach. If somebody has a great idea, we're willing to go with it.

Platt: It's all part of the dialogue, part of the enrichment of the group.

A. T. 私も好きだよ.

S. W. ウエアハウザー本社のランドスケープは同じ雰囲気です. 静寂を感じます. そこではデザインの世界がアートの世界に変わります.

W. C. アーチストとデザイナーの違いのひとつは, アーチストは自分のために, 直観的, 知的な探究をすればいいのに対して, デザイナーはクライアントの考えと自分のものとをうまく統合していかなければという点です.

A. T. 私はそれほど明快に割り切れるものではないと思うよ.

W. C. もちろん, 優秀なデザイナーは個人としての探究が不可欠ですが….

S. W. そうした夢の探究をやらせてくれるクライアントもときにはいます.

K. P. しかしクライアントに私たちと同じように考えろというのは, むずかしいことですね. それぞれのパートナーは, 個人的に親しい建築家やディベロッパーといったクライアントを抱えていることが多いんです. しかし私たちはあくまでもグループとして仕事をしています.

A. T. そうしたバウハウス的な仕事の仕方に私は大賛成だよ.

S. W. そうですね. 私たちは価値も文化も分かち合っています. けれども, それぞれの事務所で, また個々のデザイナーで異なったアプローチにより仕事を進めています. それは健全なことであり, 実際に生きている有機体のようなものです. パートナーの1人であるボブ・ジェイコブズは, ミノル・チェンという香港のクライアントの仕事をしていますが, チェン氏は南カリフォルニアにエレガントな新しいコミュニティをつくろうとしています. そこでボブは, パロスベルデスやビバリーヒルズといった, その地域に古くからあるコミュニティを詳細に調査し, これを1冊の本にまとめ, また会議でも発表しています.

K. P. コミュニティづくりには, アートや科学も含めて非常に多くの概念が含まれ, また社会的でもあります. 私たちは独自のヒーローを心の中に持っています. 私の場合はハウジングの達人のチャールズ・エイブラムズです. あなたが彼をご存知かどうか知りませんが…….

A. T. あぁ, よく知ってる. 彼の大好きなデリカテッセンに2人でよくホットパストラミを食べに行ったよ.

K. P. 彼はアーチストではありませんが, 彼の考えは卓越した才能と確固たるデザイン・フィロソフィを持って仕事に取り組めというものです. このことは, まさに私たちが話してきたこと, 「デザイナーは独自のものの見方を持て」ということなのです. この思想は, 私たちの組織の中で培っている教養のひとつです.

W. C. しかし, 強いアイデアを持つ仲間たちと共に働いていくことは, ある種の寛容さを必要としますね. 実際, 進んで違ったものの考え方を取り入れていくことは, ある意味で, 小さな会社以上に実験的であることが求められます. 私たちは, 若い人たちにまず小さなプロジェクトを取り組ませ, 違ったアプローチの仕方に挑戦させたりします. もし, 誰かがすばらしいアイデアを出せば, 私たちは喜んでそれを推進していくでしょう.

K. P. それが, 私たちの対話であり, グループを充実させている本質ですね.

Biographies　経歴

＊SWAにおける「プリンシパル」は，単なる日本語の「役員」という意味にとどまらず，チーフデザイナーとして現場を支えています．この号の作品解説ページでは担当したプリンシパルのメッセージが添えられています．ここではそのプリンシパルを紹介します．

Sausalito　From left to right: Jim Lee, Joe Runco, Juel Bortolussi, Walt Bemis, Jeff Bergfeld, Jill Gropp, Eddie Chau, Kalvin Platt, Bill Callaway, Nancy Hartwick, Larry Pearson, Lori Hjort, John Wong, Mitch Waufle, John Loomis, Elizabeth Shreeve, Donna Stolz, Joan Ehlers, Rene Bihan, Corazon Unana, Noni Mendoza, Gerry Campbell, Margaret Laible, Robyn Scheer, Sean O'Malley, Hiro Tanaka, Maureen Simmons, Dixi Carrillo,　Not shown, Roy Imamura, Dan Tuttle

Houston　From left to right: Tim Frankie, Kevin Shanley, Wilson McClain, Ed Kagi, Thad Kudela, Star Miller, Lauren Moran, John Cutler

Laguna Beach　From left to right: Leo O'Brian, Tim Harvey, Lisa Gimmy, Tom Lamb, Bob Jacob, Mike Lemm, John Taylor, Dick Law, Mike Harris, Susan Whitin, David Bickel, David Berkson, David Morgan, Rick Pariani, Lee Anne Kirby, Monica Simpson, Trent Noll, Charlene Sippie, Don Tompkins, Anne Stamper, Cathy Baranager, Theresa Clark, Bryon Ziegler, Debbie Crouch, Mark Jacobucci, Mike Major

Dallas　From left to right: Karen Koerth, Don Bounds, Chuck McDaniel, Geneva Miles, David Thompson, Lannie Hoover, Lindsey James, Chris Miller, Jim Manskey

Deerfield Beach　From left to right: Tom Fox, Bob Mulcahy, Don Murakami, Dan Mock, Bonnie Raible, Eduardo Santaella, Dan Busbin, Alyce Ptak, Bob Dallin, Mike Sardina, Jim Reeves, Dru Smyth

Principals of the SWA Group

Thomas A. Adams
Joined SWA: 1965
Education: Graduate Studies in Landscape Architecture, 1970-71 Harvard University Graduate School of Design; Bachelor of Landscape Architecture, 1967 University of California, Berkeley; Bachelor of Arts in Modern Language, 1956 State University of New York; Studies in Economics, Carleton College
Academic Activities: Visiting Critic and Lecturer, Harvard University Graduate School of Design
Professional Affiliations: Member, American Society of Landscape Architects; Associate Member, Urban Land Institute; Associate Member, NAIOP; Active in Boston Society of Landscape Architects; Affiliate Member, Boston Society of Architects

Walter P. Bemis
Joined SWA: 1974
Education: Bachelor of Science in Forestry, 1957 University of California, Berkeley; 32 Additional Short Courses taken through Continuing Education; Speech Studies, 1960 California State University, Sacramento; Certificate in Real Estate Science, 1968 American River College
Academic Activities: Instructor, Fire Science and Forestry, State Department of Forestry; Instructor, Forest Management Short Courses, State Department of Forestry; Guest Lecturer, Seminar Speaker and Moderator, U.C. Berkeley
Professional Affiliations: Member, Society of American Foresters; Past President, California Alumni Foresters; Participant on Conservation Issues, California, Speaker's Bureau, State Board of Forestry
Registration: Professional Forester

David Berkson
Joined SWA: 1982
Education: Master of Landscape Architecture, 1982 Harvard University Graduate School of Design; Bachelor of Fine Arts, 1979 Tufts University School of Special Studies; 1973-1974 School of Architecture, Washington University
Academic Activities: Lecturer, California State Polytechnic University, San Luis Obispo; Lecturer, University of California, Irvine
Professional Affiliations: Member, American Society of Landscape Architects
Registration: California

William F. Brown
Joined SWA: 1981
Education: Bachelor of Science in Landscape Architecture, 1980 Ohio State University; Study in Landscape Architecture, 1975-1977 Pennsylvania State University
Academic Activities: Guest Lecturer, Harvard University Graduate School of Design; Guest Critic, West Virginia University
Professional Affiliations: Member, American Society of Landscape Architects; Member, Urban Land Institute

Juel Bortolussi
Joined SWA: 1984
Education: Study in Business Management, 1982-1985 San Francisco State University and University of California, Berkeley Extension; Study in Science, 1975 University of San Francisco; Associate of Arts in Science, 1974 Santa Rosa Junior College
Professional Affiliations: Member, COMMON, IBM International Users Group; Member, Berkeley Macintosh Users Group; Computer Advisory Board Member, College of Marin; Member and Past Board Director of Education, ASSU

William Callaway
Joined SWA: 1967
Education: Master of Landscape Architecture, 1971 Harvard University

Graduate School of Design; Bachelor of Landscape Architecture, 1966 University of California, Berkeley
Academic Activities: Visiting Lecturer, University of California at Berkeley; Visiting Lecturer, California State Polytechnic University, San Luis Obispo; Visiting Critic, Harvard University Graduate School of Design
Professional Affiliations: Member, American Society of Landscape Architects; Board Member, Northern California Chapter of American Society of Landscape Architects; Associate Member, Urban Land Institute; Certified, Council of Landscape Architectural Registration Boards
Registration: California, Texas, Nevada, Arizona, and Oklahoma

Gerald Campbell
Joined SWA: 1967
Education: 1950 Jepson Art Institute, Los Angeles; 1946-1950 Art Barn School of Art, Salt Lake City, Utah
Academic Activities: Co-founder and Instructor, Valley Center of Arts, Van Nuys; Principal and Instructor, The Pacific Gallery, Tarzana

Bruce Cozzi
Joined SWA: 1981
Education: Studies in Business Management, Golden Gate University; Associate Degree in Business Management, 1979 College of Marin; 1972 North American School of Conservation

John E. Cutler
Joined SWA: 1979
Education: Masters Study in Landscape Architecture, 1967-1968 University of Illinois; Bachelor of Science in Landscape Architecture, 1967 Texas A & M University; 1962-1964 University of Denver
Professional Affiliations: Member, American Society of Landscape Architects; Member, NAIOP; Member, Urban Land Institute; Member, TRAPS; Member, Construction Specifications Institute; Associate, American Forestry
Registration: Texas

Tom Fox
Joined SWA: 1981
Education: Bachelor of Arts with Honors in Industrial Photography, 1981 Brooks Institute; Bachelor of Arts in Political Science, 1968 San Francisco State University
Academic Activities: Shroud of Turin Research Project, Brooks Institute

Paul Michael Gilbert
Joined SWA: 1970
Education: Graduate Study in Marine Geology and Volcanology, Research Assistant, 1963 - 1964 University of Hawaii; Graduate Study in Civil Engineering and Business, 1958 University of Nevada; Bachelor of Science in Mining Engineering, 1957 Stanford University
Academic Activities: Visiting Lecturer, Harvard University Graduate School of Design; Guest Lecturer, The Ohio State University
Professional Affiliations: Audubon Society; Wilderness Society; California Academy of Sciences; American Forestry Association; American Association for the Advancement of Sciences

Loreen Hjort
Joined SWA: 1970
Education: General Studies, College of Marin; 1957 Balboa High School
Academic Activities: Counselor, Substance Abuse Program, Marin County School System

Roy Imamura
Joined SWA: 1971
Education: Bachelor of Landscape Architecture, 1963 California State Poly-

technic College, Pomona; 1958-1960 California State Polytechnic College San Luis Obispo
Professional Affiliations: Member, American Society of Landscape Architects
Registration: Georgia, Florida, California

Robert Jacob
Joined SWA: 1979
Education: Bachelor of Landscape Architecture, 1978 University of Oregon; 1964-1957 Occidental College
Academic Activities: Guest Lecturer, University of California, Irvine; Guest Lecturer, University of California, Los Angeles
Professional Affiliations: Member, American Society of Landscape Architects; Associate Member, Urban Land Institute
Registration: California

Edmond Kagi
Joined SWA: 1963
Education: Master of Landscape Architecture, 1958 Harvard University Graduate School of Design; Bachelor of Science in Landscape Architecture, 1953 State University of New York College of Environmental Science & Forestry, Syracuse
Academic Activities: Visiting Critic, Harvard University Graduate School of Design; Visiting Critic, Louisiana State University; Guest Lecturer, University of Washington; Architectural Jury Member, Rice University
Professional Affiliations: Member, American Society of Landscape Architects; Member, American Planning Association; Director, Landscape Architecture Foundation; Member, Faculty of Landscape Architecture Advisory Council, College of Environmental Science and Forestry, State University of New York; Certified, Council of Landscape Architecture Registration Boards; Member, American Institute of Certified Planners
Registration: California, Texas, Georgia, Louisiana, New Mexico, New York, Delaware, Ohio

Gary E. Karner
Joined SWA: 1966
Education: Master of Landscape Architecture, 1961 Harvard University Graduate School of Design; Bachelor of Science in Landscape Architecture, 1958 University of California, Berkeley; 1953 - 1955 Pomona College
Academic Activities: Professor, California State Polytechnic University, San Luis Obispo; Instructor, Harvard University Graduate School of Design; Lecturer in Landscape Architecture, University of California, Berkeley
Professional Affiliations: Fellow, American Society of Landscape Architects; Certified, Council of Landscape Architectural Registration Boards
Registration: California, Washington

Thomas Lamb
Joined SWA: 1984
Education: Master of Fine Arts, 1980 Rhode Island School of Design; Bachelor of Fine Arts, 1972 Hartford Art School, University of Hartford
Academic Activities: Rhode Island School of Design; Summervail Art Workshop; Colorado Mountain College; Orange Coast College; Saddleback College
Professional Affiliations: Member and Past Board of Directors, The Society of Photographic Education; Member and Past Board of Directors, Los Angeles Center for Photographic Studies; Member, Friends of Photography
Registration: California Studio Arts/Photography; Colorado Vocational Photography/Graphic Arts

Richard Law
Joined SWA: 1963

Education: Master of Landscape Architecture, 1965 Harvard University Graduate School of Design; Bachelor of Science in Landscape Architecture, 1963 California State Polytechnic College, Pomona; Biological Science, 1959-1960 Citrus College; Industrial Design Studies, 1957-1958 Art Center School, Los Angeles
Academic Activities: Advisory Committee and Consulting Landscape Architect, University of California, Irvine
Professional Affiliations: Fellow, American Society of Landscape Architects; Certified, Council of Landscape Architectural Registration Boards
Registration: California

James Lee
Joined SWA: 1978
Education: Bachelor of Landscape Architecture, 1975 University of California, Berkeley
Academic Activities: Guest Critic, University of California, Berkeley
Professional Affiliations: Member, American Society of Landscape Architects
Registration: California

John S. Loomis
Joined SWA: 1986
Education: Bachelor of Landscape Architecture, 1977 University of Illinois
Academic Activities: Guest Lecturer, American Society of Landscape Architects; Guest Lecturer, Redwood Empire Chapter, ASLA
Professional Affiliations: Member, American Society of Landscape Architects; Member, Strybing Arboretum Society; Member, Construction Specifications Institute
Registration: California

James Manskey
Joined SWA: 1983
Education: Bachelor of Science in Landscape Architecture, 1979 Texas A&M University
Academic Activities: Guest Speaker, University of Texas, Arlington
Professional Affiliations: Member, American Society of Landscape Architects; Member, Dallas Chamber of Commerce; Member, Greater Dallas Planning Committee
Registration: Texas

Wilson McClain
Joined SWA: 1983
Education: Studies in Landscape Contracting and Landscape Architecture, 1971-1976 Mississippi State University
Professional Affiliations: Member, Texas Association of Nurserymen; Member, Construction Specifications Institute

Charles McDaniel
Joined SWA: 1979
Education: Bachelor of Science in Landscape Architecture, 1979 Texas A&M University
Professional Affiliations: Member, American Society of Landscape Architects; Member, Greater Dallas Chamber of Commerce
Registration: Texas, Oklahoma, North Carolina, Virginia

Justiniano R. Mendoza, Jr.
Joined SWA: 1980
Education: Master of Science in Landscape Architecture, 1972 University of Wisconsin; Bachelor of Science in Architecture, 1966 University of the Philippines; Studies in Painting and Sculpture AAP, 1958 Manila, Philippines
Academic Activities: Guest Lecturer, University of the Philippines
Professional Affiliations: Member, American Society of Landscape Architects
Registration: California

Chris L. Miller
Joined SWA: 1979
Education: Bachelor of Landscape Architecture, 1979 Louisiana State University
Professional Affiliations: Member, American Society of Landscape Architects; Member, Urban Land Institute; Member, Greater Dallas Chamber of Commerce
Registration: Texas

Robert S. Mulcahy
Joined SWA: 1980
Education: 1977 Conway School of Landscape Design; Bachelor of Science, 1975 University of Massachusetts
Academic Activities: Lecturer and Thesis Advisor Boston Architectural Center; Guest Juror, Site Planning Course, M.I.T. Center for Real Estate Development
Professional Affiliations: Member, American Society of Landscape Architects; Affiliate Member, NAIOP
Registration: Massachusetts

Donald S. Murakami
Joined SWA: 1981
Education: Master of Landscape Architecture, 1976 Harvard University Graduate School of Design; Bachelor of Landscape Architecture, 1973 University of Oregon; Bachelor of Fine Arts, 1971 University of British Columbia
Professional Affiliations: Member, American Society of Landscape Architects

Fredrick P. Pariani, Jr.
Joined SWA: 1982
Education: Bachelor of Landscape Architecture with Honors, 1977 University of Georgia; Art Studies Abroad Program, 1976 University of Georgia and Cortona, Italy
Academic Activities: Design Charrette Instructor, University of Georgia
Professional Affiliations: Member, American Society of Landscape Architects; Member, NAIOP
Registration: Georgia, Florida

Larry Pearson
Joined SWA: 1982
Education: Master of Landscape Architecture, 1975 University of Illinois; Bachelor of Science in Agronomy, 1972 University of Illinois
Academic Activities: Teaching Assistant, University of Illinois
Professional Affiliations: Member, American Society of Landscape Architects; Associate Member, Urban Land Institute
Registration: Washington, Ohio, Illinois

Kalvin Platt
Joined SWA: 1967
Education: Master of City Planning, 1959 Harvard Graduate School of Design; Bachelor of Architecture, 1953 University of Florida
Academic Activities: Director, Land Development Studio, Harvard University Graduate School of Design
Professional Affiliations: Associate Member, American Planning Association; Fellow, American Institute of Architects; Affiliate Member, American Society of Landscape Architects; Member, Urban Land Institute; Member, Institute of Urban Design
Registration: Florida, California

James G. Reeves
Joined SWA: 1970
Education: Master of Landscape Architecture, 1970 University of Michigan; Bachelor of Architecture, 1967 University of Texas; Sphinx Honorary Fraternity, 1960-1961 University of Arkansas
Academic Activities: Visiting Critic, Harvard University Graduate School of Design; Teaching Fellow, University of Michigan

Professional Affiliations: Member, American Society of Landscape Architects

R. Joseph Runco
Joined SWA: 1981
Education: Master of Landscape Architecture with Distinction, 1981 Harvard University Graduate School of Design; Bachelor of Science in Landscape Architecture, 1978 Oregon State University
Academic Activities: Teaching Assistant, Harvard University Graduate School of Design; Guest Studio Critic, University of Georgia
Professional Affiliations: Member, American Society of Landscape Architects
Registration: Texas, Florida

Eduardo J. Santaella
Joined SWA: 1980
Education: Master in Landscape Architecture with Distinction, 1980 Harvard University Graduate School of Design; Ingeniero Civil, Universidad Central de Venezuela; Master of Science in Civil Engineering, Carnegie Institute of Technology; Bachelor of Science in Civil Engineering, Carnegie Institute of Technology
Academic Activities: Guest Lecturer, Universidad Central, Venezuela; Guest Lecturer, Universidad Nacional Autonoma, Mexico; Approved Instructor, National Council of State Garden Clubs, Inc.
Professional Affiliations: Member, American Society of Landscape Architects; Member, American Society of Civil Engineers; Member, Sociedad Bolivariana de Arquitectos; Member, Colegio de Ingenieros de Venezuela
Registration: Registered Professional Engineer, Venezuela (Colegio de Ingenieros de Venezuela)

Michael Sardina
Joined SWA: 1972
Education: Master of Landscape Architecture, 1972 University of Michigan; Bachelor of Landscape Architecture, 1968 Michigan State University
Academic Activities: Teaching Fellow, University of Michigan; Guest Lecturer, Harvard University Graduate School of Design
Professional Affiliations: Member, American Society of Landscape Architects; Member, Urban Design Advisory Coalition; Member, Waterfronts Institute
Registration: Massachusetts, California, Connecticut, New York, North Carolina, Rhode Island

Kevin Shanley
Joined SWA: 1973
Education: Graduate Studies in Landscape Architecture, 1977-1978 Harvard University Graduate School of Design; 1969-1972 University of Santa Clara
Professional Affiliations: Member, American Society of Landscape Architects

Elizabeth Shreeve
Joined: 1984
Education: Master of Landscape Architecture, 1983 Harvard Graduate School of Design; Bachelor of Arts cum Laude in Geology, 1978 Harvard College
Academic Activities:
Guest Lecturer, University of California, Berkeley; Guest Lecturer, California State Polytechnic University, San Luis Obispo
Professional Affiliations: Member, American Planning Association

Wendy Simon
Joined SWA: 1968
Education: Bachelor of Arts, 1961 San Francisco State College; 1959-1960 University of California, Berkeley

Monica Simpson
Joined SWA: 1980
Education: Bachelor of Science cum Laude in Landscape Architecture, 1980 California State Polytechnic University, Pomona
Academic Activities: Guest Lecturer, University of Houston
Professional Affiliations: Member, American Society of Landscape Architects; Member, American Planning Association; Member, Architects, Designers and Planners for Social Responsibility
Registration: Virginia, Maryland, Texas

David Thompson
Joined SWA: 1981
Education: Bachelor of Landscape Architecture, 1981 Louisiana State University

Donald H. Tompkins
Joined SWA: 1975
Education: Master of Landscape Architecture, 1962 Harvard University Graduate School of Design; Bachelor of Science, Landscape Architecture, 1958 California State Polytechnic University, Pomona
Academic Activities: Lecturer, University of California, Los Angeles; Lecturer, University of California, Irvine; Lecturer, California State Polytechnic University; Lecturer, Long Beach State University
Professional Affiliations: President, Southern California Chapter, American Society of Landscape Architects, 1990; Member, Urban Land Institute; Member, Building Industry Association; Member, Los Angeles Headquarters Association; Member, American Society of Landscape Architects
Registration: California, Oregon

Douglas S. Way, Ph.D.
Education: Doctor of Philosophy in Applied Geomorphology, 1982 Clark University; Master of Arts in Geography, 1979 Clark University; Master of Landscape Architecture, 1968 Harvard Graduate School of Design; Bachelor of Landscape Architecture, 1967 University of Wisconsin; Studies in Civil Engineering, 1962-1965 Iowa State University
Academic Activities: Professor and Chairman, Department of Landscape Architecture, 1986 - present, Ohio State University; Adjunct Professor, Department of Landscape Architecture 1985-1986, Virginia Polytechnic Institute; Research Associate, Center for Energy and Environmental Studies, 1984-1986, Boston University; Associate Professor, Assistant Chairman and Research Associate, 1979-1985, Harvard University Graduate School of Design; Distinguished Visiting Professor, 1975, Utah State University; Assistant Professor and Research Associate in Landscape Architecture, 1970-1974, Harvard University Graduate School of Design; Instructor and Research Associate in Landscape Architecture, 1968-1970, Harvard University Graduate School of Design; Director and Faculty for over 50 short courses in Aerial Photographic Interpretation /Remote Sensing/Terrain Analysis; Member of faculty for over 20 short courses in Landscape Resource Analysis Techniques Computer Geographic Information Systems
Professional Affiliations: American Society of Landscape Architects Accreditation Board; Past Chairman, American Society of Photogrammetry/Applications Engineering Committee

Susan Whitin
Joined SWA: 1979
Education: Master of Landscape Architecture, 1976 University of Michigan; Bachelor of Arts with Honors in Art History, 1970 Connecticut College
Academic Activities: Teaching Assistant, University of Michigan School of Architecture; Lecturer and Visiting Critic, California State Polytechnic University, San Luis Obispo, California

Professional Affiliations: Member, American Society of Landscape Architects; Member, Urban Land Institute; Member, Los Angeles Headquarters Association
Registration: California

John L. Wong
Joined SWA: 1974, 1976
Education: Fellow in Landscape Architecture, 1980-1981 Rome Prize, American Academy in Rome; Master of Landscape Architecture in Urban Design, 1978 Harvard Graduate School of Design; Bachelor of Arts in Landscape Architecture with Honors, 1974 University of California, Berkeley; Associate in Arts in Architecture, 1971 City College of San Francisco
Academic Activities: Visiting Critic and Instructor, Harvard University Graduate School of Design and University of California, Berkeley
Professional Affiliations: Member, American Society of Landscape Architects; Member, Institute for Urban Design; Associate Member, Urban Land Institute; Member, City Club of San Francisco; Society of Fellows, Regional Representative, American Academy in Rome
Registration: California

MAJOR WORKS

主要作品集

THE APPROACH TO DESIGN

デザインの手法

The act of creation is a rich conversation between the creator and the thing created and those who experience the thing created.

The SWA Group professionals approach the design of our environment as a spirited act of communication: a complex, multi-layered, ongoing conversation between the natural world and the man-made world, between the past, the present and the future, between hard-driven pragmatics and the tenuous vapor of dreams. It can be a loud conversation — sometimes bordering on cacophony and chaos — between people and between ideas: builders, users, bankers, politicians, designers, technicians, artisans, theoreticians, and wise men and fools both, all whispering and shouting ideas: the mundane and the sublime, the reactive and the revolutionary, the obscure and the bold, the pragmatic and the unreal.

On occasion we may direct the entire conversation or we might only play a bit part in the interaction. We sometimes join in at the very beginning of the conversation or we just tag on at the end of the party, but we invariably bring with us a two-pronged instrument that uniquely shapes our voice in this creative act of communication.

The first prong of our tool is pragmatic problem definition and the finding of intrinsic structure in potential problem solutions. The second prong is the introduction of extrinsic structure, value, and preconception into the solution finding conversation. There is a continuous and powerful dialectic between the two throughout the conversation, with each querying, challenging and informing the other. Like a tuning fork, the two connected prongs resonate in equilibrium, creating a particular energy that would not be present in either fork alone or in forks out of balance.

In The SWA Group, which is made up of many practicing professionals working at hugely different scales, there is a strong commonality to our approach to problem solving and to our search for intrinsic structure. We have trained together to define problems in interesting and innovative ways, to consistently seek to broaden the contextual envelope, and to find order and pattern in a myriad of constraints. Educated in the 1960s and 1970s, many of the designers were taught to question and challenge the status quo, to experiment and to open the floor up to the best idea. Specific methods, tools and techniques evolve over time and are quickly shared among the designers and among the offices.

On the other hand, the very different backgrounds and current interests of our professionals lead to the introduction of widely divergent extrinsic structure. The body of our work shows the progressive development of various ideas that are clearly the result of the introduction of distinct and distinguishable values and preconceptions from each of our designers. These many philosophies enrich one another in an ongoing interplay of ideas and built form. Some designers, highly attuned to and informed by their cultural surrounds, experiment freely with first one and then another expressive form, demonstrating a remarkable range of versatility. They challenge absolute meanings and answers, exploring the periphery and subtle references around primary meanings and focal points. Others, eschewing changing values, pursue a more singular line of inquiry evolving an idea or ideas in a continuum that spans a career. It is here that landscapes of all scales have the potential to become art, for city or townscape to become community, for mere location to become place, expressing deeply rooted cultural values.

創造するという行為は，創造者と創造されるものと創造されたものを体験する者との間の豊かな会話である．

SWAは，環境のデザインを，コミュニケーションの活発な行動としてとらえてアプローチする．それは，自然と人がつくり出した世界の間で，過去，現在，未来の間で，あるいはまた確固とした合理主義と曖昧な空想や夢の間で，複雑で幾重にも重なって進められる会話である．ときには人々やアイデアをめぐって起こる不協和音や混沌に直面しながら，大きな声で交わされる会話である．それは，建築業者，利用者，銀行家，政治家，デザイナー，技術者，職人，理論家の間で，また賢者と患者の間で囁かれたり叫ばれたりするアイデアであり，世俗的なものも卓越したものも，反動的なものも革命的なものも，些細なものも大胆なものも，そして現実的なものも夢のようなものも含めて，いろいろと会話される．

私たちは，こうした会話において，その全体を指導することもあれば，そこでの交流の一部分にしか参加しないこともある．ときには，会話の最初から参加することも，あるいは最後に少しだけ参加することもある．しかし，こうした創造的なコミュニケーションの行動において私たちの意見をユニークに形づくる，どんなときも私たちが携えている2つのすぐれた武器がある．

その1つは，合理的に問題を解決することであり，潜在的な問題解決において，それぞれ固有の構造を見出すことである．2つ目は，問題解決のための会話に，外部からの構造や価値や予測を導入することである．両者はお互いに問い直し，挑戦し，知らしめることで，徹頭徹尾会話するという，絶え間ない，力強い対立がそこには存在する音叉のように，2つの関連する矛先は，ばらばらの片方やバランスしないままでは存在し得ない特殊なエネルギーを生み出しながら，釣り合って共鳴する．

さまざまなスケールの仕事に関わる，多様な専門家集団であるSWAでは，問題解決へのアプローチや，固有の構造を追求するための強力な共通点がある．すなわち，私たちは，一貫して文脈的に枠組みを広げ続けられるように，そして無数にある制約の中で秩序やパターンを見出せるように，興味深く，革新的な方法で問題を明らかにしていくという訓練を一緒に受けていた．1960年代から1970年代にかけて教育を受けた私たちデザイナーの多くは，現状に疑問を持ち，チャレンジし，試し，そして最良のアイデアに到達できるように基盤を広げておくことを教えられた．時間とともに明確な方法，手段，技術が導き出され，素早くデザイナーの間や事務所の中全体に浸透した．

他方，私たちの分野では，もっと違った背景や現在の関心事が，広く分岐した外的な構造の導入を必要ともしていた．私たちの仕事は実質的に，明らかにデザイナーそれぞれが持つ，明瞭で判別しやすい価値づけや予測の導入の結果として出てくる，多くのアイデアの発展した形となって表れる．こうした多くのフィロソフィが，進行中のアイデアの相互作用や形態の構築に次々と豊かに反映されていく．あるデザイナーたちは，文化的な状況にうまく並みはずれた多面的な才能を発揮しながら，次から次へと豊かな表現力をもって，自由に実験を続けていく．彼らは，根源的な意味や焦点を取り巻く外面的かつ微妙な関係を探究しながら，絶対的な意味や解答を引き出す努力をする．他の人たちは，それまでの仕事の経歴を通して，アイデアを発展させるという，1本のラインの延長線上で，大きく価値感を変えない範囲で仕事をしている．あらゆるスケールのランドスケープがアートとなる可能性をもっている．すなわち，文化的な価値に深く根ざした中で表現されることで，都市や街はコミュニティとなり，単なる場所が意味のある場となり得る．

PLANNING
プランニング

One goal of The SWA Group Planning is to marshal the dynamics of urban growth to create a sense of community and place. Growth can be viewed as a positive or negative part of urban life. It provides new wealth and new opportunities, and increases the element of choice and variety. It also can create sprawl, environmental degradation, chaos and social disintegration. The processes, means and techniques of SWA Planning are all designed to produce a sense of environmental suitability, a sense of community, a sense of place.

In the broadest sense, SWA Planning involves the community in matters of environmental concern. The Golden Gate National Recreation Area Plan prepared by SWA has protected an open space and environmental resource for more than 15 years while allowing its use as an escape from urban tensions. The San Diego Embarcadero Plan re-integrated the city with its waterfront. After being cut off from effective use and access for half a century, the renaissance of downtown San Diego was anchored by an urban design plan featuring civic purpose, public use and enjoyment.

Where The SWA Group has had planning presence for several decades, such as in Boca Raton, Florida, or Irvine, California, the work has produced exemplary new communities. Founded upon the dreams of their early pioneers, these communities have had integrated land planning, urban design and urban landscape design that have made them unified places with a sense of arrival, identity and community feeling that separates them from the surrounding sprawling suburbs.

In recent years SWA planning has extended to areas around the world where growth or environmental concern have come to the forefront. In such diverse terrains as found in Japan, Taiwan, Turkey or Portugal, our planners and designers are looking anew at our basic philosophy of the balance of environmental and economic concerns. Finding this balance has been a key element of our planning approach for more than 30 years. This conviction that a balance can be struck between responsible use of resources while still sustaining economic growth and social opportunity has resulted in a series of long-range plans that have established an enduring framework for land use.

SWAのプランニングの目的の1つは，コミュニティや場のセンスを創出できるように，都市の成長のダイナミックスを導き出すことである．成長は，都市生活のポジティブな部分であり，またネガティブな部分でもあり得る．それは新たな富と新しい機会を提供し，選択の要素と種類を増やす．しかし，同時にスプロールや環境悪化，混乱，社会的分裂を引き起こす．SWAのプランニングのプロセスや手法や技術はすべて，環境との調和，コミュニティや場のセンスを生み出すために作られている．

広い意味では，SWAのプランニングは環境的な関心という意味でコミュニティまで含む．ゴールデンゲート・ナショナルレクリエーションエリア計画は，オープンスペースや環境的な資源を15年以上にわたって保護し続けた一方，都市の緊張をほぐすいこいの場としての利用を可能とした．サンディエゴのエンバーカデロ計画では，街とウォーターフロントをいま一度統合した．有効な使い方やアクセスを半世紀もの間放棄していた後で，サンディエゴのダウンタウンのルネッサンスは，市民の目的や公共の用途・楽しみを中心に計画し直されたのである．

SWAは，フロリダのボカラトンやカリフォルニアのアーバインなどで，数十年にわたってプランニングに関わり続けて，模範的なコミュニティをつくり出した．初期のパイオニアたちの夢の上に築き上げられたこうしたコミュニティは，土地利用計画，アーバンデザイン，都市のランドスケープデザインなどが一体となってでき上がったものである．これらによって生み出されたコミュニティの魅力やアイデンティティが，周辺のスプロール地区との間に一線を画している．

最近のSWAのプランニング分野の仕事は，都市の成長や環境問題の関心が高まりつつある世界各地に広がっている．日本，台湾，トルコ，ポルトガルなど，さまざまな土地で展開される中で，私たちプランナーやデザイナーは，環境と経済のバランスという基本的なフィロソフィを改めて見つめ直している．このバランスを見出すことは，30年以上にわたる私たちのプランニング・アプローチの重要な要素となっている．バランスは，経済的な成長や社会的な好機を維持する一方で，資源の責任ある使い方によって達成されるという確信は，土地利用の永続的な枠組を形づくる一連の長期計画の結果生じるものである．

GGNRA-Golden Gate National Recreation Area

Marin County, California, U.S.A.

ゴールデンゲート・ナショナル・レクリエーションエリア

The GGNRA is one of the largest aggregations of public lands in a United States metropolitan area. It contains more than 40,000 ha (100,000 acres) on both sides of the Golden Gate Bridge, in San Francisco and Marin Counties. The SWA Group prepared the environmental and park studies to assist the National Park Service in planning the 36,000-hectare (90,000-acre) portion in Marin County.

The master plan that evolved from this process has worked. The fact that it did not entail the controversy of other US National Parks was due to the process that SWA designed with the Park Service team. This process included full participation of the public in more than 100 public workshops. The data was exceptional, for this was the first National Park to have a complete environmental atlas prepared as part of the initial planning process.

The park plan balanced resource preservation and public recreational goals, from the Golden Gate Headlands to Point Reyes National Seashore. It also allowed for the gradual absorption of military installations into the park.

To better serve the inner-city residents in San Francisco, the two areas of the park are linked by ferry and bus transportation. The emphasis on water transportation ensured that the waters of the Golden Gate, the Pacific, and San Francisco Bay (all bordering the parklands) would be part of the park experience. The bonus was that crossing the Golden Gate by boat reduced traffic impact on the bridge and began the recreational experience in the city. Thus, with the addition of the Bay and Gate to the park experience, the northern and southern parklands were united.

"When we convinced the Park Service that a more active community involvement was necessary, they were at first reluctant, but then launched a highly successful and exhaustive series of 100 educational and planning workshops involving every facet of the community."
– Kalvin Platt

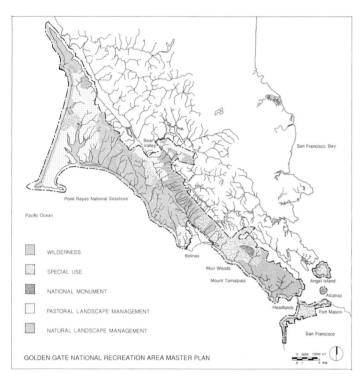

GOLDEN GATE NATIONAL RECREATION AREA MASTER PLAN

WILDERNESS

SPECIAL USE

NATIONAL MONUMENT

PASTORAL LANDSCAPE MANAGEMENT

NATURAL LANDSCAPE MANAGEMENT

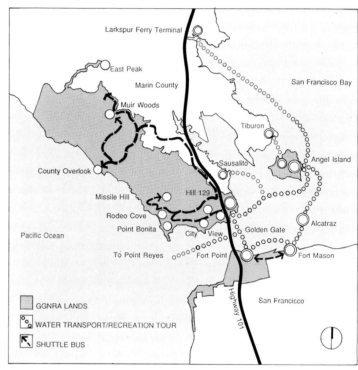

GGNRA LANDS

WATER TRANSPORT/RECREATION TOUR

SHUTTLE BUS

計画地は，アメリカの大都市の中でも最大規模の公共の土地の集合体で，金門橋（ゴールデンゲートブリッジ）を挟む両側のサンフランシスコ市とマリンカウンティにまたがる40,000ha以上の土地からなる．SWAは国立公園局の要請を受け，マリンカウンティに属する約36,000haの土地の環境および公園の調査を担当した．

このプロセスを通じて提案されたマスタープランは有効に働いた．すなわち，国立公園局と協働して計画に当たったために，アメリカ各地の他の国立公園と比較して煩雑な議論を伴わずに進めることができた．このプロセスは，100回以上のワークショップを通じて多くの市民の参加を得ている．この計画は当初からの計画プロセスの一部として，完全な環境地図を準備して着手した，初めての国立公園計画であったため，ここで得られたデータはたいへん重要なものであった．

この公園計画は，ゴールデンゲート・ヘッドランズからポイントレイズにわたり，資源の保存と市民のレクリエーションという目的をうまくバランスさせている．また，ここでは陸軍施設を公園の中にうまく取り込むことも考えられている．

サンフランシスコ市内の住民によりよいサービスを提供するために，公園の2つのエリアがフェリーとバスで結ばれている．特に水上交通の強調は，この公園をとりまくゴールデンゲート，太平洋，サンフランシスコ湾の水そのものが，公園体験の一部となることを確実にしている．さらに，ゴールデンゲートをボートで渡ることは，橋の交通量を軽減し，さらに市内の人々にレクリエーション的な体験を提供することになる．このように，公園での体験に，湾やゲートが加わることで，公園の北部と南部が一体化する．

「私たちが公園局の人たちに，もっと活発なコミュニティや市民の参加が必要だと説明したとき，最初は気の進まない様子だった．しかし，それから彼らは，好結果を生んだ徹底的な，あらゆるコミュニティの人々を含めての100回にも及ぶワークショップを始めたのである．」**カルビン・プラット**

Elkhorn at Sun Valley

Sun Valley, Idaho, U.S.A.
サンバレーのエルクホーン

Sun Valley needed to expand its recreational and lodging facilities dramatically in order to maintain its image as a first-class, year-round resort. An extensive effort to learn about the existing local development, significant national resort communities, Alpine villages and the environmental and architectural components that formulate their unique sense of place helped to enrich the design for Elkhorn.

The master plan creates a compact, pedestrian-scale, European-style village surrounded by open fields. By locating part of the golf course in the foothills of the steeper slopes, we were successful in restricting either initial or future development from the intermediate hills and ridges, thus preserving uncluttered views to the distant mountains. It was always our philosophy that views up and out were more precious than views down onto the village.

The recreational connections to Sun Valley were always perceived of as more critical than the automobile connections. For the first several months in the planning, no actual road connection was even shown on the plan. Today, this interconnection between the two resorts is multimodal. This eliminates the need to drive back and forth, saving energy and parking requirements. An efficient bus, minibus and carriage system further supports this program.

The design complements the environment by locating the village in the central bowl. The contrast of the compact village in the center of the treeless open basin further emphasizes the open space to development ratio.

"The mission to create a contemporary, complete resort in a pristine mountain valley hidden from any existing development and that would complement historic Sun Valley development was indeed a unique challenge."
— **Kalvin Platt**

"The design's most successful mark on the landscape is in the myriad of recreation connections established between the sister resort communities."
— **Thomas Adams**

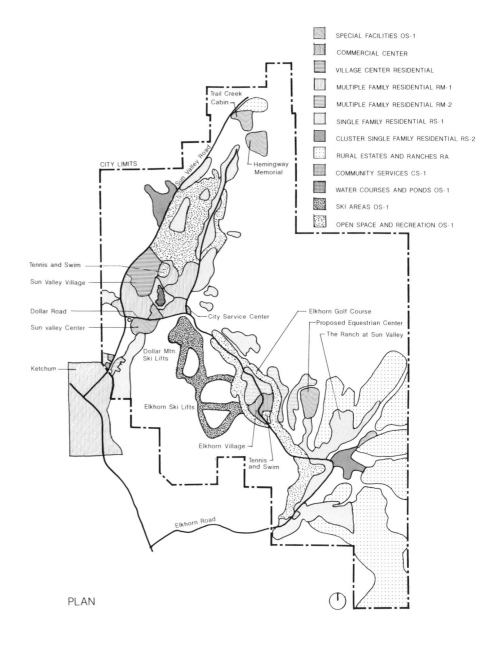

SPECIAL FACILITIES OS-1
COMMERCIAL CENTER
VILLAGE CENTER RESIDENTIAL
MULTIPLE FAMILY RESIDENTIAL RM-1
MULTIPLE FAMILY RESIDENTIAL RM-2
SINGLE FAMILY RESIDENTIAL RS-1
CLUSTER SINGLE FAMILY RESIDENTIAL RS-2
RURAL ESTATES AND RANCHES RA
COMMUNITY SERVICES CS-1
WATER COURSES AND PONDS OS-1
SKI AREAS OS-1
OPEN SPACE AND RECREATION OS-1

PLAN

サンバレーでは，最高級の，通年型のリゾート地としてのイメージを保持しつつ，レクリエーションや宿泊施設を大幅に拡充する必要が生じてきた。既存の地域的な開発や重要な全国規模のリゾート施設，アルパインビレッジ，それぞれの場のユニークなセンスを引き出す環境的・建築的な構成要素などを調べ，そこから学ぶという広範な調査が，エルクホーンのデザインを充実させるのに大いに役立った。

　マスタープランでは，オープンスペースに囲まれるかたちでコンパクトな歩行者スケールのヨーロッパスタイルのビレッジを配置している。急斜面の丘の麓にゴルフコースを配置することで，遠くの山の眺望を失わずに，その途中の丘や尾根を，現在も将来的にも乱開発から守ることに成功している。ビレッジの中から見上げたり，遠くを見晴らしたときの眺めの方が，丘の上からビレッジを見下ろしたときの眺めよりずっと大切であるというのが，私たちがいつも考えているフィロソフィである。

　サンバレーにおけるさまざまなレクリエーション活動の相互の結びつきは，自動車の動線より重要である。計画初期の数か月は，全く自動車道路は図面に現われなかったくらいである。現在では，2つのリゾート地を結ぶ手段はバスやミニバス，馬車など何種類もあり，いままでのようにマイカーで行ったり来たりすることもなく，エネルギーの節約や駐車場問題の軽減に役立っている。

　谷間の中央の盆地にビレッジを配置して環境づくりのデザイン的な要としている。樹木のない広大な盆地の中心に建てられたコンパクトなビレッジは開発面積率以上に，かえってオープンスペースを強調する結果となっている。

　「これまでのいかなる開発にも影響されることなく残った，自然そのままの山間の谷間に，由緒あるサンバレーの開発を補完し得るような最新かつ完全なリゾート施設をつくり出すという仕事は，実にユニークなチャレンジであった。」
**　　　　　　　　　　　　　　カルビン・プラット**
　「ランドスケープにおいて，デザイン的に最もうまくいくための秘訣は，周辺の複数のリゾートコミュニティ間で，いかにうまく数多くのレクリエーションの連携ができるかということにかかっている。」
**　　　　　　　　　　　　　　トーマス・アダムス**

San Diego Embarcadero Master Plan

San Diego, California U.S.A.

サンディエゴ・エンバーカデロ

In 1977 The SWA Group prepared a master plan for the redevelopment of San Diego's downtown waterfront. The Unified Port District is a jurisdiction separate from the city. Thus, the master plan had to address the port's goals of generating tourist revenue, the city's goals of spurring downtown renewal with a striking civic edge, and the California Coastal Commission's goals of opening the waterfront to people. In accommodating these multiple goals, the plan has endured, largely intact, over the 15 years since its inception. It is still being implemented in close conformance to the SWA guidelines and long-range design goals.

Downtown San Diego has prospered and grown substantially with the development of the Embarcadero. The marinas, piers, parks, walkways, promenades, and amusement areas have given a new life to a previously run-down, derelict area with little civic use. The linear nature of the plan allowed a series of functional areas to be related to downtown use areas. The design integrated these different functions into an overall civic concept and provided a green setting for downtown with spectacular views of the city.

"San Diego, like so many port cities had turned their back to their water's edge. We were successful in reorientating the growth of downtown back to Embarcadero and the bay."

– Jim Reeves

SWAは1977年にサンディエゴ・ダウンタウンのウォーターフロント再開発のためのマスタープランを作成した．それまで港湾地区は市とは別の管轄下にあった．そこでマスタープランは，観光収入の獲得，ダウンタウンの活性化，ウォーターフロントの市民への開放など関係各署の目的を満たすものでなければならなかった．こうした多くの目的を充足しながら，マスタープランは大きな変更もなく，現在も，ほとんどそのままの形で整備されつつある．

サンディエゴのダウンタウンの成長・繁栄は，エンバーカデロ，つまり船着き場としての発展に同調していた．衰弱し，ほとんど放棄されてしまった地域が，マリーナ，桟橋，公園，歩道，プロムナード，アミューズメント施設などの整備によって新たな命を吹き込まれた．計画地は海岸に沿って線状に延びており，それぞれの機能をもつ地区がダウンタウンと密接に結びつけられた．デザインは，異なる機能をもつ地区を，包括的な市のコンセプトに沿ってまとめ上げ，すばらしい都市景観を生み出すとともにダウンタウンに緑の環境を提供した．

「他の港湾都市の多くがそうであるように，サンディエゴもウォーターフロントに背を向けて発展していた．私たちの成功は，いま一度エンバーカデロや湾に向けてダウンタウンが発展するように再調整したことによる．」 ジェームズ・リーブズ

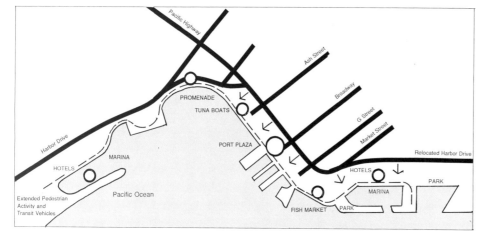

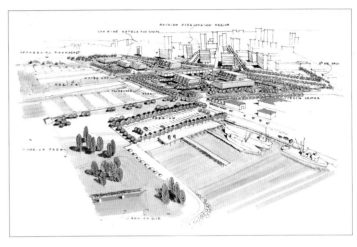

Village

Arvida Resort Community at Boca Raton

Boca Raton, Florida, U.S.A.

アーバイダ・リゾートコミュニティ

Boca Raton was an early, prestigious Florida beachfront resort — a product of the 1920s boom and the creative energies of Addison Mizner, a legendary architect of those times. After the depression, the hotel and much of the land around it languished until Arthur Vining Davis, founder of Alcoa Aluminum, bought them in the fifties, founded Arvida and brought in a California-based development team headed by Chuck Cobb of Kaiser-Aetna in the seventies.

The SWA Group was called upon, then, to conceive of a resort community for the 2,000 ha (5,000 acres), including the legendary Hotel and Club. As most of the land was far removed from the beachfront that had been the focus of all Florida resorts, the plan created a connection by continuity of resort image, landscaped roadway and thematic environmental and urban design elements. These elements included setbacks, lakes and waterways, golf frontage, graphics, entries and thematic wall structures.

Natural hammocks and drainageways were planned into a series of villages' connected by bicycle and pedestrianways. The City of Boca Raton adopted many of the Arvida urban design elements and added special facilities at the beaches. Residents could participate in the Florida environment and sense that Boca Raton was a "special place."

The SWA Group's role over an 18-year period that saw much of the lands developed was that of overall environmental quality control, innovation in Town Planning and interface with the Boca Raton community. This combination of land planning and landscape design follows from the unique approach of the firm. Land planning involved establishing overall goals and guidelines for the physical development of the land. It included identifying programmatic aspects of housing projects, retail, office, special use, recreation and civic needs. It also involved relating these to the environmental character of the land and balancing these with the economic

demands of the real estate marketplace. Social requirements of transportation, education and civic needs were worked out with a team of consultants. Finally, the plans had to be coordinated with the operating goals of the Arvida Corporation and receive the approval of the local public agencies.

Landscape design followed this planning effort, to implement the guidelines for infrastructure of roads, parks, open space, waterways, community facilities and recreation. Key items were designed by SWA directly. Many other elements were designed by local architects, engineers and landscape architects under the design review of SWA. By designing key elements such as the Beach Club and the Park of Commerce and villages at Boca West, Les Jardins and Millpond, SWA demonstrated the community building approach and character desired for the entire community. Consistency with other projects was assured by review and guidelines, creating an overall community quality.

ボカラトンはフロリダの海浜リゾートの中でも、初期にできた最高級のもので、1920年代のブームの産物であり、当時の伝説的な建築家アディソン・マイズナーが創出した傑作である。大恐慌以降、その周辺のホテルや土地の多くは見捨てられ、さびれていたが、50年代にアルコア・アルミニウム社の創設者であるアーサー・バイニング・デイビスが一帯を買い取った。その後、70年代にアーバイダを設立し、カリフォルニアを本拠として活躍していたチャック・コッブを代表とするディベロッパー、カイザー・エトナ社に、この開発を依頼した。

SWAは、伝説的なホテルやクラブハウスを含む2,000haの敷地にリゾートコミュニティをつくる計画を依頼された。敷地のほとんどは、かつてはフロリダのリゾートの中心であった海岸から離れているため、計画は、リゾートのイメージを連続できるよう、ランドスケープを施された道路やテーマごとの環境デザイン、アーバンデザインの要素を結びつけている。デザインの要素としては、

建物のセットバック、湖や水路、ゴルフ場の見晴らし、グラフィックス、入口、そしてテーマ別の壁面などが挙げられる。自転車路や歩行者路でつながった連続するビレッジの中に既存の大木が保存され、また、排水路が計画された。ボカラトン市は、アーバイダのアーバンデザインの要素を数多く採用し、海岸に海水浴客用の施設を追加した。住民は、フロリダの環境に溶け込み、ボカラトンを特別な場所として感じとることができる。

過去18年間の開発の様子を見ると、SWAの果たした役割は、環境全体の質的なコントロール、そして新しいタウンプランニング手法の導入、ボカラトンのコミュニティとの接点づくりである。土地利用計画とランドスケープデザインの結合は、SWAのユニークな計画手法に基づいている。土地利用計画では、全体的な目標を設定し、実際の開発のためのガイドラインを作成した。そして、住宅、商業、業務、特殊用途、レクリエーション、そして公共用途などのすべてを計画的に関連づけ

ていく。また、これらの施設をそれぞれの敷地の環境に関連づけ、さらに不動産としての経済的な価値づけにも合致させていくことでもある。交通、教育、公共施設等社会的な要請に対しては、コンサルタントとチームを組んで作業した。最終的には、計画はアーバイダ社の目指す業務目標と一致させなければならないし、ローカルな公的機関の承認も得なければならない。

このプランニング・プロセスに続いて、ランドスケープデザインは、道路、公園、オープンスペース、水路、コミュニティやレクリエーション施設などのインフラのためのガイドラインを具現化していく。重要なアイテムはSWAによって直接デザインされた。その他の多くのエレメントはSWAの監修の下で、地元の建築家や技術者、ランドスケープ・アーキテクトによってデザインされた。ビーチクラブ、パーク・オブ・コマース、レ・ジャルダンやミルポンド、ボカウエストのビレッジなどの重要な構成要素をSWAがデザインすることで、コミュニティ全体に求められている建物の特徴を示すことができた。他のプロジェクトとの一貫性は、デザイン監修やガイドラインによって可能となり、それらが全体として質の高いコミュニティの創出を可能にした。

計画が連続的に立てられ、質的なコントロールがうまくいった結果、フロリダにユニークなコミュニティが誕生した。ランドスケープデザインが質をさらに高め、いまやボカラトンの特徴である「場のセンス(sence of place)」を生み出した。

「開発においては、よいプランだけでは充分ではない。開発基準への厳しい、徹底した執着もまた必要である。開発期間を通しての、主たるデザイナーによる途切れのない指導が、適切なマーケットを獲得する質の高い環境を生み出すと同時に、その他のまだ開発されていない部分にまで、付加価値を与える。」　　　エドアルド・サンテーラ

「ボカラトンは、フロリダに残された最も魅力のある生活および仕事の場である。アーバイダ開発のビジョンやその模範的なプランニングやデザインの実施は、東海岸ではユニークな価値ある生活を可能にした。いろいろな意味で、ボカラトンの成熟した多様性は、将来の大いなる模範となる。」　　　フレデリック・パリアニ

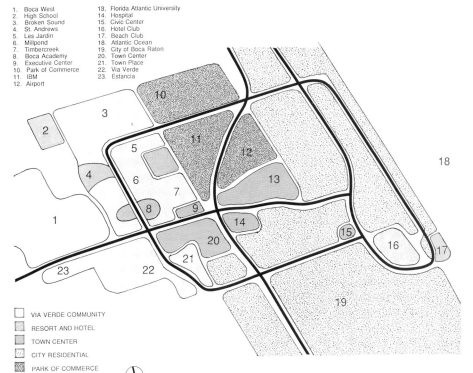

1. Boca West
2. High School
3. Broken Sound
4. St. Andrews
5. Les Jardin
6. Millpond
7. Timbercreek
8. Boca Academy
9. Executive Center
10. Park of Commerce
11. IBM
12. Airport
13. Florida Atlantic University
14. Hospital
15. Civic Center
16. Hotel Club
17. Beach Club
18. Atlantic Ocean
19. City of Boca Raton
20. Town Center
21. Town Place
22. Via Verde
23. Estancia

☐ VIA VERDE COMMUNITY
▨ RESORT AND HOTEL
▨ TOWN CENTER
▨ CITY RESIDENTIAL
▨ PARK OF COMMERCE
☐ UNIVERSITY / SCHOOL

ARVIDA VILLAGES AT BOCA RATON

The results of the planning continuity and quality control have created an unique community in Florida. Landscape design has enhanced this quality and provided for a sense of place that is now a recognized aspect of Boca Raton. *"In development, a good plan is not enough. Strict and consistent adherence to a good set of development criteria is also essential. Uninterrupted guidance provided by the main designer during the development period not only results in quality environments that will capture the available markets, but will also create additional value for the unbuilt portions of any development."* **– Eduardo Santaella**

"Boca Raton remains one of the most attractive places to live and work in Florida. Arvida's development vision and its commitment to exemplary planning and design has created a quality of life unique on the east coast. In many ways, the maturing diversity of Boca Raton is a great model for the future." **– Rick Pariani**

Irvine Ranch Story

Irvine, California, U.S.A.
アーバインランチ

Introduction to the Irvine Ranch Story:

The Irvine Ranch has established itself as one of the most desirable places to live in Southern California. This reputation is principally due to the fact that The Irvine Company had the foresight to recognize the importance of design in the creation of new communities.

The SWA Group has provided land planning and design consultation to The Irvine Company on many of their most noteworthy projects such as Newport Center, Fashion Island, Mariner Square Apartments, Baywood Apartments, Promontory Point Apartments, Woodbridge, the Newport Coast, MacArthur Court, Jamboree Center and University Park.

The Irvine Ranch has gone through several distinct periods in its transition from a vast ranching and farming enterprise on more than 36,000 ha (90,000 acres) to one of the premier urban areas of the country.

The Early Period - Mid '60s to Mid '70s

The period from the mid '60s to mid '70s was one great opportunity for us. Management of The Irvine Company was dominated by people with great idealism about the kind of place they could build. For us it was a case of being at the right place at the right time. Projects like Newport Center, Fashion Island, University Park, Mariner Square, Baywood, Promontory Point, and Woodbridge were planned, designed, and, for the most part, built during this period. There was an opportunity and desire to be innovative on all of these projects. We all wanted to do great things.

University Park

University Park was an early experiment. The central ranch was beginning to develop the suburban sprawl pattern typical of Southern California. A more rational pattern of clustered, identifiable villages was begun with University Park. Community planning really had not advanced much since before the second World War. Radburn and the Greenbelt communities of the New Deal were still the best models. This community model has an internalized greenbelt amenity system which includes recreation facilities, schools, pedestrian circulation and open space. Around this greenbelt framework, the residential units are arranged.

University Park is based on these planning principles. In a similar way the residential units are arranged along streets and around auto courts with large open spaces on the other side away from the automobile. These interconnected green areas accommodate pedestrian circulation, recreation, parks, schools and a variety of human activities. A significant first for University Park was the introduction of townhouses which raised the residential density, but also allowed a great increase in the amount of green open space. This community stands as a highly successful example of innovative community design uncommon in Orange County during the 1960s.

Irvine Ranch　アーバインランチ

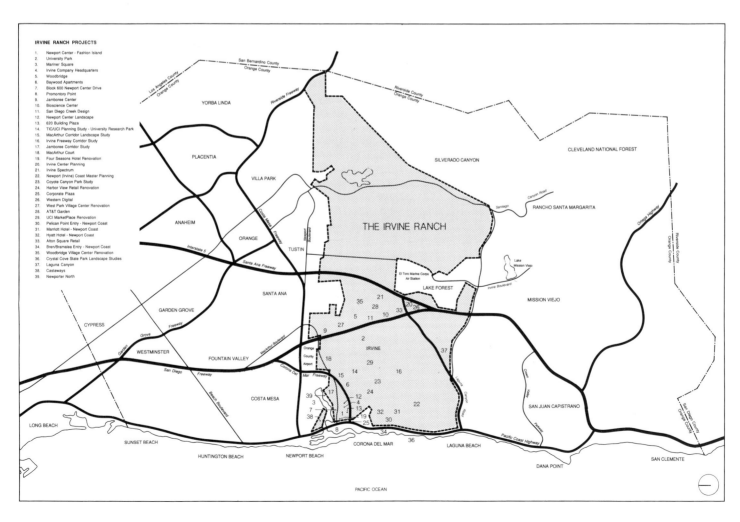

IRVINE RANCH PROJECTS

1. Newport Center - Fashion Island
2. University Park
3. Mariner Square
4. Irvine Company Headquarters
5. Woodbridge
6. Baywood Apartments
7. Block 600 Newport Center Drive
8. Promontory Point
9. Jamboree Center
10. Bioscience Center
11. San Diego Creek Design
12. Newport Center Landscape
13. 620 Building Plaza
14. TIC/UCI Planning Study - University Research Park
15. MacArthur Corridor Landscape Study
16. Irvine Freeway Corridor Study
17. Jamboree Corridor Study
18. MacArthur Court
19. Four Seasons Hotel Renovation
20. Irvine Center Planning
21. Irvine Spectrum
22. Newport (Irvine) Coast Master Planning
23. Coyote Canyon Park Study
24. Harbor View Retail Renovation
25. Corporate Plaza
26. Western Digital
27. West Park Village Center Renovation
28. AT&T Garden
29. UCI MarketPlace Renovation
30. Pelican Point Entry - Newport Coast
31. Marriott Hotel - Newport Coast
32. Hyatt Hotel - Newport Coast
33. Alton Square Retail
34. Bren/Bramalea Entry - Newport Coast
35. Woodbridge Village Center Renovation
36. Crystal Cove State Park Landscape Studies
37. Laguna Canyon
38. Castaways
39. Newporter North

1. はじめに

アーバインランチは，南カリフォルニアの最も理想的な住環境の1つであるとの評価を得ている．この評価は，主にアーバイン社が，新しいコミュニティをつくる際のデザインの重要性を認識する先見の明があったことによる．

SWAはアーバイン社に依頼されて，数多くの主要なプロジェクトの土地利用計画，デザイン監修を担当した．たとえば，ニューポートセンター，ファッションアイランド，マリーナスクエア・アパート，ベイウッドアパート，プロモントリーポイント・アパート，ウッドブリッジ，ニューポートコ

ースト，マッカーサーコート，ジャンボリーセンター，そしてユニバーシティパーク等である．

アーバインランチは，この36,000ha以上にわたる広大な農場地域が，国内有数のアーバンエリアへと変身するまでに，いくつかの明確な時期を経ている．

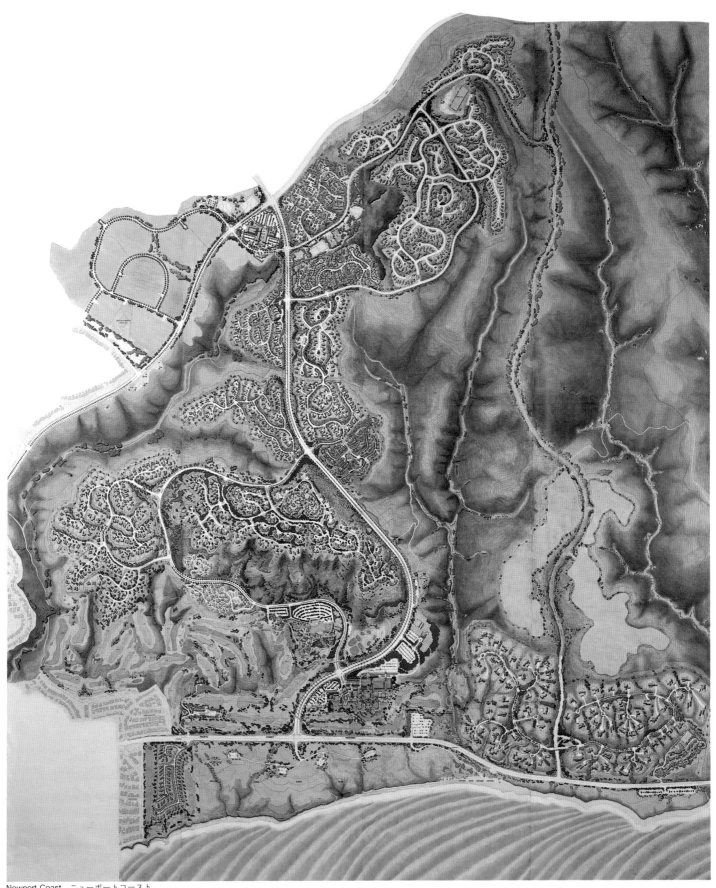

Newport Coast　ニューポートコースト

Baywood Apartments

Baywood Apartments is a significant milestone with more than 400 units and represents a high point in creating an inseparable relationship between the site, the buildings, and the landscape. Everything is in harmony. This design approach contrasts sharply with other communities built at the same time. In these projects, the buildings sit on engineered pads surrounded by 2:1 slopes. The landscape is applied like cosmetics. It's an afterthought.

At Baywood, we completely reshaped the site — sculpted it to accommodate and merge with the buildings. The success here is that the site appears to have never been touched. The great, gently rolling meadow is the central focus. Everything relates to the meadow. The landscape is a woodland. The buildings are nestled in the woods. The feeling of Baywood is that of a preexisting wooded site with a great meadow in the middle and buildings carefully placed in the trees.

Promontory Point

By contrast, the Promontory Point Apartments are very urban. It's a Mediterranean hill town with lush Mediterranean planting, rich paving, and fountain courtyards. The hill was made even higher by scooping out a new waterway connecting to Newport Bay. This allowed stepping the units down the hill and providing fantastic views for all. At first, the more than 500 units were overwhelming. But, as the Mediterranean landscape began to grow and flourish, Promontory Point took on the quality of a hillside village.

Mid '80s to Present

The period from the mid '80s to the present has been another period of tremendous opportunity for us with the Irvine Company. Unlike the earlier periods where we were working on a largely undeveloped ranch, we are now working within a mature community with everything in place, the cities and their governments. People live, work, and raise families here. Many of our projects deal with redevelopment or infill on remaining parcels. Working on these specific sites, our focus is more on creating a strong sense of place rather than structuring large, multiple land-use developments.

Some notable accomplishments: the complete renovation of Fashion Island and Newport Center, MacArthur Court, Jamboree Center, and the Newport Coast.

Photo by Steve Proehl

University Park　ユニバーシティパーク

Baywood Apartments　ベイウッドアパート

Promontry Point　プロモントリーポイント

2.　開発初期－1960年代中期から70年代中期まで

この時期は、私たちにとって絶好の機会であった。アーバイン社の経営は、これからつくり上げようとする都市について、偉大な理想をもった優秀な人々によって占められていた。私たちにとっては、まさに正しい場と時期を得た仕事であったといえる。ニューポートセンター、ファッションアイランド、ユニバーシティパーク、マリーナスクエア、ベイウッド、プロモントリーポイント、ウッドブリッジといったプロジェクトがこの時期に計画・設計され、そのほとんどがこの時期に完成している。これらのプロジェクトはいずれも革新的であることが求められ、また、そうしたいと願ってできたものである。私たちすべてが偉大な仕事を遂行したいと願っていた時期である。

●ユニバーシティパーク●

これは、ごく初期の試みである。敷地の中央部の農場地帯では、南カリフォルニアによくある典型的な郊外型のスプロール現象が起き始めていた。もう少し合理的なクラスター型の、アイデンティティをもったビレッジとして開発された最初の例がユニバーシティパークである。コミュニティ計画は、第2次世界大戦の前からほとんど進展していなかった。ニューディール政策の結果生まれた

ラドバーンやグリーンベルトといったコミュニティが、当時はまだ最良のモデルであった。このコミュニティ・モデルは、レクリエーション施設、学校、歩行者動線、オープンスペース等を含む内部のグリーンベルト、アメニティシステムを有するものである。このグリーンベルトの骨格の周辺に住宅が配置されていた。

ユニバーシティパークは、この計画理論に則っている。よく似た手法で、住戸ユニットは通り沿いに、あるいは駐車場広場に面して配置され、その反対側には車の入らない広いオープンスペースがつくられた。相互に連結した緑地帯は、歩行者動線、レクリエーション、公園、学校、あるいはさまざまな活動の場として利用される。ユニバーシティパークでの重要な初めての試みは、住居の密度を上げるだけでなく、緑地を飛躍的に増加させることにもつながるタウンハウスの導入である。ユニバーシティパークは、1960年代のオレンジカウンティではまだ一般的でなかった革新的なコミュニティのデザインとして、たいへんうまく成功した例といえる。

●ベイウッドアパート●

ベイウッドアパートは400以上の住戸群からなり、敷地と建物とランドスケープがみごとに調和した

例として画期的な作品である。すべてが調和を保っている。デザイン・アプローチは、同時期に建てられた他のコミュニティと比較して、対照的である。他のプロジェクトでは建物は2割勾配の斜面に囲まれた平らな造成面に建てられ、ランドスケープは化粧のように後から加えられていた。

しかしベイウッドでは、環境と建物が一体化するように、敷地を完全につくり直している。そして、ここでの成功は完成後に敷地が全く手を加えられなかったかのように見えることである。広大な、ゆるやかにうねる草原が中心に位置し、すべてがこの草原に結びついている。ランドスケープは森林を形成し、その中に住宅が点在する。ベイウッドから受ける印象は、中心に広々とした草原が広がり、そして木々の間に注意深く建物が配された既存の森林のようである。

●プロモントリーポイント●

対照的にプロモントリーポイント・アパートは、たいへん都市的で豊富な緑、鮮やかな舗装、そして噴水のあるコートヤードなどをもつ地中海風のヒルタウンである。丘はニューポート湾につながる新しい水路を掘削した際の土砂によって造成された。したがって段状に住戸ユニットを配置でき、どの住宅からもすばらしい眺めが可能となった。

MacArthur Court

Located across from the John Wayne Airport, MacArthur Court represents the desire to intensify land-use densities on previously developed property. Phase II proposes the addition of twin 15-story office towers and a parking structure to an existing low rise office complex. The design issues revolved around the need for identity, quality and integration.

Our attitudes were as much influenced by a context of randomly ordered, disparate developments as by the desire to create in concert with the new buildings a place with a sense of urbanity, elegance and quiet beauty.

The project takes an architecturally formal approach with the landscape. Tree hedges scribe its perimeter, blocks of Canary Island palms give a sense of monumentation to its corners and entries, and rows of Fan palms silhouette in the skyline highlighting its entry drive. The landscape is bold and revealing. As one approaches and moves through the complex, there is a clear sense of the individual landscape components, their relationship to one another and a sense of the larger whole they form.

The Newport Coast

The Newport Coast represents a milestone in accommodating both public and private interests. This is environment building of the highest order, creating a community and its setting while preserving and enhancing vast areas for the enjoyment and use of everyone.

The Newport Coast is 4,000 ha (10,000 acres) of California Coastline and foothills planned as a community, with more than 75% remaining in permanent open space and parkland. There will be more than 2,600 houses, two 18-hole golf courses, and five resort hotels. The Newport Coast is an example of the overwhelming importance of the landscape in community building.

What we are doing here with landscape on the Coast will create the character and image of this community in the tradition of the great California landscapes like that of Rancho Santa Fe, Carmel, Palos Verdes, Montecito, and Beverly Hills where buildings are nestled within the trees and the forest seems to have always been there.

"We are creating landscape on a grand scale. It is bold and simple: the natural landscape of the arroyos and hillsides, the groves of pines and Eucalyptus. This is a program of forestation, not landscaping." – ***Dick Law***

◀▲MacArthur Court　マッカーサーコート

▼Newport Coast　ニューポートコースト

Newport Center　ニューポートセンター

当初は500戸以上の住宅が他を圧倒していたが，地中海風のランドスケープの木々が成長して茂った現在は，ヒルサイド・ビレッジとしての特質を備えている．

3．80年代中期から現在まで

この時期は，アーバイン社と私たちにとって，もうひとつの絶好の機会であった．未開の農場地帯に計画を実現していくという初期とは異なり，街や行政施設も含めた必要なものが的確に配置されて，すでにでき上がったコミュニティの中に，なにかを計画していくという段階である．人々はここに住み，働き，そして家族を育てている．プロジェクトはこれまで以上の時間と労力を要するが，どの仕事の機会もそれぞれ意味深いものばかりである．プロジェクトの多くは，再開発か，残された土地へのインフィル型の開発である．こうした特殊な敷地への計画であるため，大規模で多目的な土地利用開発を構築するというより，より強い場のセンスを生み出すことを主眼としている．

特筆すべきものとしては，ファッションアイランドの全面改修，ニューポートセンター，マッカーサーコート，ジャンボリーセンター，そしてニューポートコーストが挙げられる．

●マッカーサーコート●

ジョン・ウェイン空港に相対するマッカーサーコートは，以前の施設をより高密度化することが求められていた．そこで第2期計画では，ツインの15階建オフィスビルと駐車場棟を既存の低層のオフィスビル群に追加することが提案された．デザイン的には，アイデンティティの確立，質の確保，そして全体をいかに統合するかが主眼とされた．

この計画に対する取り組みは，不規則かつ異種雑多な開発のコンテクストと同時に，都市的でエレガントで美しい環境につくり上げたいという欲求にも影響を受けた．

この計画は，ランドスケープの面でも建築的な秩序立ったアプローチがとられた．生け垣は境界を形づくり，一団のカナリーヤシが角地や入口の象徴的な雰囲気を醸し出し，スカイラインにシルエットを映し出すオウギヤシの並木が進入路を際立たせている．ランドスケープは大胆で啓発的である．人々がここを訪れ，この複合施設内を歩き回る時，それぞれ個別の景観要素や相互の関係，そして全体がつくり出す一体感をはっきりと読み取ることができる．

●ニューポートコースト●

ニューポートコーストは公共と民間双方の関心をうまく適合させた例として画期的なものである．広大な土地を保全し，多くの人々の利用に供するために整備しつつ，高度に秩序立てられた環境をつくり，コミュニティとその背景を創出している．

ニューポートコーストはコミュニティとして計画された約4,000haのカリフォルニアの海岸線および背後の丘陵地からなり，全体の75%以上が永久的なオープンスペースあるいは公園として保存される．2,600戸以上の住宅，2つの18ホールのゴルフコース，5つのリゾートホテルが計画され，コミュニティづくりにおいてランドスケープがいかに重要かを示す好例である．

SWAは，ランチョ・サンタフェ，カーメル，パロス・ベルデス，モンテチト，ビバリーヒルズなどに見られるような，建物が木々や林の間に隠れて，ずっと昔からそこに森があったような，偉大なカリフォルニア特有の景観の伝統に則って，コミュニティの性格やイメージを生み出すことを目指した．

「ここでのランドスケープは，渓谷や丘陵地の自然の景観，マツやユーカリの林など，すべて大きいスケールで大胆にかつシンプルに計画された．これは，ランドスケープというより，むしろ植林計画といったほうがふさわしい．」**リチャード・ロウ**

Baywood Apartments　ベイウッドアパート

COMMUNITIES
コミュニティ

Development of very large tracts of land under some form of physical master plan has been accounting for more and more of the recent expansion of American towns and cities. These range from several hundred to several thousand acres.

More recent post-World War II large-scale new community projects have ranged from remote-location, second-home and resort communities to close-in or even in-town locations of higher density and sophisticated-use mixes. What makes a new community a "good place to live?" Newness itself — raw, unfinished and unlovely — is a difficult condition to overcome. How has SWA approached this task? New community projects designed by SWA in the period of 1969-1991 have been selected as having achieved in different contexts, and in differing ways, an important quality of amenity. These are: Regency on 182 ha (450 acres) in Omaha, Nebraska; Woodbridge on 650 ha (1,600 acres) in Irvine, California; Green Meadows-Phase 1 on 160 ha (400 acres), Green Meadows Phase II on 160 ha (400 acres), both in Johnston (Des Moines), Iowa; and Victoria on 890 ha (2,200 acres) in Rancho Cucamonga, California.

Five of these six projects are located on land originally devoid of natural beauty in the form of lakes, streams, woods and dramatic views. Even the exception is still mostly on "ordinary" environmentally undifferentiated land. This means that the emphasis is upon *creation* of a landscape rather than upon its *preservation*. To speak of "creation of a landscape" is to raise some important questions as to what community design involves and what are the means of design expressions. These projects are offered not just in terms of their "greenness," (i.e., the successful introduction of nature into a very large cultural artifact), but also in terms of their "scale."

Aiming at a merely "green" new community has become commonplace. Achieving "scale" is not so easy, because it demands a great deal more of both the designer and the developer. The following selected project descriptions will investigate the interrelationship between plan, greenness and scale and how the quality of amenity has been achieved. In addition, four newer Southern California communities are discussed in the context of that region's heritage as an incubator of new communities.

SWA creates plans that try to create a more livable environment by promoting an overall sense of community. This is achieved primarily through the physical design of the community. Creating a simple, clear community structure by linking important community elements is a fundamental principle of this approach. Strongly relating the community open space and circulation systems to one another in positive ways is a typical means. Landscape is also critical to reinforcing the overall unity of the community. SWA's community plans try to ensure that the landscape design and physical plan express the same overall idea. Community structure is also expressed in a clear spatial hierarchy set by the scale of important community elements such as streets and other public space. Elements designed to address the automobile scale look very different from elements designed to accommodate pedestrians. Creating identity for a community is an important aspect of physical design that often involves subtly incorporating historical or cultural references into both the physical layout of the community and the design of landscape and architectural elements.

マスタープランに基づく広大な土地の開発計画は、アメリカの都市や街をどんどん大きく拡張している。数百エーカーからときには数千エーカーにも及ぶ。

第2次世界大戦後の大規模な新しいコミュニティプロジェクトは、市街地と離れたセカンドハウス的、リゾート施設的なコミュニティから、市街地の周辺や内部にある高密度で洗練された複合用途のコミュニティにいたるまで、さまざまである。新しいコミュニティを「住みよい環境」にするにはどうしたらいいのだろう。開発されていない、未完成な、魅力のない、新しい土地はそう簡単には征服されない。SWAはいかにしてこの課題に取り組んできたか。ここでは、SWAによって1969年から1991年の間にデザインされた、異なるコンテクストと異なる方法で実現し、アメニティという重要な特質をもった新しいコミュニティ計画を選んで紹介している。それらは、ネブラスカ州オマハの182haのリージェンシー、カリフォルニア州アーバインの650haのウッドブリッジ、それぞれ160haずつのアイオワ州デモインのジョンストンに位置するグリーンメドウズの第1期と第2期、カリフォルニア州のランチョ・クカモンガの890haのビクトリアである。

6つのプロジェクトのうちの5つまでが、湖や小川や森やドラマチックな眺めなどの自然の美がなにもない土地に計画された。唯一例外のものでも、その土地のほとんどは環境的には画一的な土地である。したがって、ランドスケープを保存するというより、ランドスケープそのものを創出することに重点が置かれた。そこでの「ランドスケープの創出」とは、すなわちコミュニティデザインとは何を意味するのか、あるいはデザイン表現の意味するものはといった重要な疑問を提示することであった。これらのプロジェクトには、たとえば非常に大きな文化的な人工の環境にうまく自然を導入するような、「緑化」ということだけでなく、スケールという観点も導入された。

もちろん、緑の豊富な新しいコミュニティを目指すことは共通している。しかし、そこで適切なスケールを追求することは、デザイナーとディベロッパーの両者のより多くの努力を必要とするという点で、たいへんむずかしい。ここに紹介したプロジェクトは、プラン、緑化とそのスケール、アメニティの特質がどのように付加されたかといった点について、相互の関連を調べながら言及している。さらに、4つの新しいサザンカリフォルニアのコミュニティについては、その地域独特の伝統を新しいコミュニティのインキュベーターとして考えるというコンテクストの中で論じられている。

SWAは、もっと住みよい環境をコミュニティ意識を醸成することでつくり出そうと考えてデザインしている。これは根本的には、コミュニティの実際のデザインを通して実践される。重要なコミュニティの構成要素と関連づけながら、シンプルで明快なコミュニティの構造を創出することは、私たちのデザイン手法の基本的な原則である。相互に強くポジティブに関連し合うコミュニティ・オープンスペースおよび歩行者動線のシステムは、典型的な手法である。ランドスケープは、コミュニティ全体を強く結びつけるために必須である。SWAのコミュニティ計画は、ランドスケープデザインと実際の計画が全体として同じアイデアを表現するようにしている。コミュニティの構造は、道路や公共空間といった、重要なコミュニティの構成要素のスケールによって制定された、明快な空間の序列として表現される。自動車用のスケールをもってデザインされた要素は、歩行者用のスケールのそれとは全く異なるものになる。コミュニティの個性を生み出すことは、しばしば歴史的な意味と文化的な意味を統合して、配置計画、ランドスケープ、建築デザインの中に投影していくという、実際の設計の重要な一面を担うことになる。

Village of Woodbridge

Irvine, California, U.S.A.
ウッドブリッジ住宅地

Developed over a period of more than 15 years, Woodbridge is a 9,000-unit mixed-use residential community located on 700 ha (1,750 acres). The landscape challenge was to create topographic relief from the virtually flat site while solving flooding problems from San Diego Creek, which bisected the site, and to give the neighborhoods intimate scale, identity, greenery and open space. The planning challenge was to provide a truly balanced community, linked visually and economically to the city and the region, and to provide a wide variety of housing types, finely integrated throughout each neighborhood.

Woodbridge has a cross-axial plan. The Village Center lies at the intersection of two corridors: an east-west activity corridor and a north-south corridor composed of lakes. Yale Loop Road links the four quadrants, and a landscaped berm provides an edge to the Village. Visible from the road are a network of neighborhood parks and open spaces and, beyond, the fine-grain mix of houses.

The best way to understand Woodbridge is to walk through the community: start at the Village Center; have a hamburger and a beer on the outdoor terrace overlooking the lake (what a great view!); then stroll across the bridge to the lake and walk along the trail. Kids ride their bikes there while, in spring, baby ducks paddle after their mothers. Ask a passerby what he (or she) thinks of the community. "A great place . . . people are friendly" is a typical response. Walk to the swimming lagoon where kids splash while their mothers sunbathe. Walk past the impromptu sand volleyball game and continue on to the Tennis Club and into a neighborhood park, with its elementary school in the center. School's out, but a softball game is in progress. That's what Woodbridge is all about.

"Woodbridge is a community in the truest sense of the word."
– Dick Law

"At Woodbridge we incorporated the Radburn concept of pedestrian separation around the lake with a recognition that the greenways would move from the back of homes to the street for safety and to make the roads more livable."
–Kalvin Platt

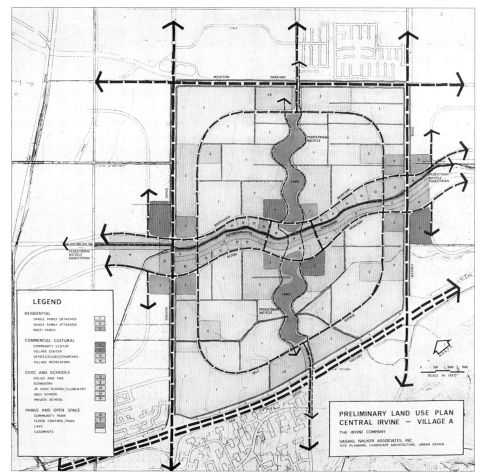

LEGEND

PRELIMINARY LAND USE PLAN
CENTRAL IRVINE – VILLAGE A
THE IRVINE COMPANY

SASAKI, WALKER ASSOCIATES, INC.
SITE PLANNING, LANDSCAPE ARCHITECTURE, URBAN DESIGN

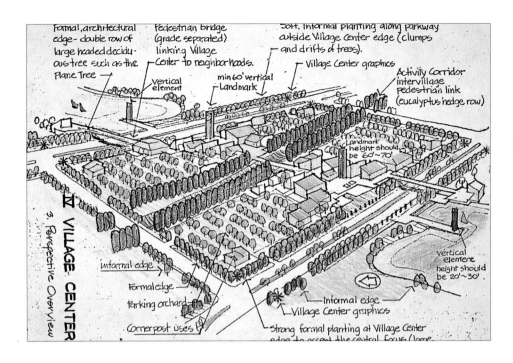

Formal, architectural edge- double row of large headed deciduous tree such as the Plane Tree

Pedestrian bridge (grade separated) linking Village Center to neighborhoods.

Vertical element

min 60' vertical Landmark

Soft, informal planting along parkway outside Village Center edge (clumps and drifts of trees).

Village Center graphics

Activity Corridor intervillage pedestrian link (eucalyptus hedge row)

Landmark height should be 60~70

Vertical element height should be 20'~30'

Informal edge

Formal edge

Parking orchard

Cornerpost uses

Informal edge. Village Center graphics

Strong formal planting at Village Center edge to accent the central focus (lame

Ⅳ VILLAGE CENTER
3. Perspective Overview

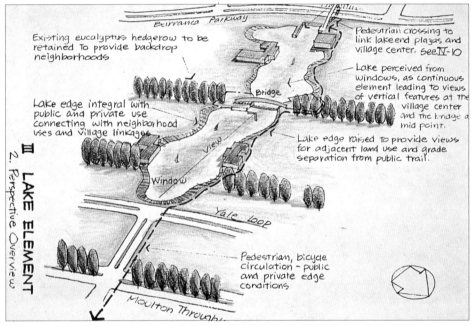

Burranca Parkway

Existing eucalyptus hedgerow to be retained to provide backdrop neighborhoods

Pedestrian crossing to link lake end plazas and village center. see Ⅳ-10

Lake perceived from windows, as continuous element leading to views of vertical features at the village center and the bridge a mid point.

Bridge

Lake edge integral with public and private use connecting with neighborhood uses and village linkages

View

Lake edge raised to provide views for adjacent land use and grade separation from public trail.

Window

Yale Loop

Pedestrian, bicycle circulation - public and private edge conditions

Moulton Throughi

Ⅲ LAKE ELEMENT
2. Perspective Overview

ウッドブリッジは，南カリフォルニアのアーバインランチを構成するコミュニティの１つで，700haの敷地に9,000戸の住宅を含むさまざまな施設からなり，15年以上かけて開発が進められてきた．ランドスケープデザイン上の試みとして，敷地を二分して流れるサンディエゴ川の洪水氾濫対策を施した上で，ほとんど平坦な敷地を少し起伏のある地形に変え，周辺の住宅地に，親しみのあるスケール感，アイデンティティ，緑地，オープンスペースを提供するよう計画した．プランニング上では，視覚的にも経済的にも市や地域に結びついた，実際にバランスのとれたコミュニティを形成し，また，さまざまなタイプの住宅を用意し，精巧に統一のとれた近隣住区をつくり出すことを目指した．

ウッドブリッジは十字型のプランで，ビレッジセンターは２つの軸線の交点に位置している．東西方向はアクティビティ・コリドー，南北方向は湖で構成している．環状道路が４つの四分円状の住宅地をつなぎ，路傍の植栽がビレッジの領域を区切っている．道路からは，近隣住区の公園やオープンスペースのネットワークが見え，その向こうにさまざまな住宅の連なりが見える．

ウッドブリッジを理解する最良の方法は，コミュニティの中を歩いてみることである．ビレッジセンターからスタートし，湖に張り出した屋外のテラスでハンバーガーとビールで休憩．それから湖にかかる橋を渡り，小道を辿る．子供たちが自転車を乗り回し，春にはアヒルの親子がスイスイと泳いでいる．通りかかる人々にこのコミュニティをどう思っているか聞いてみよう．「すばらしい場所よ，みんな仲良しだし．」といった返事が返ってくる．水遊び用の池では，子供たちは水しぶきを上げ，母親たちは日光浴．砂地で即席のバレーボールゲームをやっているところを通り過ぎ，テニスクラブを過ぎると，中央に小学校のある近隣公園に出る．学校はもう終わっていたが，ソフトボールの試合の真っ最中．これがウッドブリッジのすべてである．

「ウッドブリッジは本当の意味でのコミュニティがあるところだ．」　　　　　リチャード・ロウ
「ウッドブリッジでは，それぞれの住宅の裏から緑道で安全に表通りに行くことができ，さらに道路を一層住み心地のよい場所にするという利点のために，湖のまわりでは歩行者と自動車を分離するという，ラドバーン方式を採用した．」
　　　　　　　　　　　　　カルビン・プラット

Southern California Community Planning

California, U.S.A.

サザンカリフォルニア・コミュニティ

In the course of preparing master plans for new communities in Southern California, The SWA Group has developed an approach that purposefully brings together landscape design and land planning in a way that creates better integrated, more coherent community plans. The essence of the approach is a belief that the landscape design and physical site plan should complement one another on a structural level. In practice, this means that the landscape plan and land plan are developed simultaneously and must positively reinforce each other throughout the design process. In SWA's approach, road hierarchy, neighborhood design, grading, plant material selection and other design elements should all be an expression of the fundamental community design concepts.

An important aspect of SWA's approach to community planning in Southern California over the past ten years has been to understand and build upon the local context when developing plans for new communities. Southern California has a unique natural, cultural, and historical environment that provides a surfeit of precedents for landscape design and land planning. As one of the fastest-growing metropolitan areas of the United States since the late 19th century, Southern California has been an ideal place for the development of new communities. The finest of these — Rancho Palos Verdes, Rancho Santa Fe and Beverly Hills, among others — have provided inspiration for much of SWA's work. To document these places and the forces that shaped them, Robert Jacob, a Southern California SWA Principal, recently completed a study of Southern California communities entitled *The Southern California Town Planning Heritage*. Several communities exemplify SWA's recent Southern California community planning work:

Victoria (1979–1985) is a 850-hectare (2,100-acre) planned community located in Rancho Cucamonga, 40 miles east of Los Angeles. Responding to the initial question of whether or not it was even possible to create an integrated community given the landowner's fragmented ownership, SWA proposed a classic parkway in the tradition of Palos Verdes Drive. Victoria Parkway links the four villages and provides a consistent open-space armature that unifies and identifies the community.

Heritage (1984–1986), an 450-hectare (1,100-acre) community located several miles east of Victoria in neighboring Fontana, relies on a strong physical form and complementary landscape planting to create identity. The two villages focus on centrally located neighborhood schools that are tied to the surrounding residential neighborhoods by a system of trails. Traditional landscape plantings of palms and Eucalyptus windrows create a distinctly Southern California identity.

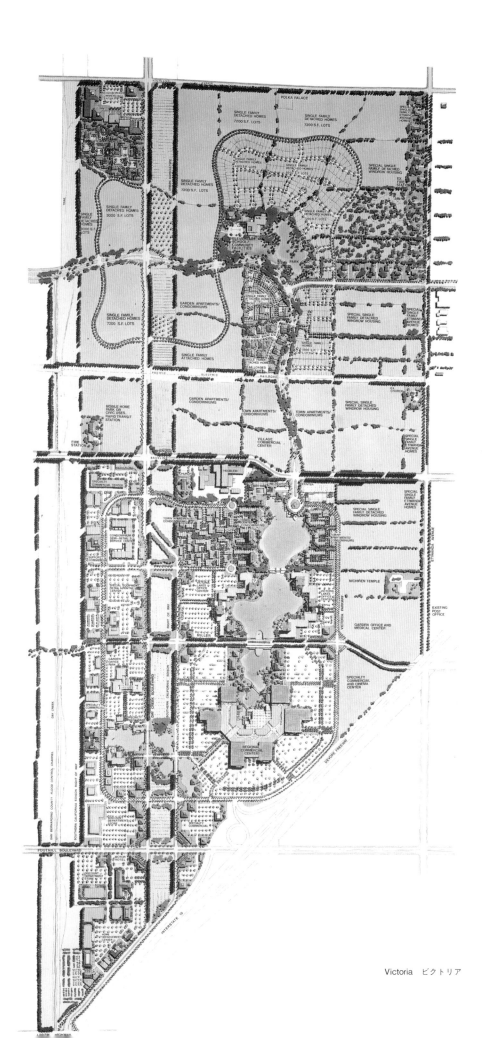

Victoria　ビクトリア

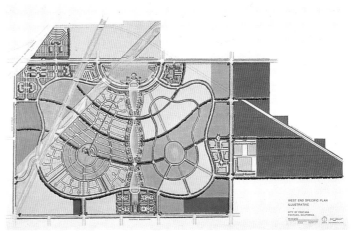

Heritage　ヘリテイジ

Heritage　ヘリテイジ

サザンカリフォルニアにおける新しいコミュニティのマスタープランを準備する中で，SWAはランドスケープデザインと土地利用計画が一体になって，より一層まとまりの良い，整合性のあるコミュニティをつくる手法を生み出した．そのポイントは，ランドスケープデザインと敷地計画は，本来お互いに補完し合うべきものであるということである．実際，デザインプロセス全般を通して，ランドスケープと土地利用計画や敷地計画が，同時に相互に関連し合いながら進められた．SWAの手法では，道路の体系，近隣住区のデザイン，造成計画，植栽樹種の選別，その他のデザイン要素など，すべてがコミュニティの基本的なデザインコンセプトを具象化していく．

このプロジェクトにおいてSWAが過去10年間にわたって採用した手法の重要な点は，新しいコミュニティ開発計画において，その地方独自のコンテクストを理解し，その上に立って計画することである．サザンカリフォルニアはランドスケープデザインや土地利用において数多くの先例を生み出したユニークな自然，文化，そして歴史的な環境をもっている．19世紀末以降のアメリカにおいて，最も早いスピードで発展した大都市のひとつであるため，サザンカリフォルニアは，新しいコミュニティ開発にはうってつけの場所であった．周辺のランチョ・パロスベルデス，ランチョ・サンタフェ，ビバリーヒルズといった良い先例が，SWAの仕事に多くのインスピレーションを与えてくれた．これらの事例やその都市形態に影響を与えた要因について調査した，SWAサザンカリフォルニア事務所のプリンシパル，ロバート・ジェイコブは，最近，この調査の結果を「サザンカリフォルニアのタウンプランニングの遺産」として本にまとめた．いくつかのコミュニティがSWAの最近のサザンカリフォルニアにおけるコミュニティ計画への取り組みを例証している．

ビクトリア（1979－1985年）

ロサンゼルスの東約60kmのランチョ・クカモンガに計画されたコミュニティである．所有地がばらばらに点在する当計画地で，まとまりのあるコミュニティを創出できるかという難しい問題に対して，SWAは元来この地域にあったパロスベルデス・ドライブという道路の伝統を踏襲して，古典的なパークウェイを提案した．ビクトリアパークウェイは，4つのビレッジを結びつけ，コミュニティを一体化し，アイデンティティを付与する一貫したオープンスペースの枠組をつくり出している．

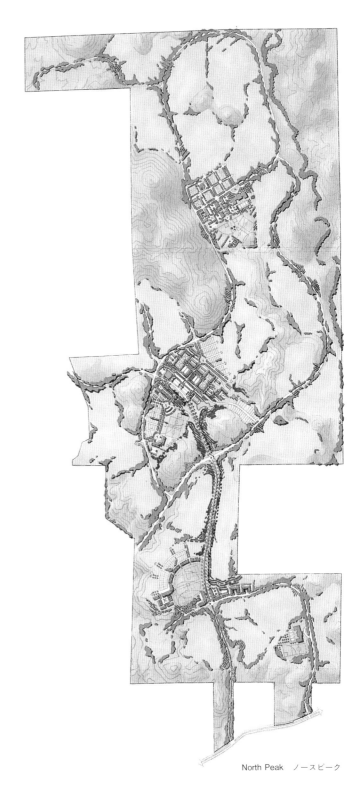

North Peak　ノースピーク

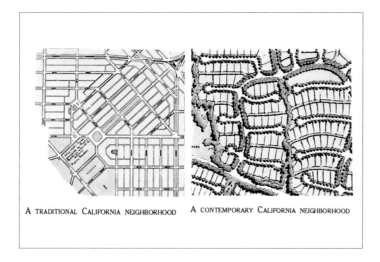

A TRADITIONAL CALIFORNIA NEIGHBORHOOD   A CONTEMPORARY CALIFORNIA NEIGHBORHOOD

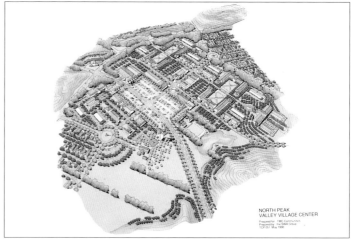

NORTH PEAK
VALLEY VILLAGE CENTER
Prepared for: TMC Communities
Prepared by: the SWA Group
TGP 051 May 1990

North Peak　ノースピーク

North Peak　ノースピーク

North Peak　ノースピーク

Porta Bella　ポルタベラ

North Peak (1988–1991) is a 800-hectare (2000-acre) community located in Lake Elsinore, 96 km (60 miles) southeast of Los Angeles. SWA's plan proposes an integrated mix of traditional and contemporary development patterns focusing on three traditional town centers. The landscape plan proposes retention of significant areas of natural landscape, traditional Eucalyptus plantations along major roads, processional rows of palms, and citrus orchards to recall the Southern California landscape tradition.

Porta Bella (1990–1991), a 390-hectare (960-acre) hillside community located within the Santa Clarita Valley, lies approximately 56 km (35 miles) north of Los Angeles. The 3,200-home community incorporates SWA's "livable environments studio" notions of town design, which include identifiable systems of the environment, mobility, and lifestyle. The Porta Bella plan proposes a series of interactive neighborhoods, including a traditional hilltop Town Center and a mixed-use rail station district. The landscape plan creates a unifying character for the area reflective of early California landscapes.

ヘリテイジ(1984－1986年)

ビクトリアの東数キロ，フォンタナに隣接する445haの土地に計画されたコミュニティである．力強い形態とそれを補完する植栽計画がアイデンティティを生み出している．2つのビレッジが，周辺の住宅地と緑道システムで結ばれた近隣の学校を中心に配置され，ヤシやユーカリの並木といった伝統的な植栽がサザンカリフォルニアらしい景観をつくり出している．

ノースピーク(1988－1991年)

ロサンゼルスの南東約90km，エルシノア湖に面した800haの敷地に計画されたコミュニティである．SWAは，3つの伝統的なタウンセンターを中心とした，伝統的かつ現代風な開発をミックスしたコミュニティを提案した．ランドスケーププランでは，特定地域の自然植生の保護，主要街路沿いの伝統的なユーカリ並木，整然と並ぶヤシの並木，サザンカリフォルニアのランドスケープの伝統を思い起こさせるオレンジ畑などを提案した．

ポルタベラ(1990－1991年)

ロサンゼルスの北50km，サンタクラリタバレーに位置する約390haの丘陵地に計画されたコミュニティである．3,200戸の住宅からなるコミュニティは，SWAのタウンデザインの「住みよい環境のスタジオ」という意図通りに，個性的な環境，動線，ライフスタイルを具現化している．この計画では，伝統的な丘の上のタウンセンターと複合用途の鉄道駅周辺施設群を含む，相互に関連する一連の近隣住区の形成を提案した．ランドスケーププランは，初期カリフォルニアのランドスケープの特徴を生かして地域の統一的な特徴を生み出す．

Regency and Green Meadows

Omaha, Nebraska; and Des Moines, Iowa, U.S.A.

リージェンシーとグリーンメドウズ

Three projects offer a study of two community design theories. In this article, the dominant Master Planned Community (MPC) model is discussed by example of the Regency and Green Meadows communities. A more recent Neo-Traditional Neighborhood model is studied by evalation of the Green Meadows West community plan.

In comparing these two very different approaches, questions of scale, pedestrian versus automobile orientation and the role of architectural theme predominate. Perhaps most important however, is the question of market and financial possibility. In this critically important dimension, the standard MPC is well proven while the Neo-Traditional challenger is not. What is likely to happen is that the two community design approaches will be blended in such a way as to capture the advantages of each.

Regency

The plan for Regency, prepared in 1969, combined the Olmstedian tradition of curving street patterns that follow topography with the contemporary ideal of multi-use, master-planned community. Our client, the United Benefit Life Insurance Company of Omaha, Nebraska, had purchased 200 ha (500 acres) of eroding farmland, treeless and hilly, with some flood plain. On this site (after much earth-moving, grading, and the construction of a man-made lake) we located the high-density area of offices, retail stores, motels, restaurants, and low- and mid-rise apartments at the base of the uplands. On higher ground we located the low-density, single-family residential neighborhoods. Between these two broad areas, we laid out a curving parkway boulevard.

Such a boulevard — or collector road — became a familiar structuring device of that era's larger new communities. Like similar master-planned communities, Regency represented a pastoral, "soft-space" environment. The mix of urban uses in the higher-density areas was <u>not</u> achieved within a grid of streets; instead, Regency was organized around larger sub-units of land that tended to segregate uses. This segregation was deemed essential by many community developers because it allowed maximum land use flexibility over time and allowed land use parcels to be developed with a variety of architectural definitions. Such flexibility is not as available in a Neo-Traditional community where land uses are closely related in proximity and where consistent architectural theme and character are much more important.

Regency's amenities were focused not on architectural but on *landscape* elements — trees, grass, parks, lakes, recreation areas and pedestrian greenways. These elements, installed prior to development, formed the image of Regency and accounted, in large part, for Regency's success, both financially and visually. A truly multi-use community, Regency is now home to about 4,000 people. It is also a destination for thousands more — for working, shopping, dining, and social activities.

When viewed through the lens of the emerging "neo-traditional" community design model, Regency may appear flawed. There are no architecturally distinguished buildings or themes. Pedestrian movement through the entire community, while well accommodated, is beyond convenient scale. The contrast, variety, convenience, charm and community focus expected in neo-traditional models are largely missing. Such judgments, while valid, should be tempered by two important criteria that engage the community designer and the client: 1) consumers' preferences and 2) what community builders can actually deliver.

以下のプロジェクトは，相反する2つのコミュニ
ティ・デザイン理論を理解する上で，たいへん好
対照をなしている．リージェンシーと，それに影
響を受けたグリーンメドウズ第1期が伝統的なマ
スター・プランド・コミュニティ（MPC）を，グリ
ーンメドウズ第2期が最近の新しい傾向であるネ
オ・トラディショナル・コミュニティ・モデルを代
表している．ここでは，SWAのコミュニティ・
デザイン手法の変遷をたどる．

リージェンシー

1968年に作成された計画は，オルムステッド以来
の伝統的な手法である，地形に沿ってうねるよう
にカーブした街路と現代の理想的な多目的利用に
供するコミュニティを組み合わせたものである．
クライアントのネブラスカ州オマハを本拠とする
ユナイテッドベネフィット生命保険会社は，木の
ない丘陵地の，ところどころに氾濫原を含む，約
200haの浸食谷間の広大な農地を購入した．この土
地を大規模に造成し直し，人工湖をつくり，敷地
西側の低地にオフィス，商業施設，モーテル，レ
ストラン，そして低層・中層のアパート群を配置
して高密度なエリアとした．敷地東側のやや小高
い部分には低密度の独立住宅による住区を配置し
た．ゆるやかにカーブする大通りがこれら2つの
エリアを分けている．

　こうした大通り（またはコレクター道路）は，当
時の大規模な新しいコミュニティの一般的な構成
要素であった．よく似た計画のコミュニティの中
でも，リージェンシーはとりわけ牧歌的でのどか
な環境となっている．高密度地区の都市的な施設
の混在は，グリッド状の道路パターンでなく，そ
れぞれ機能別にいくつかグルーピングされてでき
る比較的大きなサブユニットをとり巻くように組
み合わされている．この機能分離は，コミュニ
ティづくりには重要である．時間の経過とともに現
われる用途変更などへのフレキシビリティを最大
に確保でき，さらに多様な施設の併置による混在
を，建築的に明確に表現する必要もなくしている．
　リージェンシーのアメニティは，建築的にとい
うより，樹木，草地，公園，湖，レクリエーショ
ン地区，歩行者用の緑道といったランドスケープ
的な要素により創出されている．これらのアメニ
ティ構成要素が開発のどんなものにも優先された
結果，リージェンシーのイメージが形づくられ，
それが結局は財政的にも視覚的にも，この計画を
成功に導いた．リージェンシーは人口約4,000人の
複合用途のコミュニティである．そこでは仕事を
はじめ，ショッピング，食事，社会活動などのさ
まざまな活動が展開される．
　リージェンシーは，現在話題に上がっている「ネ
オ・トラディショナル・コミュニティ」のデザイン
モデルとしてみれば，多くの欠点を抱えている．
建築的に際立った建物もテーマもない．コミュニ
ティの中の歩行者動線は充分確保されているもの
の，便利なヒューマンスケールからはほど遠い．
「ネオ・トラディショナル」モデルにみられるコン
トラストと多様性，利便性，魅力，そしてコミュ
ニティの象徴といったものは，ここでは見られな
い．しかしながら，この計画では，消費者の好み，
また，開発する側が実際になにを提供できるかに
ついて，デザイナーとクライアントが一体となっ
て探究した結果，こうした判断が適用された．

REGENCY PLAN

0 100 200 400M
0 200 400 800FT

Green Meadows

The first and second phases of Green Meadows illustrate the evolution in community designers' thinking, both within The SWA Group and among other planners and designers in America.

Phase One began in 1978, when Pioneer Hi-Bred International of Des Moines, Iowa, commissioned SWA to prepare a development plan for some 160 ha (400 acres) of flat, treeless land near a major flood plain. Regency was selected as the model. Our plan for Phase One thus incorporated a parkway boulevard and dispersed facilities and amenities. We developed an attractive pedestrian greenway system that also functioned as a channel for storm-water drainage. Overall, we focused on the "middle scale" landscape; as a result, the grading and small lakes, small trees, shrubs, walkways, lighting and signage provide a friendly, garden-like appearance.

Phase Two began in 1989. Rejecting the standard model of a golf course-oriented community, Pioneer's new young president requested a neo-traditional community that would reflect the scale and charm of Iowa's older small towns and villages. SWA then produced and refined the plan, in collaboration with William Johnson of William J. Johnson & Associates, a landscape architectural firm with a tradition of concern for such communities.

The plan for Phase Two embodies the trend toward more formal and community-enhancing patterns, while preserving a close association with the natural environment. The emphasis is on a scaled-down grid of streets, an overlap of uses, structures as focal points, and strong, formal spatial design. Pedestrians, not automobiles, are favored. Different housing types are mixed. The village green is the focus of the community, easily accessible to a church, small offices, retail stores, a school and a central park.

In the large-scale expansion of the 1960s through the 1980s, suburban development obliterated the country while not offering the town. Green Meadows is now combining green amenity with traditional village streets and a village green. Perhaps its greatest advance is the move from automobile to pedestrian scale, a move which encourages convenient, frequent and friendly encounters among people.

"The design of residential environments in America is perhaps the most important and most neglected-category of new development. It has been SWA's privilege for many years to participate with some very responsible developers in the design and building of some very wonderful new communities. Unfortunately, most of these serve primarily the affluent. It is time that the kind of amenities associated with upper income housing and community environments were made more widely available. Community designers do not lack for ideas of how to do this. Rigid zoning conventions and traffic engineering dominated street improvement requirements are keeping good things from happening. Putting the environmental movement and community builders together with good community designers and agency planners is an idea whose time has come. The results would be superlative."
– **Edmond Kagi**

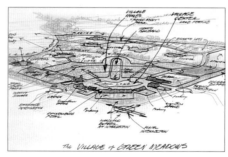

グリーンメドウズ

グリーンメドウズの第1期と第2期は，SWAだけでなくアメリカ中のプランナーやデザイナーに，コミュニティの新しい考え方を提示した．

第1期は1978年に，アイオワ州デモインを本拠地とするパイオニア・ハイブリッド・インターナショナル社が，川の氾濫原に近い，木のない約160haの土地に対する開発計画をSWAに依頼してきたことから始まる．その際，リージェンシーがモデルとして取り上げられた．第1期計画では，並木のある大通りと，散在する施設やアメニティをつなぎ合わせ，悪天候時の排水路ともなる，魅力的な歩行者用の緑道システムを提案した．全体的に，ここでは中間的なスケールのランドスケープにデザインの焦点を当てている．その結果，敷地の高低，小さな湖，低い木々，灌木，緑道，照明やサインなどが，親しげな，庭園のような景観をつくり出している．

第2期は1989年に始まった．クライアントのパイオニア社の若い社長は，元来ゴルフコースであったところに標準的なコミュニティを計画するのでなく，アイオワ州独特の古い小さな町や村のスケールや魅力を反映した，「ネオ・トラディショナル・コミュニティ」の建設を望んだ．SWAは，伝統的なコミュニティづくりに経験の豊富なランドスケープ事務所であるウィリアム・J・ジョンソン事務所と共同でこの計画に当たった．

第2期は，自然環境との密接な関連を保護しながら，より一層格式の高い，コミュニティの形成を高めるパターンを具体的に表現している．特に，スケールダウンしたグリッド状の通り，中心的施設における用途や構造の多重性，力強い，格式のある空間デザインなどが強調された．自動車でなく歩行者が優先され，また，さまざまな住戸タイプが用意された．ビレッジグリーンは，コミュニティの中心であり，そこから教会，小さなオフィス，店舗，学校，そして中央公園に簡単に歩いて行くことができる．

1960年代から80年代にかけての大規模な郊外の開発によって，アメリカからカントリーがなくなり，かといってタウンができたわけでもなかった．グリーンメドウズは，グリーンアメニティと伝統的なビレッジストリートやビレッジグリーンをうまく結合させている．おそらく最も重要な進歩は，自動車から歩行者中心のスケールへの転換であろう．このことが，そこに住む人々の利便性とより頻繁かつ密接な出会いを可能にした．

「アメリカの居住環境のデザインは，最も重要でありながら，最も無視されてきたカテゴリーである．すばらしい新しいコミュニティの計画や建設に責任をもつディベロッパーたちと一緒になって，何年にもわたってこうした計画に参加してきたのは，SWAの特権でもある．残念ながら，これらの多くは裕福な人々へのサービスとなっている．高収入の人たちの住宅やコミュニティの環境でつくり出されたアメニティは，もっと広く普及するべき時期にきている．コミュニティ・デザイナーが，どうすべきかのアイデアを持っていないわけではない．厳しいゾーニング規制や自動車交通優先の道路改善の要求などが，より良いコミュニティづくりを妨げている．環境保護運動やコミュニティを建設する人たちがコミュニティ・デザイナーやプランナーと一緒になることで，何かができる時期にきている．結果は最高のものになるだろう．」

エドモンド・ケーギ

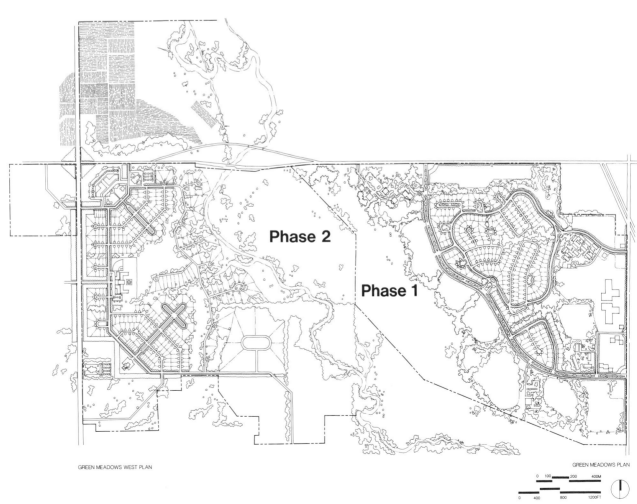

Phase 2

Phase 1

GREEN MEADOWS WEST PLAN

GREEN MEADOWS PLAN

0 100 200 400M

0 400 800 1200FT

PLACES
プレイス

The character of a place is determined by its public spaces, its landscape, its environment — not its skyline. People experience life at street level, building memories that are shaped by the everyday as much as by the remarkable. We remember Paris for its grand boulevards, Rome for its piazzas and fountains, and Boston for its emerald necklace of parks.

Memorable places create strong, emotion-provoking images. They enrich and transform, engaging the imagination, stimulating the senses and invigorating the spirit. They have personality: Memorable places may reveal beauty and allow us to see the world with fresh eyes, or they may be mysterious, evoke silence and cause us to wonder, "What's going on here?"

Places that are memorable resonate and reverberate with their context. The elements of placemaking may embrace the historical context, cultural influences, the climate, an evocative site condition, or civic sensibility. Discovering the personality of a place is an exciting journey on which we search, with the client, for a special quality and a fresh response. In this quest, we reach for the creation of an idea and for meaning, not a borrowed style. The meaning evolves from a spatially specific and site-specific dialectic which is made visible.

場の性格は，スカイラインからでなく，そこにある公共的な空間やランドスケープ，環境といったことから決定される．人々は，毎日の生活やちょっと目立った特徴などから，その場の性格を通りのレベルや建物の記憶から体験する．パリはあの大通りを思い出し，ローマは広場や噴水を，ボストンはエメラルドネックレス公園を思い出すようにである．

記憶に残る場所には，強い，感情を揺り動かすようなイメージがある．それらは，イマジネーションを豊かにし，変化させ，引きつけ，感覚を刺激し，精神を鼓舞する．そこには個性がある．美しく，新鮮に映り感動させることができ，ミステリアスで，沈黙を導き，「ここでは一体何が起きているのだろう？」という不思議な気持ちを起こさせる．

記憶に残る場所は，そのコンテクストに共鳴し，反響する．場を形成する要素は，歴史的なコンテクストや文化的な影響，気候，その土地の状況，市民の意識を包含したものである．場の個性を見出すことは，特別な質と新鮮な反応を求めて，私たちがクライアントと一緒に追求し続ける刺激的な旅のようなものである．こうした探究の中で，私たちは，借り物のスタイルでない，アイデアの創造や意味に到達できる．意味は視覚化された空間的な特性や敷地特有の論理から引き出される．

Hampton Road

Lexington, Massachusetts, U.S.A.
ハンプトンロード

Nestled into a heavily forested hillside in historic Lexington, Massachusetts, are six individual luxury houses designed by Robert A.M. Stern. His six designs recall the New England estate homes of the early 1900s.

To locate the homes on the granite-ledged hillside, SWA created small clearings in the hardwood and pine forest. Minimum grading creates the country lane that penetrates the site. A fieldstone wall follows along one side of the lane recalling the familiar scene of stone walls running through the New England countryside.

"Each home has its own landscape setting. The notion of individuality and personal character is recognized."
— ***Michael Sardina***

マサチューセッツ州の歴史的な街レキシントンの
ゆるやかな丘陵の林の中に，ロバート・スターン設
計の6軒の大邸宅が建っている．スターンの設計
した6軒の家のデザインは，まるで今世紀初めの
ニューイングランド地方特有の大邸宅のようである．

花崗岩の岩棚からなる丘陵地に邸宅を配置する
ため，広葉樹やマツの林の中に小さな敷地を設け，
最小限の造成で，敷地を貫く道路をつくり出して
いる．道路の片側には，ニューイングランドのい
なかでごく普通に見られるような自然石積みの石
垣が連なっている．

「どの家もそれぞれ固有のランドスケープをもっ
ている．そこには個人と個性という概念が認めら
れる．」
マイケル・サーディナ

Magee Ranch

Danville, California, U.S.A.
マギーランチ

The SWA Group has been involved with the development of this 220-hectare (540-acre) ranch from conception through implementation. Throughout this process, we have sought to design a community which engages and preserves the essential beauty of the site. With the active participation of the nearby communities, we determined that the site's unstable side slopes and visible ridgelines should not be built on. Thus we developed a scheme that concentrates development onto hidden terraces and canyons and dedicates 2/3 of the site for regional park use.

The development pattern creates a broad interface between developed areas and an enveloping naturalized landscape. We believe that the "magic" of this development lies not only in the preservation of open space, but also in the rich, varied interactions between the cultivated, developed areas and the wild, naturalized ones. To this end, we have preserved, enhanced and re-established the broad, naturalized and agrarian landscapes along these interactive zones, and have begun a dialogue with the initial phases of development.

"As the community grows, we hope to see the dialogue expand and develop into a lasting and endearing relationship."   **– Jim Lee**

"Magee Ranch is mass graded but the end result looks as if it were always there. The challenge was to contour the slopes and to save all the oaks on the hillsides."   **– Larry Pearson**

SWAは，カリフォルニア州ダンビルにある200haのマギーランチ開発に際し，そのコンセプトづくりから施工監理まで関わってきた．このプロセスを通じて，敷地が有する本質的な美しさを引き出し，保存していくようなコミュニティデザインが模索された．周辺のコミュニティの人々もこの段階で計画に参加し，敷地の不安定な斜面上や，よく見える稜線上に建物をつくらないということを申し合わせた．そこで，敷地を目立たないテラス状の土地や谷沿いに設定し，そして敷地の3分の2を地域的な公園としての利用に供することとした．

開発のパターンは，新たに開発される地域と，それを囲む自然のランドスケープを，広い範囲で融合させている．この開発地区の魅力は，単にオープンスペースの保存に基づくものではなく，開発された地域と，原生の自然，また作り出された自然とが，豊かにかつ多様に結びついていることから生まれるものと考える．2つの要素が融合するゾーンに沿って広がる，新たにつくり出された広大な自然景観を保護し，魅力を高め，再構築した．それが，開発の重要な第1段階となったのである．

「コミュニティの成長につれ，(そこに生まれた)会話が広がリ，さらに長く慕われる関係へと発展していくことを望む．」　　　ジェームズ・リー
「マギーランチは，広範囲な造成によりできあがったが，結果的には，以前からずっとそこにあったかのようである．ここでの試みは，斜面の形を造り直す一方，斜面に生えているカシの木をすべて保護することであった．」　　　ラリー・ピアソン

Liliore Green Rains Housing at Stanford University

Palo Alto, California, U.S.A.

スタンフォード大学リリオア・グリーンレインズ住宅地

The environment of the Stanford campus sets the overall context for the project and establishes the basis for reinterpretation of the architectural and landscape traditions of the University. The original campus was conceived as an axial and open quadrangle interwoven with a series of linking courtyards. The overall spatial organization is formal and sequential, and the landscape design and plant materials create a play between formal and informal, open and enclosed, and native and ornamental. Given these historical precedents, it is the intent of this

design to reflect the same spirit and tradition both in spatial form and in use of material.

The campus axial organization provided the basic framework for the building and layout for the new housing site. The personality of the project was further developed through the preservation and renovation of the Buttery Building, the oldest structure on the Stanford campus. This structure was incorporated as the focus of the project.

The courtyards along the main axis are formal in character, complementing the build-

ing layout and creating spaces of varying scale. A central open space runs the length of the project and offers a variety of areas where students may meet for informal social gatherings or participate in active and passive recreation.

"The design links Spanish-style architecture with a series of formal courtyards, while the landscape reflects the project's natural setting."
*– **John Wong***

スタンフォードのキャンパスの環境は，プロジェクトの包括的なコンテクストとなり，大学の建築やランドスケープの伝統を再解釈するための基礎となる．オリジナルなキャンパスは，軸線に沿って配置された四角い建物からなり，それぞれが囲む中庭により互いに結びつけられている．全体の空間的な秩序はフォーマルで連続的である．そしてランドスケープデザインや植栽素材が，フォーマルとインフォーマル，オープンと囲われた部分，自然とつくられた環境のそれぞれをつなぐ役割を果たしている．こうした歴史的な先例にしたがっ

て，新しいプロジェクトのデザインも，空間的にも材料的にも，同じ考え方と伝統を踏襲することとなった．

キャンパスの軸線は，新しい住宅地の建物や配置の基本的なフレームとなっている．このプロジェクトの性格は，スタンフォードのキャンパスの中で最も古い建物であるバッテリービルの保存修復によって，いちだんと個性化される．バッテリービルは，プロジェクトの中心的な存在に位置づけられたものである．

メインの軸線に沿った中庭は，フォーマルな性

格を有し，建物の配置を誘導し，さまざまなスケールのスペースをつくり出す．中央の広いオープンスペースは，プロジェクト全体にわたる長さをもち，学生たちがインフォーマルに集まったり，さまざまなレクリエーションに参加したりする場所となる．

「敷地計画がスパニッシュスタイルの建築と一連のフォーマルな中庭をつなぎ，一方，ランドスケープはキャンパスの自然環境を反映したものとなっている．」
ジョン・ウォン

Photo by Steve Proehl

Andover Companies Corporate Headquaters

Andover, Massachusetts, U.S.A.

アンドーバー社本社

Photo by Eric Roth

The building and landscape reflect the client's desire for an image of stability, permanence, and timelessness — qualities appropriate for an insurance company.

The site posed some constraints. Wetlands lay between the existing road and the prime riverfront building area. Three different vegetation zones covered the site. The sloping ground also demanded careful siting and grading for the new access road, parking and building footprint.

A certain amount of inspiration for the design derived from the spatial characteristics of European chateaux. It was an opportunity to try to achieve entry sequence and spatial relationships which were created by tall trees, making what open space we created instantly precious.

A simple country lane was laid out to approach the building. Observing the local vernacular of fieldstone walls that border country roads and enclose fields and forest, a single stone wall was employed to wind alongside our lane. The single stone wall created a contemporary tension associated with simple restraint and the surrounding woodland.

The preserved woodland surrounding the building courts and gardens creates densely forested edges and reinforces the building's axial relationship to the landscape. The mature trees preserved near the building give an immediate sense of the secure and mature relationship of building to site. In spring, a double row of flowering cherry trees give cheerful evidence that the harsh New England winter is finally past.

The architecture and landscape for the Corporate Headquarters blend into the age of the surrounding landscape. The mark of the new project is difficult to perceive.

"My first reaction upon walking the site and experiencing the quiet, beautiful, mature white pine forest along the river was twofold: We ought to play the dense, existing woodland against open space; and we should make the project seem as if it had been there for years."
– Michael Sardina

建物もランドスケープも，保険会社特有の，クライアントの希望である「安定，永続，時間の超越」を反映したものとなっている．

敷地には，いくつかの規制があった．既存の道路と川に面した建物の計画地の間には沼地があり，さらに，敷地は3種の異なった植生のゾーンからなっていた．傾斜地であるという点も，アクセス道路や駐車場，建物用地のための，注意深い配置計画と造成計画を必要とした．

デザインのためのインスピレーションは，多分にヨーロッパのシャトーの空間的な特質から得ている．この計画は，閉ざされた森の中にオープンスペースを創り出すことにより，入口までのシークエンスや空間の相互関係を劇的に演出する良い機会であった．

建物へのアプローチ道路はシンプルな田舎道として計画された．この地域では一般的な，自然石積みの石垣で道路を緑どり，周辺の草原や林と区画する手法を，ここでもそのまま引用している．一重の石垣は，シンプルな建物と周辺の自然と一体となって，新たな緊張を生み出す．

建物の中庭や庭園の保護された自然林は，密度高く茂る自然の垣根を形成し，建物のランドスケープとの軸線的な関係を強調する．建物近くの大きく成長した樹木は，安心感を人々に与え，かつ建物と敷地を密接に結びつける．春には，2列のサクラ並木が見事な花を咲かせ，ニューイングランドの厳しい冬が去ったことを，楽しげに教えてくれる．

建築とランドスケープは，時間とともに，周辺の環境に溶け込んでいく．新しいプロジェクトを示す目印を見つけるのはむずかしい．

「計画の初めに，敷地を歩きまわり，川に沿った静かな，美しい，大きなホワイトパイン（北米産ストローブマツ）の林を体験して私の反応は倍加された．私たちは，高密な既存の自然林とオープンスペースとのコントラストを強調し，さらに新たなプロジェクトがあたかも何年も前からそこにあったようなものとなるように計画すべきであると考えた．」
マイケル・サーディナ

IBM Almaden

San Jose, California, U.S.A.
IBM社アルメイデン研究所

IBM has long been concerned about the environmental quality of its facilities and the well-being of its employees. For the scientists who would work at this West Coast research laboratory, the company chose a 230-hectare (580-acre) cattle ranch in the Almaden Valley, south of San Jose. There SWA and architects MBT Associates sited the facility on a 6-hectare (15-acre) hilltop, leaving the remainder of the property in its agrarian state. In fact, we convinced IBM to lease much of the land so that the ranching could continue and the fine old orchards would remain.

One enters the site from the valley floor through blooming fruit trees and ascends among hills covered with grazing cattle. The building first comes into view after one rounds a hill. Native grasses were seeded to come right up to the building's edge, so that the building looms like a castle in the distance. The approach road spirals around the complex, ending on a high point, with views of the adjacent valley.

Rows of hedges screen the parking from the building. A series of open-ended courtyards offer views to the hills. Boulders uncovered during the grading were used to extend the existing rock outcrops and to provide seating for the scientists taking breaks in the courtyards. Elsewhere, a small grove for the scientists' use recalls the old orchards down in the valley. Beyond are trails leading to meadows for picnicking and sporting events.

"The research facility is an 'Ivory Tower' perched on a hilltop. The landscape is meant to inspire as well as offer respite to the resident scientists."
– William Callaway

IBM社は，長年にわたって，同社の全施設の環境的な質の向上と社員の福祉に強い関心を払ってきた．西海岸地域の研究所で働く科学者のために，同社は，カリフォルニア州サンノゼ市の南，アルメイデンバレーにある230haの放牧場を入手した．そこで，SWAと建築設計事務所のMBTは丘の上の6haの用地に建物を配置し，それ以外の敷地はすべて牧場のままで残すことにした．実際，IBM社にその土地を貸すことを納得してもらったため，現在もそのまま牧場として使われ，古く，すばらしい果樹園も残されている．

ここを訪れる人々は，谷間から花咲く果樹の間を通り，草を食む牛たちのいる丘をアプローチする．丘をひと巡りしてから建物が目の前に現れる．外壁に沿って，その土地固有の牧草が植え込まれ，遠目には城郭のように見える．アプローチ道路は，施設を螺線状に取り巻き，隣接する谷間のすばらしい眺めを与えつつ，いちばん高いところで終わっている．

生垣が駐車場を囲み，建物からの目隠しとなっている．片側が開けた中庭からは丘陵のすばらしい眺めが得られる．敷地を造成する時に出てきた岩を，あたかも一部露出している既存の岩盤に連なっているかのように配置し，科学者が休憩するときのベンチを提供している．中庭のあちらこちらに配置された，科学者のための小さな林は，谷間の古い果樹園を思い起こさせる．遊歩道はさらにピクニックやスポーツなどのイベントにも使われる広い草原に続いている．

「研究施設は，丘の上の象牙の塔である．ランドスケープは，研究者たちに刺激と同時に安らぎを与える．」
ウィリアム・キャラウェイ

Meridian

Aurora, Illinois, U.S.A.
メリディアン

With literally thousands of acres similar in character surrounding the Meridian Business Campus — a mixed-use office, research and industrial development — it was to be a challenge posed by CMD Midwest, Inc., for The SWA Group to create an environment that would attract companies desiring a high-quality sense of place for their employees. The land use area had to be able not only to change to reflect market demand, but to co-exist adjacent to one another without lowering the quality of the environment.

With these challenges in mind, a meandering parkway (romantic in character and form), a series of lakes (slicing diagonally across the property), and an open space and trails system (linking a commuter rail station with the business campus) were designed to create an upscale

"front yard" for offices.

The design vocabulary of Meridian is simple, yet bold. The play of formal allees and street trees against symbolically reforested parkways provides enough contrast to make the view from the street interesting while unifying the campus.

Other design details include a vertical monument which identifies the entry into the campus; monumental, high-tech, white walls encircling and embracing the major intersection of the arterial streets; and a double allee of trees which draws the line of the collector street through the campus.

Meridian is a project where a set of stringent, yet not overbearing, development guidelines had to be followed to ensure the long-term success of this upscale environment. The results of this

dedication to detail included the creation of contiguous berming within landscape easements; landscape planting that worked in concert with the streetscapes; and signage, site lighting, and building setbacks which further enhanced the campus' contrasting theme. A number of national or international companies such as Nissan, Hyundai, JVC, Rockwell International, Sears and Amocan have come to Meridian and adopted the design elements.

"The streetscape, lakes, monuments and trails create a setting into which a variety of buildings can be placed, rather than placing landscaping around the buildings."

– Larry Pearson

イリノイ州シカゴの西方にある工業都市オーロラでは，メリディアン・ビジネスキャンパスを取り囲むように，同じような特徴の土地が何千エーカーにも渡り広がっている．メリディアンはCMDミッドウエスト社によって開発された，多様なオフィス，研究施設，工業施設からなる開発である．SWAは，従業員に質の高い環境を望んでいる企業を誘致するための環境づくりを行なった．各区画の土地利用は，マーケットの需要に応じて変化できなければならないが，同時に環境の質的低下を伴わずに，隣接区画と共存していかなければならない．

このことを念頭に置いて，形も特性もたいへん魅力的な曲がりくねるパークウェイ，敷地を斜めに横切る湖，オープンスペース，そして通勤用列車の駅と開発地をつなぐ小道などが，オフィスのスケールの大きい前庭としてデザインされた．

メリディアンのデザインボキャブラリーは，シンプルかつ大胆にである．シンボリックに再植林されたパークウェイと，規則正しい並木道や街路樹の対比が，通りからの眺めをおもしろく演出し，同時にキャンパス全体を一体化している．

他のデザイン・ディテールとしては，キャンパスへの入口を示す直立したモニュメント，幹線道路の交差点を取り巻いて環状に配置されているモニュメンタルでハイテクの白い壁，キャンパスを通り抜けるコレクターロードを際立たせている2重に植えられた並木の3つが挙げられる．

メリディアンという，スケールの大きな環境を長い時間をかけて成功に導いていくためには，説得力のある，しかし威圧的でない開発のガイドラインを遵守する必要があった．ディテールへのこだわりが，道路際の一連のランドスケープ用地を生み出している．そこには，キャンパスのテーマを一層引き立たせる道路景観と協調する植栽，サイン，照明，そして建物のセットバックなどがみられる．数多くの国内外の企業，たとえば日産自動車，韓国の現代自動車，JVC（日本ビクター），ロックウェル・インターナショナル，シアーズ，アモカンなどの企業がメリディアンに進出し，そのデザイン要素を採用している．

「道路景観，湖，モニュメント，小道などが環境をつくり，そこにさまざまな建物が配置されるのであり，建物が先にあって，その周囲にランドスケープを施すわけではない．」 **ラリー・ピアソン**

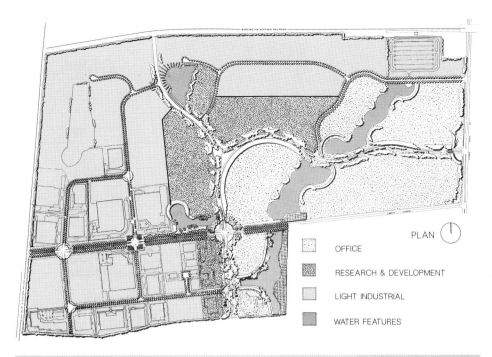

PLAN

- OFFICE
- RESEARCH & DEVELOPMENT
- LIGHT INDUSTRIAL
- WATER FEATURES

Westwood Gateway II
Los Angeles, California, U.S.A.
ウエストウッド・ゲートウェイ II

This office and park project is located at the entrance to the Westwood area of Los Angeles from the San Diego Freeway.

This project went through numerous designs and more than one architect before a final site plan and design parti were accepted. We entered late in the process but profoundly influenced the design. The landscape concept is a large open space defined by the two office towers and two major streets. A 180-meter-long (600-foot-long) pedestrian way, or plaza, beautifully refined and detailed, connects the office tower with the parking structures. Rectangular pools filled with Koi fish and water lilies accent this linear plaza. The edges of the pools are defined by crisp hedges and green Verde marble. Mature Phoenix reclinata palms rise in the center of the space, while formal palm courts on either side of the office towers provide a contrast from the groomed, informal park area. Large specimen ficus trees and rolling lawn offer a green, seemingly mature and pastoral setting for the office towers, within the larger urban context.

"The interaction between client, architect, landscape architect, and other members of the team can be an additive process; each good idea then contributes to making the whole greater than the sum of its parts. This is a very rewarding experience."
　　　　　　　　　　　　　　　– **Dick Law**

ロサンゼルスの, サンディエゴ・フリーウェイから ウエストウッド地域へのエントランスに位置する オフィスと公園の計画である.

このプロジェクトでは, 最終的な配置計画やデ ザインが決まるまでに, 実にさまざまな案が検討 され, 何人もの建築家が関係していた. 私たちは 計画の遅い段階で参画したが, デザインに充分に 大きな影響を与えることができた. ランドスケー プのコンセプトは, 2棟の高層オフィスビルと2 本の主要街路によって明確に区画された広いオー プンスペースである. 美しくデザインされたディ テールをもつ180mの長さの歩行者用広場がオフ ィスタワーと駐車場を連結している.

コイが泳ぎ, スイレンの咲く長方形の池が, 細 長いプラザにアクセントを添えている. 池の周囲 は, 刈り込まれた灌木と, 緑色のヴェルデ大理石 で縁取られている. 大きく繁ったフェニックスが 池の両サイドに並び, 高層オフィス棟の両側にあ るフォーマルなヤシの木広場は, インフォーマルな 公園部分と対照をなしている. さまざまな高木や 芝生の緑が, 大都市のコンテクストの中にある, オフィスタワーに緑と成熟した牧歌的な表情を与 えている.

「クライアント, 建築家, ランドスケープデザイナ ー, そしてチームの他のすべての人々の相互作用 が, プロジェクトをよりよいものとした. それぞ れの優れたアイデアが, それぞれの積み重ね以上 の効果を発揮した. それは, たいへん価値のある 体験であった.」
　　　　　　　　　　　　　　リチャード・ロウ

Fountain Court at Curtis Center

Philadelphia, Pennsylvania, U.S.A.

カーチスセンター・ファウンテンコート

This project offered a unique challenge: to re-design a major interior space — an atrium — for a building listed on the National Registry of Historic Places. We were thrilled with the opportunity, one landscape architects don't often get.

At our first meeting, we were told that the developer's program required three items: a fountain, a stone floor and some retail uses bordering the atrium. Then, on our first visit to the atrium (which was originally roofless), we were struck by the height of the space relative to its length and width. The pedestrian was overwhelmed! As a service court — 55 m (180 feet) by 18 m (60 feet), and 55 m (180 feet) high — the space had accommodated a loading dock and large vehicles. Our major task was to adapt the space to pedestrian scale, humanize it, and make it elegant.

Viewing the atrium as a Great Room, we focused attention at one end with a sensuous fountain, composed of six curvilinear terraces that appear to "flow" from the source of water. Leading the eye toward this fountain, and also providing a transitional scale from the structure to the individual, are the flanking rows of tall pedestal planters. The foliage sprouting from the tops of the planters creates a lowered translucent ceiling. The marble flooring pattern, inspired by Pennsylvania Dutch quilts, is a counter to the building's simple facade and fenestration. It leads the eye toward the source of its pattern, the fountain. The focus of the eye remains low: on floor and fountain. The woven stone is also colorful textural linkage tying together fountain to pedestals, pedestals to urns and urns to pedestrians.

"We developed the sensuous fountain to counterbalance the straight-line geometry of the floor, walls and rows of pedestals. In effect, the fluid forms ease the rigidity of the space and became the origin, or source, for the whole design."
— ***Michael Sardina***

この計画は，アメリカの歴史的建造物に指定されている建物の，インテリアの主要空間であるアトリウムを改装するという，ユニークな挑戦であった．ランドスケープアーキテクトにとって，このような仕事はめったにないチャンスなので，私たちは非常に感動した．

打ち合わせの席で，ディベロッパーに3つの要素，噴水，石の床，そしてアトリウムの周囲の店舗によってアトリウムを彩ることを依頼された．そこで，まず最初に実際にアトリウムを訪れて（当初はここは屋根のないスペースであった），アトリウムの広さに比して高さが非常に高いことに驚き，その高さに圧倒された．54m×18mの平面に高さが54mという空間は，かつて大型自動車が入って荷積みをするサービスコートとして使われていた．私たちは，ここを歩行者のスケールに合った，人間的な，エレガントな空間に変えることを目指した．

アトリウムを大きな部屋としてみることで，一方の端に洒落た噴水を配置して1つの焦点とし，そこからちょうど噴水の源から流れ出るように，曲線状の6つのテラスをつくり出した．一列に並んだ，高い台の上のプランターが視線を噴水のほうに導き，同時に大きな建物のスケールを個人のスケールに移行させている．プランターから伸びるヤシの葉が，低い透かしの天井をつくり出している．床の大理石のパターンは，ペンシルバニアのダッチキルトからヒントを得たもので，建物のファサードや窓割りのパターンに対抗している．床のパターンは，その根源の噴水に視線を導く．視線の焦点は，床と噴水という低いところに止まる．織り込まれた石のパターンは，さらにカラフルに，噴水からプランターを支える柱脚へ，柱脚から床に置かれた植栽用の壺へ，壺から歩行者へと連なっていく．

「私たちは，床や壁やプランターの高い柱脚の列といった，直線的な幾何学模様に釣り合う，美しい噴水を考えた．実際，水の流れのつくり出す形は，空間の固さを和らげ，デザイン全体の源泉となる．」

マイケル・サーディナ

International Jewelry Center

Los Angeles, California, U.S.A.

国際ジュエリーセンター

This small urban park is really a modernist garden, in the tradition of Guevrekian and other experimenters of the 1920s. In a tough urban setting, the garden is a respite. It extends the interior restaurant space, spilling out of doors. It is also an abstract, three-dimensional space which can be considered in purely sculptural terms — as a large cubic volume set within three planes.

Our challenge was to create an urban park in Los Angeles, a city where people don't often stroll or sit in parks. This particular section of the city had not yet been developed; so the park was designed for future use by the urban population that will work in the Pershing Square area.

When we arrived on the project, the location of the garden was a given — the gloomy north side of the building. Our most critical problem, then, was to bring light into the garden. We chose materials for their cheerful, practical and sensual qualities: a gravel floor (for texture and sound); the ferns at the base of the glass block wall (for fine texture and movement in light breezes); the honey locust trees (for consistency in matching, seasonal yellow color, leafless structure in winter, dappled light in summer); and glass block (for reflective, ambiguous light).

"At the time we began to design this garden, PPG had just begun to manufacture solar block. The block has an intriguing quality that I thought would be fun to work with. The block's surface coating creates an ambiguity about the size and depth of the garden because of its fuzzy, reflective character."
— ***Susan Whitin***

この小さなアーバンパークは，1920年代のゲーブルキアンや他の実験的な人々の伝統的手法によるモダニスト庭園である．ロサンゼルスの活発な都市構造の中にあって，この庭園はひとときの休息の場を提供している．室内のレストランがドアから外へはみ出してきたようなこの空間は，また抽象的な3次元的空間でもある．「3つの平面によって構成された大きな立方体」という純粋な彫刻的表現によってもとらえられるであろう．

ここでの挑戦は，ロサンゼルスという，人々が公園の中でゆっくり散策したり座ったりすることの少ない街に，アーバンパークをつくり出すことであった．計画地は現在でも開発の進んでいない特殊な地域にあったため，将来的にパーシングスクエア地域で働く人々を想定して，この公園を設計した．

敷地は建物の北側の薄暗い場所だったので，庭園に光を導入することを目的として，材料に楽しげで実用的，そして美しいものを選び出した．たとえば小石敷きの床(質感と音響)，ガラスブロックの壁の前にはシダの茂み(繊細な質感と微風にもそよぐ動き)，アメリカサイカチの植栽(秋の黄葉，冬の落葉，夏の木漏れ日などがこの場所に最適)，そしてガラスブロック(光を反射したり拡散する)である．

「この設計を開始したときに，PPGがちょうどソーラーブロックを生産し始めた．このブロックは私が使ってみたいと思う魅力を充分に備えていた．ブロック表面のコーティングが，均一でなく反射する性質をもち，この庭園のサイズや奥行きにほどよいテクスチュアだったのである．」

スーザン・ホワイティン

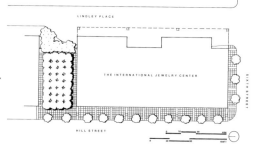

Worldwide Plaza

New York, New York, U.S.A.
ワールドワイドプラザ

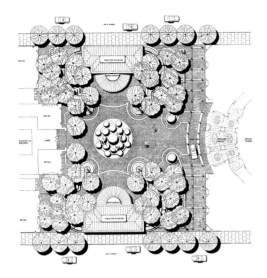

In order to make his numbers work (that is, to realize a reasonable profit on the project), the developer Norm Zeckendorf, of ZCW Associates, needed a floor-area-ratio (FAR) of 12 on this Midtown Manhattan block, once the site of Madison Square Garden. By New York's planning codes, the allowable FAR was 10. The City of New York would allow a bonus of one FAR, however, if the total reconstruction of the Eighth Avenue/49th Street subway station was funded by the project. In addition, one FAR might be granted if the "public amenities" (or public open space) met stringent requirements established by the Planning Department. SWA's design for the mid-block plaza succeeded in

getting the necessary approvals, after going through the lengthy Urban Land Use Requirement Permit approval process.

The plaza lies between a 49-story office tower to the east, and a 38-story tower of residential units to the west. The ground floors of both towers are occupied by retail uses. Architect David Childs, of SOM, designed the office tower to recall classic New York skyscrapers of the 1920s. To complement this, the street-level on-structure plaza is paved in Roman brick. Gently curving retaining walls of Roman brick with limestone caps accommodate a 1.8-meter (6-foot) grade change between 49th and 50th Streets, while separating pedestrians from the mid-block

driveway. These low walls also provide much of the required 240 linear meters (800 linear feet) of seating. Two groves of sycamores offer shade in summer, and moveable chairs near the central fountain serve office workers, residents and patrons of the six-theatre complex below the plaza.

"The plaza is a refreshing oasis in this gritty New York neighborhood. It also is a common meeting place between residents and office workers and is used seven days a week for many hours of the day and night."

– Michael Sardina

ディベロッパーであるZCWアソシエイツのノーム・ゼッケンドルフは、かつてマジソンスクエアガーデンの敷地であったミッドマンハッタンのこのブロックで、充分採算性のあるプロジェクトを計画するには、1,200％の容積率が必要と考えた．が，ニューヨークの計画コードは1,000％しか許可していなかった．ただしニューヨーク市は、もし8番街と49丁目の交点にある地下鉄駅も含めた全体地域を再開発するならば、容積率を100％緩和し，また、市の計画局の厳しい基準に合致する公共のためのアメニティ（公共のオープンスペース）をつくるなら、さらに100％の上乗せを認めるとの

条件を出した．長い開発許可申請プロセスを経て、SWAのデザインによる敷地中央の広場は必要な許可条件を手に入れることに成功した．

広場は、敷地東側の49階建てのオフィス棟と西側の38階建ての住居棟の間に位置する．建物の1階は両棟とも店舗が専有している．設計者であるSOMのデイビッド・チャイルズは、オフィス棟を1920年代のクラシックな摩天楼のようにデザインした．これを補完するように、道路レベルの広場の床はローマれんがで舗装された．ゆるくカーブを描く、石灰石を冠するローマれんがの低い壁が49丁目と50丁目の約1.8mの高低差を吸収し、ブロ

ックの中央を横切る自動車道と歩行者を分けている．この一連の低い壁は、同時にまた長さ240mのベンチにもなる．プラタナスの2つの林が夏には気持ちのよい木陰を提供し、中央の噴水周辺に置かれた可動のイスが、ここに働く人々、住民、そして広場下にある6つの劇場の関係者たちにいこいの場を提供する．

「広場は、ニューヨークのほこりっぽい街中のオアシスである．住民と働く人が出会う場であり、また1週間に7日昼も夜も24時間使われる場所でもある．」
マイケル・サーディナ

Arizona Center

Phoenix, Arizona, U.S.A.
アリゾナセンター

Downtown Phoenix was dead. Everyone thought The Rouse Company was crazy to join the city in trying to do its usual magic. There were no historic buildings, no waterfront, not even a history of downtown retail. The main attraction of this eight-block project of retail, office and a hotel would be its desert gardens — an oasis.

At the center, the oasis would be cool, wet and tranquil. To achieve this effect, the center is 2.4 m (8 feet) lower than street level, water is concentrated there, and the shade is dense. From this sunken oasis, one looks out to the tiered stroll gardens, intricately patterned with desert plants and flowers. Date palms give structure to the spaces and provide an overstory

of shade. Mesquites and jacarandas provide understory shade along the walkway. Several experiences are offered, in tranquil stroll gardens, on eating terraces, in intimate parterre gardens, in the children's maze garden, and along the promenade overlooking the gardens. Embellishments include Henry Beer-designed arbors and a trio of frogs in foggy grottoes.

Materials include three colors of Arizona sandstone in paving and walls, decomposed granite walks, precast concrete steps, painted steel railings and teak hand rails. Desert plants include agave, insegnite, sage, hesperaloe, peppers, yucca and palms.

"The tranquil gardens contrast with the bustling Festival Market, full of shops, bars and eateries. At night the mood changes to a more dramatic urban scene. People now stay downtown after work to meet, eat and drink. Suburbanites come on weekends to shop, and teenagers hang out in the gardens."

– William Callaway

"We tried to think of the eight blocks as a whole and struggled to activate the entire 'canvas' it represented. It was important to us to find a level of intimacy and delight in each piece as we worked to orchestrate and weave together the larger experience."

– Jim Lee

アリゾナ州フェニックスのダウンタウンは荒廃が進んでいた．誰もが，ラウス社がいつもの魔法で市と協働してこの地域の再開発に取り組むとは狂気の沙汰だと噂した．歴史的な建物もなく，ウォーターフロントもない．さらにダウンタウンの商業集積さえない状態であった．商業施設，オフィス，ホテルを含む8ブロックからなるこのプロジェクトの売り物は，その砂漠の中の庭園，すなわちオアシスであった．

オアシスには，涼しさ，適度な湿り気，そして静けさが必要である．この効果を得るために，センターは道路レベルから約2.4m低くし，水がここに集中し，影が濃く差すように計画された．一段低いオアシスから，砂漠の木や草花が植えられた

テラス状の散策できる庭園に続く．高いナツメヤシが庭園に空間の広がりを与え，長い影を落とす．メスキートやジャカランダが散策路に低い影を落とす．静かな散策路をはじめ，食事用のテラス，色とりどりの花木庭園，子供用の迷路庭園，庭園を見下ろす散策路などが用意され，さまざまな体験を味わえる．また，ヘンリー・ビア設計のあずまややや小さな洞窟の中の3匹のカエルなどの楽しい装飾もある．

アリゾナ産の3色の砂岩による舗装や壁，花崗石の道，プレキャストコンクリートの階段，塗装仕上げのスチール柵，チーク材の手すりなどが用いられ，また，リュウゼツラン，セージ，ペッパー，ユッカ，ヤシなどの砂漠の植物が植えられた．

「静かな庭園は，さまざまな店舗やバー，レストランからなる賑やかなフェスティバルマーケットとは対照的である．夜は，さらにドラマチックに都会的な雰囲気へと変化する．人々は仕事が終わってからもダウンタウンに滞在して，人と会ったり，食事を楽しんだりするようになった．郊外居住者も週末には買い物にくるようになり，若者は庭園に集い楽しんでいる．」ウィリアム・キャラウェイ

「私たちは，この8ブロックをひとつのまとまりの空間と考え，その全体をキャンバスと見立ててデザインした．どの部分にも親密で楽しい雰囲気を創出することが大事であった．それらを調和させ，相互に関連させることで，さらに豊かな体験を可能にすることを目指した．」 ジェームズ・リー

Fashion Island

Newport Beach, California, U.S.A.
ファッションアイランド

More than 20 years ago, The SWA Group began to work on the development of Newport Center, the business nucleus of south coast Orange County. This 180-hectare (450-acre), mixed-use project, including hotel, office, residential, commercial and civic uses, was designed as the heart of the developing Irvine Ranch. Newport Center was viewed as the gateway to the Irvine Ranch; and Fashion Island — a shopping mall — was to be the Center's commercial core.

At that time, Fashion Island was unique. Built when indoor malls were in vogue, this mall was the only major outdoor regional shopping center of its kind, surrounded (and supported) by office development, including the Irvine Company headquarters, and the residential development beyond. The original design of Fashion Island combined courtyards with public open spaces, expressing the civic quality of the mall. In time, however, the Irvine Company decided that this mall needed a new image and character.

One of the most significant struggles with the development of the mall's renovation was in maintaining the owner's personal vision for Fashion Island while observing all the traditional rules of retail design, demanding, perhaps, a distinctly different design aesthetic.

The new image, derived from the dry, subtropical climate of Southern California, was to be Mediterranean. The mall was conceived as a series of neighborhoods within a European village that appeared to have been built over time. A main street runs through the village, linking the neighborhoods, each with its distinct character. The major tenants would occupy large "villas" with forecourt plazas fronting on the main street. A story, or script, was written to describe the atmosphere of each neighborhood, the elements to be found there, and the events to occur there each month, throughout the year. Having developed these ideas in close collaboration with the Irvine Company, SWA redesigned the landscape spaces and renovated the plantings, introducing bold combinations of Mexican fan palms, Canary Island date palms, oleanders and Indian laurels.

"Fashion Island is the crown jewel of Newport Center. To have been a part of this successful team was personally the most satisfying aspect of the work."
– David Berkson

SWAが，カリフォルニア州オレンジカウンティの南部海岸沿いのビジネスの中心であるニューポートセンターの開発を始めてから，もう20年以上が経つ．この180haの広さの，ホテル，オフィス，住宅，商業，公共施設などからなる，複合用途施設は，開発中のアーバインランチの中心地区として設計された．ニューポートセンターは，アーバインランチへの入口であり，ショッピングモールのファッションアイランドはニューポートセンターの商業施設の中心となるものである．

当時，ファッションアイランドはユニークであった．室内型のモールが流行であった当時，オフィス(この開発を手がけているアーバイン社の本社を含む)や住居棟などに囲まれた，大規模な屋外型の広域ショッピングセンターは，ここが唯一のものであったからである．最初の計画では，公共のオープンスペースと中庭による構成で，モールはごく普通の公共的な性格であった．しかし，時間の経過とともに，アーバイン社はこのモールには，全く新しいイメージと性格が必要であると判断した．

モールを刷新する上での最も難しい課題は，伝統的な商業デザインの規則を尊重し，明らかに異なるデザインの趣味を満足させる一方で，いかに

オーナーの個人的なファッションアイランドに対するビジョンを反映させていくかであった．

新しいイメージは，サザンカリフォルニア特有の乾燥した亜熱帯気候から考慮して地中海を基本とした．モールは，長い時間の中で形成されてきたヨーロッパの街に見られるようなものをイメージして設計している．メインストリートは各地区をつなぎながら，それぞれ個性的な各ビレッジを貫いて走っている．主なテナントは，メインストリートに面した前庭つきの大きなビラという区画を占めている．それぞれの地区ごとに異なる雰囲気や，そこに見出す要素，年間を通じて毎月催されるイベントなどを描いた脚本が準備された．SWAは，アーバイン社と密着してこれらの計画を進め，ランドスケープ計画を見直し，植栽計画を一新し，メキシコのオウギヤシ，カナリーアイランドのナツメヤシ，オレアンダー，インディアン・ローレルなどを植えた．

「ファッションアイランドは，まるでニューポートセンターの宝石である．この開発チームの一員として計画に参加したことで，個人的にたいへん満足のいく仕事ができた．」**デイビッド・バークソン**

NEWPORT CENTER
AERIAL PERSPECTIVE

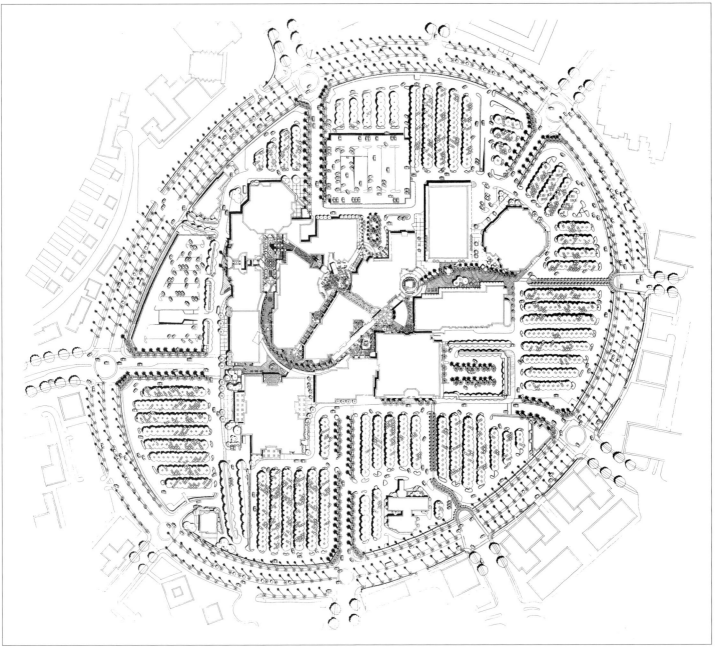

Hyatt Regency Scottsdale Gainey Ranch

Scottsdale, Arizona, U.S.A.
ゲイニーランチのハイアットリージェンシー

Like the grand old resort hotels, modern resort hotels are escapes from urban daily life. Many new hotels have become fantasy lands, as well, combining a "Disneyland" atmosphere with water parks. At the Hyatt Regency/Gainey Ranch, we wanted to integrate modern requirements into the model of a grand old hotel — quiet, informal, elegant — where one would be tempted to dress for dinner, play croquet, or take an evening stroll (while the kids are using the water slide).

A series of garden courts are formed by the wings of the building and groves of date palms. Each garden offers a different character and experience. The Entry and Fountain Garden Courts combine to form the entry processional, leading to the Water Gardens. The Entry Court is surrounded by palms and hedges with a cooling central fountain. Moving on axis through the open-air lobby, one looks to the mountains rising beyond the Fountain Court. This court is flanked by palms and water runnels that frame the view and lead one gently down to the main cross-axial promenade and the Water Garden East. In the cool evenings, a bonfire punctuates the view.

The swimming pools, in the East and West Water Gardens, are connected by an "aqueduct" from which bougainvillea hangs and water falls in the form of spouts and cascades. The Water Garden West is the active pool, with a sand beach, water slide and water temple. The Water Garden East is a calmer, more traditional pool. One swims around and under grotto pavilions that house hot spas and cold plunges. Other gardens include the quiet, secluded Garden Court and the more animated Lawn Court, used for games and outdoor receptions.

"The design, with its formal, axial compositions and temple-like structures, recalls pre-Colombian civilizations." **–William Callaway**

"Building an oasis in the desert is a challenge; building this complex and interactive system of plants, pavements, fountains and pools pushed us to our limits . . . it was a grand time!"
– John Loomis

かつての大規模なリゾートホテルがそうであったように、現代のリゾートホテルもまた、都市の日常生活からの逃避地となっている。今日、多くの新しいホテルは、水を配した公園にディズニーランド的な雰囲気を加えた、いわゆるファンタジーランド化している。アリゾナ州スコッツデイルに建つハイアットリージェンシーでは、かつてのリゾートホテルがもっていた、静けさ、親しさ、優雅さといった特徴(夕食に正装し、クロケットを楽しみ、子供たちはプールのすべり台で遊び、夕べの散歩を楽しむといった)に、現代的な要求を統合することを試みた。

連続した中庭が、建物とナツメヤシの木立ちによって形づくられている。それぞれ特色があり、異なる体験を提供する。正面玄関アプローチとこれに続く噴水のある庭は、玄関であると同時に人々を水の庭に導く。ここは、中央に噴水があり、ヤシの木と生垣に囲まれている。吹き放しのロビーの軸線に沿って進むと、噴水の向こうに山並みが見えてくる。水の庭は、ヤシの並木と水路が眺望を縁取り、ゆるやかな下り坂が人々を、主軸と交差するプロムナードや東の水の庭に導く。涼しい夜などはかがり火が焚かれて、また別の景観を呈する。

東と西の庭には水泳プールがあり、2つのプールはアクアダクトで結びつけられている。アクアダクトにはブーゲンビリアが咲き乱れ、水がしぶきをあげたり滝になって流れ落ちている。西の水の庭は活動的なプールで、砂浜やすべり台、水上の寺院などもある。東の水の庭は、より静かな、伝統的なプールである。内部に温泉や飛び込みプールのある洞穴のまわりを人々は泳ぎまわる。他にも静かな閉ざされた庭や、さまざまなゲームや野外のレセプションなどに使われる芝生の庭もある。

「フォーマルで軸線的な構成、寺院のような建物というデザインは、コロンブス以前の文明を思わせる。」
ウィリアム・キャラウェイ

「砂漠にオアシスをつくることは、1つの挑戦である。建物をつくり、植栽や舗装、噴水、プールなどを配して相互に関連づけていく。それは私たちの限界への挑戦であり、たいへん満足のいく仕事であった。」
ジョン・ルーミス

Williams Square

Las Colinas, Texas, U.S.A.
ウィリアムズスクエア

At Williams Square, bronze sculptures of wild mustangs gallop across an open granite plaza and through an abstract running stream, capturing a spirit which has come to symbolize this new Texas community.

The client, developer Ben Carpenter, wanted to convey an impression of stability and permanence. Together with sculptor Robert Glen, The SWA Group responded with a composition of varying hues and finishes of granite, enlivened by running water and built to last forever.

"Williams Square exists as a symbol of one man's concept of what life for all of us should be — free and unburdened by rope or bridle, free to be who we choose to be. Around this abstract idea the whole design effort revolves. Horses bigger than life, running on a flat, scaleless plain, allow each of us to draw our own conclusion about their meaning and their relationship to us."
— ***Jim Reeves***

テキサス州ラスコリナスのウィリアムズスクエアでは，テキサスの新しいコミュニティを象徴するかのように，野性馬のブロンズ像が花崗岩の広場を横切り，抽象化された川の流れをしぶきを上げて駆けている．

クライアントであるディベロッパーのベン・カーペンターは，安定と永続を表現したいと考えた．彫刻家ロバート・グレンと一体となってSWAは，さまざまな色調の構成と花崗岩の仕上げを決定し，流れる水によって活気づけ，永続的な環境をつくり出した．

「ウィリアムズスクエアは，すべての人々にとって人生とはどうあるべきか，ロープや手綱で繋がれることなく，自分の人生を自由に選べるべきであるという，ある人物のコンセプトをシンボルとして表現したものである．この抽象的なアイデアを巡って，デザイン全体が展開された．実物以上に

大きい馬たちが，フラットでスケールのない広場を駆けている姿は，私たちすべてに，その意味するところと私たちとの関連を想起させ，結論づける方向に導いてくれるだろう．」
ジェームズ・リーブズ

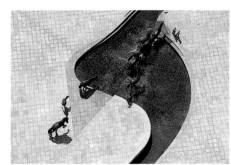

Dallas West End Historic District

Dallas, Texas, U.S.A.
ダラス・ウエストエンド歴史地区

The SWA Group consulted to the Dallas Department of Public Works on the development of an urban master plan for this 20-block district of historic warehouses in downtown Dallas. The plan's objectives were to encourage diverse yet compatible uses, to improve vehicular circulation, and to provide a sense of identity for the district. The project successfully stimulated interest in private redevelopment as well as public sector support for opportunities to revitalize the district.

"It makes little difference whether streets are paved of stone, dirt, asphalt or gold; it is the merchant that rules. Streets are about merchants. Streets returned to merchants are streets of life and vitality."
— **Jim Reeves**

"When we designed Dallas Alley we tried to put a bright cap on this end of the Historic District"
— **Chuck McDaniel**

SWAはテキサス州ダラス市の公共建築計画局に，ダウンタウンの20ブロックにわたる古い歴史的な倉庫が残る地区の市街地のマスタープランの作成に関するコンサルティングを行なった．このマスタープランの目的は，多様でありながら一体感のある土地利用を促進し，自動車交通事情を改良し，地区独自の個性を確立することであった．この計画は，みごとに公共セクタの支持ばかりでなく，民間開発の関心も促すことになった．

「道路を石で敷くか，泥のままかアスファルトか金で敷くかといったことは大して問題ではない．それを決めるのは商人である．道路は商人とともに存在する．商人に返された道路は，生き生きとした活力に満ちたものとなる．」
ジェームズ・リーブズ

「私たちがダラスの通りをデザインしたとき，この歴史的な地区の端に，『明るい帽子』を被せようと計画した．」
チャック・マクダニエル

National Bank of Commerce Plaza
San Antonio, Texas, U.S.A.
ナショナル商業銀行プラザ

In the design of this project, the seminal thought was pure river: everything was to be one with the river, from the soft and gentle curves of its walks and planters to the soft, grassy overlook with its cypress, emulating a thousand such scenes throughout Texas. Everything leads either to or from the river's edge. In this great and ancient city we are at once reminded that the river — every drop of its flowing waters — is a giver of life.

"We wanted to honor and respect this river. We wanted to create a place where we could visit our beginning and perhaps glimpse our future."
– Jim Reeves

"Our vision was to create a garden of surprise and mystery which enriched the urban tableau of Riverwalk."
– Chris Miller

この広場は，有名なテキサス州サンアントニオの川沿いに位置しているため，デザインの中心は川に置かれた．すべてのものが川と一体になるようにデザインされた．ゆるやかにカーブして流れる川や歩道，プランターの植物も頭上のサイプレスや足元の灌木もやさしくカーブを描き，テキサスのどこにでもある光景となっている．すべてが川辺に向かい，川辺から戻ってくる．この偉大な古い都市で，川は流れる水の一滴一滴が命あるものであることを思い出させてくれる．

「私たちは川を讃え，尊重したいと考えた．ここを訪れることが，根源を知り，また未来を垣間見ることになるような場所を創出したかった.」
ジェームズ・リーブズ

「私たちのビジョンは，リバーウォークの劇的な都市空間をさらに豊かにする，驚きとミステリーの庭をつくることであった.」
クリス・ミラー

The Fountain Plaza, Broward County Convention Center

Fort Lauderdale, Florida, U.S.A.

ブロワードカウンティ・コンベンションセンター

The centerpiece for the Broward County Convention Center and the proposed adjacent mixed-use development is a monumental sculpture fountain set in a 1.3 acre entrance plaza. In collaboration with renowed wildlife sculptor, Kent Ullberg, the fountain depicts abstractly an uplifted segment of the ocean. The main thirty (30') feet high bronze Sailfish and two additional support pieces are represented in "Three Stages of Ascent" and are set on a black granite wedge simulating a wave form. Diorama elements including the Dolphin, Kingfish, and Ballyhoo portray the ocean community. The Ridley Sea Turtle sculpture pays homage to the endangered species and draws public attention to environmental awareness.

The water effects are sequenced to simulate the Sailfish jumping out of the ocean and "tail-walking". Water cascades over the entire granite wedge and flows down all four sides. Spray mist jets at the granite wedge base and the introduced pier further evoke the idea of the ocean scenario and shoreline.

"The Fountain Plaza uniquely captures the spirit and essence of the locale and the Sailfish and Plaza are becoming a symbol and landmark for the City of Fort Lauderdale. The project also represents the best collaborative talents of the firm."
— **Don Murakami**

コンベンションセンターと隣接地に計画された複合施設のセンターピースは，約5,000㎡のエントランスプラザに設けられた，モニュメンタルな彫刻のある噴水である．有名な野生生物の彫刻家ケント・ウルバーグと協働したもので，ダイナミックな海を抽象的に描写した噴水を配置している．中心となる高さ9mの背びれの大きいバショウカジキと，それをサポートする他の2つの彫刻は「上昇の3段階」を表わしている．彫刻は波を型どる黒御影石の台座に載っている．イルカ，キングフィッシュ（サバの一種），バリフー（サヨリの一種）をあしらったジオラマ風の作品は，海洋のコミュニティを表わしている．リドリー海亀の彫刻は，絶滅の危機に瀕している種族への敬意を表わし，環境問題への人々の注意を促してもいる．

　水面はカジキが海面からジャンプし，尾びれで立ちながら泳いでいく一連の動作を効果的に演出している．黒御影石の台座全体から水が滝のようにあふれ，四周に流れ落ちる．水煙が台座の底部に向けて噴き出し，そこに差し込まれた桟橋がいっそう海洋と海岸の雰囲気を高める．

「ファウンテン・プラザは地域のもつ精神や特質を独特な形で捉えたものであり，バショウカジキや広場はフォート・ローダーテイル市のシンボルとなり，ランドマークとなりつつある．このプロジェクトは，SWAの専門家たちの英知を結集した最高の共同作業であったともいえる．」

ドナルド・ムラカミ

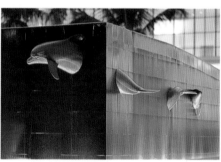

Sparks Street Mall

Ottawa, Ontario, Canada

スパークスストリートのモール

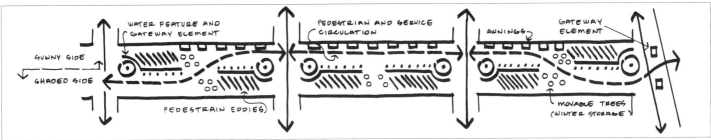

The design for Sparks Street builds on a theme of tradition, elegance and distinction, while offering new opportunities for pedestrian and commercial use. The main entry to the Mall offers views of the historic Parliament House beyond. The traditional character of Sparks Street is emphasized by revealing views to the many heritage buildings on the Mall and by the location of light standards, sidewalks, and a central street pavement to reflect the layout of a traditional urban street. High quality materials, formal patterns, and classical forms and details contribute to an atmosphere of elegance.

"Of all the problems in urban design, finding a solution that everyone can understand and support remains number one. It took twenty-eight review agencies, four competitions, any number of later designs, hard-core pragmatics, strong debate, disagreement, and more debate, to find a solution. It always does — most of the time."

–Jim Reeves

カナダの首都オタワにあるスパークスストリートのデザインは、伝統、優雅さ、気品をテーマとし、また歩行者や商業的な使用に新たな機会を与えるように計画された．モールへの主入口の向こうには、歴史的な国会議事堂が見えている．通りの伝統的な特色は、モールに面した数多くの歴史的な建物をよく見えるようにしたこと、照明灯や歩道の配置、伝統的な都市の通りのレイアウトを反映した中心街路の舗装などによっていっそう強調されている．質の高い材料、フォーマルなパターン、クラシックな形態やディテールの採用などが、エレガントな雰囲気づくりに貢献している．

「アーバンデザインの大きな問題は、だれもが理解し、支持してくれる解決を見出すことである．このプロジェクトでは、28回の見直し作業、4回のコンペ、その後の数々の設計、根強い実用主義、激しい議論、意見の不一致、さらに議論、そしてようやく解決を見出した．どんな場合もだいたい似たようなものだ．」　ジェームズ・リーブス

Burnaby Metrotown Resource Library

Burnaby, British Columbia, Canada

バーナビー・メトロタウン資源図書館

The plan features a civic lawn, parterre gardens in a series of flat tiers with fountains, two double allees of honey locusts trees, a children's garden and a native flower garden. In order to dramatize the building exposure to the front door of the space, the central area was planned as forced perspective. The effect gives a stronger sense of civic grandeur; and the illusion of a bigger, lengthier and prominent civic focus.

The design idea for Burnaby's central space parallels the idea of the Lawn at the University of Virginia designed by President Thomas Jefferson. In Jefferson's rectangular lawn space, the buildings are located on the four sides and provide a column arcade border for the Lawn. At Burnaby, the Central Lawn is also a rectangle, and the buildings are placed on three sides. The double allees of honey locust trees recall the colonnade border and lend a sense of structure for the whole design. The central lawn in both examples, represents democracy by suggesting qualities of openness, flexibility and availability for all to use.

"A civic space should be inviting, functional, grand, wonderful, and multi-purposed. A space that one can look into and look out of. A place that encourages participation."

– John Wong

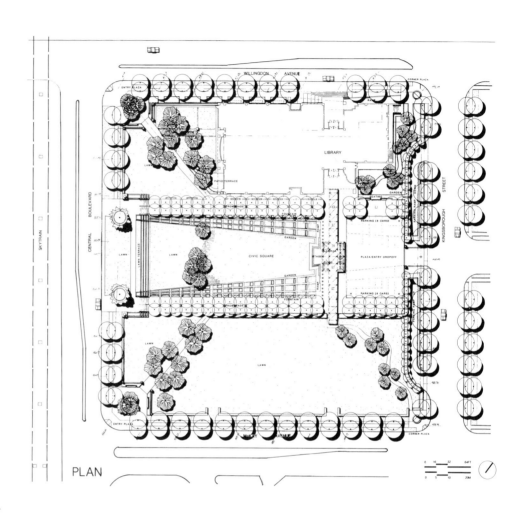

PLAN

この図書館はカナダ・ブリティッシュコロンビアのバーナビーに建つ．計画は芝生の市民広場と，平坦で段状につながった噴水のある花壇，2列のニセアカシアの並木，子供広場，野性の花畑などを特徴としている．空間の正面に建物をドラマチックに据えるために，中央の広場はパースをつけてデザインしている．この効果は，都市の威厳を強く表現し，空間をより大きく，奥行をより深く見せ，都市の際立った中心を形づくる．

　バーナビーの中央広場のデザインは，大統領トーマス・ジェファーソン設計のバージニア大学の芝生広場に相通じるものである．ジェファーソンの長方形の芝生スペースにおいては，建物はその四周に配置され，芝生との境に列柱のアーケードがある．バーナビーでも中央の芝生は長方形で，3方に建物がある．2列のニセアカシアの並木が列柱のアーケードを思わせ，また，全体の中である種の構造物のような役割を担っている．両者とも，中央の芝生は，あらゆる用途への開放性，柔軟性，適応性などの点で民主主義を象徴したものである．

「市民のための空間は，人々を招き入れ，機能的で，広く，楽しく，多様に使えなくてはならない．それは内部が覗けたり，外部が見通せる空間である．人々の参加を促す空間だ．」　ジョン・ウォン

Lantern Bay Blufftop Parks

Dana Point, California, U.S.A.
ランタンベイ・ブラフトップ公園

The site was steep — a leftover borrow pit from the construction of Dana Point Harbor. Originally, the ocean met the land in beautiful tide pools at the base of bluffs. These bluffs, or palisades, were once popular vista points. After the borrow pit had been carved into the site, however, there were no sustaining natural systems on the site. The blufftop was a totally disfigured and abandoned landform. Thus, the entire site had to be completely regraded to recapture the lost grandeur and use of the blufftops. This was the first design concept.

The construction of Golden Lantern Road between the harbor and Pacific Coast Highway had divided the site into two natural use areas. This suggested our second design concept: to have two distinctly different parks, each with its own character and relationship to the sea.

The western park accommodated the surrounding communities' desire to be directly tied to the blufftop edge and Dana Point Harbor. For several neighborhoods, then, we provided connections, accentuated by frequent grade changes and pedestrian ramps. The eastern park was designed as a large open space reminiscent of the dramatic blufftops of the unaltered California Coast. The shape and form of this park was purposely simplified, flattened, and tilted to accent the visual connection between the blufftop and the sea.

Both parks bring people as close to the edge of the blufftop as possible without endangering them. The eastern park edge experience is long and smooth, with slowly changing panoramic views. The western park leads directly to the bluff edge, then back into the park, rhythmically incorporating the handicapped access ramps. The sensation of being right at the edge of the blufftop without falling is the most dramatic experience within the parks.

The third concept was to keep the park equipment, lighting and furniture to a minimum and to remove them from the coastal periphery. With grading and plant materials, we emphasized the uninterrupted vistas of land and sea.

"When we finished the grading and planting plans, this project was done. With a natural setting like this, we were searching for the least obvious appearance of design with the most human impact."
                                        – Don Tompkins

敷地は，急峻なカリフォルニア州ダナポイントの港を建設した際の土取場の名残りである．元来ここは太平洋が，崖の下の潮の満ち引きする美しい入江で陸地と出会う場所であり，これらの崖，あるいは断崖は，かつては人々の恰好の展望台であった．しかし，敷地がいまのように窪地になってからは，かつての自然の魅力もなくなり，見捨てられた場所になっていた．このため，敷地全体を造成し直し，失った壮麗さや，崖の上という特徴を取り戻す必要があった．これが第1のデザインコンセプトであった．

港と太平洋沿岸ハイウェイの間にゴールデン・ランタン道路を建設することで，敷地は大きく2分された．このことがそれぞれ独自の特徴と海への関係をもつ，2つの全く異なる公園をつくるという第2のデザインコンセプトを示唆した．

西側の公園は，周辺のコミュニティの要望で，崖や港に直接接するように計画された．周辺の近隣住区のために連絡路をつくり，段差を細かく刻んでアクセントをつけ，歩行者用の斜路をつけた．東側の公園はカリフォルニアの海岸地帯にいまも変わらず存在する断崖上の劇的な空間に似た，広いオープンスペースとしてデザインされた．公園の形態は，崖と海を視覚的に関連づけるために意図的に単純化，平坦化され，傾斜をつけられている．

東西の両公園とも，危険のない範囲内で，崖の端ぎりぎりまで人が近づけるようになっている．東の公園の端は，ゆっくりと眺望を変化させながら，長くなだらかに続いている．西の公園はまず人々を崖の端へ導き，そこから公園に入っていく．この導入路は途中で障害者用の斜路とリズミカルに交差している．今にも落ちそうな崖の縁ぎりぎりにいるという感覚は，公園の中でも最もドラマティックな体験である．

第3番目のコンセプトは，公園の諸設備，照明や備品類は必要最小限に止め，特に海岸沿いの周縁部には何も置かないようにしたことである．造成や植栽計画では，特に陸と海の両方の眺望を損なわないことを主眼に決定した．

「私たちが造成計画や植栽計画を終えたとき，このプロジェクトは完了した．このような自然環境においては，人々に強い印象を与える．しかし人為的に行なわれたと気付かれないようなデザインを追究している．」
                                        ドナルド・トンプキンズ

Refugio Valley Park

Hercules, California, U.S.A.

レフュージオバレー公園

In the late 1970s, when we became consultants to the City of Hercules, that master-planned community was still developing. In its subdivisions lived some 4,000 people — mostly young, middle-income, and racially mixed — with a certain "pioneer" spirit. It would take some 15 years for the town to grow to its projected population of 20,000. Meanwhile, the town manager and an ad-hoc citizens group hoped that the park we were to create, Refugio Valley Park, would be the major catalyst for the town's development.

It was. Part of the park's success lies in its natural setting: a valley among the coastal ranges of the San Francisco Bay Area, with eucalyptus-covered slopes leading up to ridges with fine views. Gradual, sensitive development had not yet broken the valley's link to the East Bay Regional Park system. And the nearest freeway, winding among the foothills, was not seen or heard until a strategic moment when all the valley opened up to view — briefly. The valley park was well placed, then, to serve as the identity of the town.

Named for the old company town of the Hercules Powder Company, Hercules has a new source of prosperity — the local life science and technology firms. Our design for the park, too, combines a sense of history, tradition, and new technology. Taking as our model the English landscape garden, we shaped the land to accommodate a meadow for active sports, a lake, picnic areas, a community garden, a play hill, and a grass amphitheatre. The structures and furnishings are bold expressions of modern technology: we used cast-in-place concrete, fabricated steel pipe (painted white), and other materials. The basic form of the domed pavilion recalls a temple in an English garden, but its materials and expression are modern.

"The design of the park was heavily oriented toward community use, so public participation through informal sessions was crucial. Even school children participated in the design. They also helped in the construction of tile work and painted murals."
– ***William Callaway***

1970年代後半，SWAがカリフォルニア州ハーキュリー市のコンサルタントになったとき，マスタープランで計画されたコミュニティはまだ開発中であった．計画された区画の住区には，比較的若い世代で，中流階級の，そしてさまざまな人種からなる，パイオニア精神をもった人々が4,000人ほど住んでいた．計画人口の2万人が住む町に成長するまでには，それから15年あまりかかった．市の担当者やそこに住む市民グループは，私たちがつくりつつあった新しい公園が，その間の街の発展の触媒となることを期待していた．

この公園は期待に沿うものであった．うまく成功した理由は，その自然のすばらしさにある．サンフランシスコ・ベイエリアの海岸に沿った谷間にあり，ユーカリの生える斜面を上ると，眺めのいい崖の上に出る．イーストベイ地域のパーク・システムに連結する谷間を壊さないよう，公園は少しずつ，注意深く開発が進められた．谷間全体が見える端までいかない限りは，丘の斜面の下をうねるように走る最も近いフリーウェイの姿は見えず，騒音も聞こえてこない．このようにバレーパークはうまく配置され，街のアイデンティティを示す場となっている．

ハーキュリー市はハーキュリー・パウダー社から名付けられた街であるが，いままた地元に生命科学や技術に関する企業が進出するという，新しい繁栄の源を見出した．私たちの公園のデザインも，こうした歴史や伝統と新しい技術の統合を意図した．イギリス庭園を参考に，活動的なスポーツのための草原，湖，ピクニックランド，コミュニティ庭園，遊びの丘，そして芝生の円形劇場などを生み出すように土地を造成した．建物やファニチュアは現代技術の大胆な表現となっている．素材にはコンクリート，白く塗ったスチールパイプなどが使われた．ドーム屋根のパビリオンの形態は，イギリス庭園のテンプルのようであるが，素材や表現はまったく新しい．

「公園のデザインは，地域住民の利用を第一に考えたため，非公式にではあるが，さまざまな形で市民がこの計画に参加している．学校の生徒までデザインに参加した．彼らは，公園のタイルや壁画の制作にも参加してくれた．」

ウィリアム・キャラウェイ

Photo by Simo Neri

Photo by Steve Proehl

Photo by Simo Neri

Shethar Memorial Garden

Tacoma, Washington, U.S.A.

シェザー・メモリアルガーデン

The Weyerhaeuser Company retained The SWA Group to design a memorial in honor of John Shethar, a much-loved executive based at the company's corporate headquarters. Knowing of Shethar's appreciation for nature — especially its woods and lakes — his colleagues, friends and family had set aside a wooded area adjacent to a lake and the headquarters facility. Within this woodland they wanted to construct an intimate memorial garden, where individuals could withdraw in solitude or small groups could gather informally.

We selected a clearing near the edge of the woodland, with vistas overlooking the lake. In our minds, we wanted to bunker the garden into the gentle slopes to minimize the intrusion of off-site road noise. The scheme suggests that, in excavating, native granite outcrops were encountered and that the material excavated was reconstituted and used to construct the seating terrace, steps and decomposed granite paths throughout the woodland.

The resulting granite ledge reflects the drilling and splitting process. A spring emerges from the outcrop, quietly drawing attention to the edge we have set and the lake it flows to meet.

"On our first site visit, we saw that they had reserved a beautifully wooded site with wonderful vistas of the lake. We came away intending to develop a garden rooted in a spirit of reverence, of being at one with nature. The memorial garden would be at once a creation and a product of its natural environment."

– Jim Lee

ウエアハウザー社は，本社で長く活躍し，多くの人々に愛されたジョン・シェザーの記念碑のデザインをSWAに委託した．シェザーは自然，特に森や湖を愛していたので，彼の仲間や友人，家族は，ここワシントン州タコマにある本社近くの，湖に隣接した森の中にメモリアルガーデンを設置することにした．森の中の敷地に，そこを訪れる人々が静かに孤独を楽しめ，かつ少人数が気軽に集まったりできる，親しみのあるメモリアルガーデンを望んだ．

敷地には，森のはずれの，湖を見下ろす，眺望の開けたところを選んだ．私たちは敷地脇を通る道路の騒音を排除するために，この庭をゆるやかな傾斜の窪地に配置したかった．この計画は以下の物語を示唆している．

敷地を掘ってみると，そこには花崗岩床が現われた．掘り出した花崗岩を再構成して座席となるテラスや階段をつくり，また森の中の小道の舗装に利用した．

その結果，花崗岩は穴を開けられたり，割られ

たりした痕跡をとどめている．この岩棚から湧き出した水が，人々の注意を敷地の境界やその水が流れ込む湖へと，静かに引きつける．

「最初に敷地を訪れたとき，そこには湖へのすばらしい眺望をもった，たいへん美しい森が保全されていた．そこで自然を敬う精神に基づいて庭園を創出することにした．メモリアルガーデンは，人間の創作であると同時に，自然環境がつくり出した産物でもある．」

ジェームズ・リー

CURRENT WORKS

最近作・計画案

East Highlands Ranch

Highland, California, U.S.A.

イーストハイランドランチ

East Highlands Ranch was established in the late 19th century in the foothills of the San Bernardino Mountains 96 km (60 miles) east of Los Angeles. Originally one of Southern California's premier citrus ranches, it was acquired by Mobil Land in the early 1980s for the purpose of creating a planned community. SWA was brought into the project in 1987 to prepare site plans and landscape plans for the final phases of development which included over 200 ha (500 acres), many of which were still producing oranges.

For the land at the north end of the project above Highland Avenue, SWA's design concept was to integrate both the surrounding natural chaparral landscape and the existing citrus orchards into the new, predominantly single-family development by preserving portions of the citrus orchards and developing strong connections with the surrounding natural landscape. The citrus orchards contain many old stone walls and stone water courses that were part of the original gravity-flow irrigation system. The most attractive of these walls will be preserved and will become the focus of the trail and open space system in the community. Roads were carefully aligned to emphasize visual connections to both the citrus orchards and the dramatic natural landscape.

At the southern end of the project, SWA created three small traditional residential neighborhoods, each with a small park at its center. The circulation system was designed to create a clear, three-level hierarchy. Neighborhood streets typically contain ten to twenty dwellings, often located on cul-de-sacs that open physically to a trail or visually to open space. On collector streets, dwellings with specially treated side yard elevations face the street to create the image of a traditional, large-lot, single-family neighborhood. Arterial roads reinforce the overall landscape identity with broad setback plantings of citrus orchards and views into the adjacent natural open space.

イーストハイランドランチはロサンゼルスの96km東にあるサンベナディノ山脈の麓の丘陵地に19世紀に設立された．元来は南カリフォルニア地方有数の果樹園農場であったが，1980年代初めに計画的なコミュニティとして開発するために，モービルランド社によって買収された．SWAは1987年にこの計画に参画し，200haに及ぶ，まだほとんどオレンジの果樹園である敷地の開発計画の最終段階で，敷地計画とランドスケープ計画を担当した．

私たちは敷地の中央を走るハイランドアベニューの北側部分を計画したが，そこでのコンセプトは，周辺の低木の茂みや既存の柑橘類の果樹園という自然環境と，新しい，比較的高級な独立住宅が並ぶ開発地域を一体化し，さらにほとんどの果樹園をそのまま維持しつつ，周辺の自然の景観に新しい開発を馴染ませることを目指した．果樹園には多くの古い石垣や石の水路があり，これらは自然流下の排水路となっていた．このすばらしい石垣は残され，新たにできるコミュニティの散策路やオープンスペースのアクセントとして活用された．道路は果樹園および周辺の自然環境との視覚的な関係を強調するように，注意深く再配置された．

SWAは敷地の南でも，中心に小公園をもつ3つの小さな伝統的な住区を計画した．道路計画は明快な3層構造としている．近隣道路は10～12軒の住宅を結んでおり，実際に散策路につながっていたり，視覚的にオープンスペースに開けているクルドサックがしばしば用いられている．コレクター道路沿いでは特別に意匠の施された建物が，伝統的な，比較的敷地の規模の大きい，戸建住宅地特有の雰囲気をつくり出している．幹線道路では，広々とセットバックして植えられたオレンジの果樹園や隣接する自然のオープンスペースへの眺望によって，全体的な景観のアイデンティティを強調している．

ORCHARD HIGHLANDS

SYCAMORE VALLEY

ORCHARD TERRACES

RED HILL

HIGHLAND AVENUE

HIGHLAND GARDENS

LEGEND

SYCAMORE

CAMPHOR

CALIFORNIA PEPPER

CITRUS GROVES

CITRUS STREET TREES

RESIDENTIAL STREET TREES

PALMS

EXISTING PARKLAND TREES

CHAPARRAL

EXISTING LANDSCAPE

EAST HIGHLANDS RANCH

Mayaluum

Cancun, Mexico

マヤルム

SWA is currently preparing the Master Plan for Mayaluum. This international resort is located along the 200-kilometer (130-mile) Cancun-Tulum corridor, an area recently designated by the government of Mexico for high-quality resort development.

The Master Plan responds comprehensively to all the site sensitivities and amenities to create a highly imageable resort that offers the visitor a broad array of accommodations, facilities and activities. This design approach could serve as the prototype for all future resort development in the Cancun-Tulum corridor.

To preserve the quality and character of the site, development of the resort is proposed primarily in areas that have been previously impacted by agriculture, grazing or hurricanes. The Master Plan calls for the preservation of almost 50% of the total site area as an environmental preserve. In addition, significant forest stands within developed areas will be saved, beach, dune and mangrove areas will be carefully protected, and unique underground caverns and cenotes will be preserved and enhanced as botanic gardens and wildlife sanctuaries. The enhancement of the existing landscape and site conditions is proposed by the cultivation of indigenous forest plants.

A heightened awareness of the cultural heritage and the unique environment is experienced as a visitor moves throughout the resort and the site amenities. The rich heritage of Mayan, Spanish, Mexican and Caribbean cultures can be seen and experienced at each of the four hotels of the resort. The hotels provide accommodations that range from the traditional style of Spain and Mexico, the informal feeling of the Caribbean, and clustered bungalows at the marina, to jungle treetop rooms. The more frequent visitor may enjoy ocean-front, marina, lagoon and golf course residences and villas.

The rich environment of Mayaluum provides a great variety of outdoor activities that take advantage of the site's natural beauty, excellent climate, and diverse water resources. These resources include more than a mile of white sand beaches, clear ocean waters, extensive clear water lagoon systems, and a network of underground limestone caves and underground rivers that offer diving for both the experienced and the beginner. Also offered is a marina, 36 holes of golf, a tennis club, fitness center and spa, conference facilities many restaurants, nightclubs, shops of all kinds, and a museum and cultural center. These landscapes and site amenities are connected with a pedestrian open space network linking the Yucatan jungle to the coastline.

"The Master Plan for Mayaluum demonstrates how tropical resort development can be enriched by an environmentally responsive design approach. The Plan blends the sensitivity of the land, the respect of cultural heritage, and the exotic resort experience."

– Bob Mulcahy

Pool at Lagoon

Harbour Village

Hotel Entry Drive

Lagoon

SWAは現在マヤルムのためのマスタープランを作成している．マヤルムは，高級リゾート地としてメキシコ政府によって開発された，200kmにおよぶユカタン半島のカリブ海に面したカンクン・ツルムの一角に位置する国際的なリゾート地である．

マスタープランは全体として，敷地の特徴やアメニティを最大に生かして，思い出に残るリゾート地を創出することを目指した．すなわち，ここを訪れる人たちに各種多様な宿泊，その他の施設を提供することであった．このデザインアプローチは，カンクン・ツルム一帯の将来のリゾート開発のモデルケースとなり得るものである．

敷地の特質や個性を保持しつつ，このリゾート開発は，かつては農業，牧畜，そしてハリケーンによって影響を受けていた土地において展開された．マスタープランでは，敷地全体の50%を環境保全地区として現状のまま残す方針を立てた．さらに，施設用地の中に存在する重要な林を残し，海岸，砂丘，マングローブの林なども注意深く保護し，ユニークな洞窟などはそのまま，植物園や野性動物のサンクチュアリとして利用する．既存のランドスケープや敷地の魅力は，この土地固有の植物を栽培することでさらに高められる．

文化遺産やユニークな環境は，リゾートや敷地のアメニティの中を動き回ることによって，強く体感される．マヤの豊かな文化遺産，スペイン，メキシコ，カリブ沿岸の文化などが4つのホテルでそれぞれ鑑賞でき，体験できる．ホテルは，伝統的なスペイン風，メキシコ風から，くだけたカリビアン，マリーナ周辺にクラスター状に配置されたバンガロー，さらにジャングルの木上住居のようなスタイルまでいろいろ取り揃えられる．頻繁に訪れる客には，海岸，マリーナ，ラグーン，ゴルフコースなどに隣接したレジデンスやビラが用意される．

マヤルムの豊かな環境は，敷地の自然の美，気候のすばらしさ，さまざまな水辺環境という，恵まれた利点によって，さまざまなアウトドア活動の場を提供する．さらに1マイル（約1.6km）以上続く白い砂浜，きれいな海水，澄んだ真水のラグーン，地下でネットワークする鍾乳洞，うまい人から初心者までのダイビングの場となる地下を流れる川などもある．マリーナ，36ホールのゴルフ場，テニスクラブ，フィットネスセンターと温泉，会議施設，レストラン，ナイトクラブ，あらゆる種類のショップ，美術館，文化センターまで設置される．

「マヤルムのマスタープランは，熱帯のリゾート開発が，いかに環境に呼応したデザイン手法で豊かに計画され得るかを証明するものである．計画は敷地に対する感受性，文化遺産に対する敬意，そして異国風なリゾート体験を融合させている．」

ロバート・モケーヒ

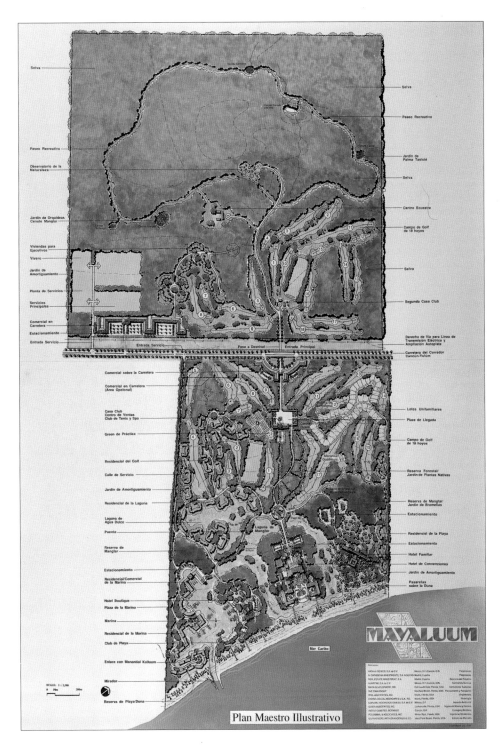

Plan Maestro Illustrativo

Hidiv Beldisi Villas

Kanlica, Istanbul, Turkey

ヒディブ・ベルディシビラ

Forty villas perch on a bare ridge-top overlooking the Asian side of the tree-lined Bosphorus, crowding one another, each appearing to be straining for the best view of the blue waters of the Turkish capital.

The landscape design was conceived to counter the destructive rhythms and geometries of the view-exploiting site plan. There are two parts: the internal, street environment, and the exterior, or view-oriented, pool-side environment. The softer "interior" forms and textures seem to be crying out against the harsh geometries outside while singing a soothing song for the village residents inside. The materials and movements of the "exterior" walls, pools and terraces were designed to address time and place: the ancient and complex history around these hills, and the unique vantage of this ridge.

The street is posed as a public seam, with articulating details, special lights, walls, fountains, and pavements stitching the villas together. The line of the street is sinuous, in contrast to the march of the villas, and the color white is in contrast to the dark green ground covers. The tree planting is a soft fluff of birch, a myriad of trunks and twigs to fade out the tight cadence of the architecture. Evergreens provide wintertime privacy, and fruit trees add color and flavor to the gardens.

The rear, view-oriented gardens are torn by a rough stone wall that runs continuously as an edge to the world. It separates the near, private garden from the distant, and public, vistas; it rips apart earth from earth and ties the garden vista to the sky, the waters of the pools and the waters of the Bosphorus. Each terrace has a pool and each pool has a fountain, a traditional element for a garden and a practical one for its privacy-giving splashing sounds.

"We are hoping that the very high standards of this project will act as a beacon for the re-establishment of a garden tradition in modern day Turkey."
– Kevin Shanley

"In Turkey the contrasts between the very, very old and the very new are extreme. The challenge is to incorporate western design experience while respecting Turkish cultural and historical references."
– John Culter

PLAN

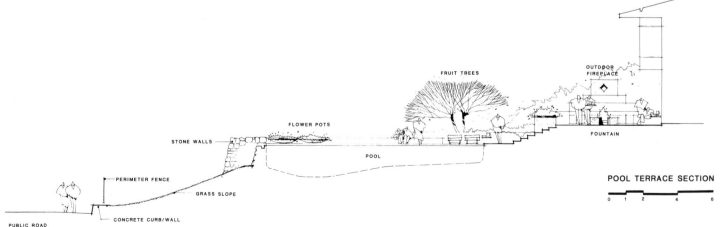

POOL TERRACE SECTION

トルコのイスタンブールのボスポラス海峡に面し、木々の間からアジア側を見下ろす崖の上に、それぞれ紺碧の海のすばらしい眺望をもって、肩を寄せ合うように40軒のビラが建っている。

ランドスケープデザインは、眺望を重視した堅苦しい配置計画を和らげるよう計画された。全体は道路を中心とする内部の囲まれた環境と、各戸のプールサイド側の眺望のいい外側の環境の2つからなる。内側の環境を形成するやわらかい形や素材が、外側の厳しい幾何学的配置と対照をなし、住民に潤いを与えている。石垣、プール、テラスといった外側の環境を形成する素材やその動きは、この周辺の古代からの複雑な歴史や崖の上という

ユニークな地形を活かして、デザインされた。

街路は、はっきりしたディテール、特別な照明、壁、噴水、舗装などで整備され、各ビラを結んでいる。曲がりくねって走る道路は、びっしりと並ぶビラと対照的であり、白い道路は地面を覆う植栽の緑と対照的である。やわらかで軽やかなカバの木の植栽が、その無数の小枝で、ぎっしりとつまったビラを消してくれる。常緑樹が冬のプライバシーを確保し、果樹が庭園に彩りや香りを添える。

各ビラの裏にある眺めの庭の外側は、粗石の垣根で区画されている。この石垣はまた、近くのプライベートな庭園と少し離れたパブリックな眺めを分け、さらに地面と敷地を分け、庭園の眺めを

空に導き、プールの水面をボスポラスの水面にむすびつける。どのビラもテラスにプールを有し、プールの手前には噴水がある。これは、伝統的な庭園の要素であり、その水音でプライバシーを守るという実用的な意味ももっている。

「このプロジェクトのたいへん高級な規範が、現代トルコにおける庭園の伝統を再構築する指標となることを望んでいる。」　　　　**ケビン・シャンレイ**

「トルコでは、新旧のコントラストが極端である。トルコの文化的、歴史的な事柄を尊重しつつ、西洋のデザイン体験を統合するのが、この計画における挑戦であった。」　　　　**ジョン・カトラー**

All photos are view of under construction　写真は建設中風景

Hyatt Pelican Hill

Orange County, California, U.S.A.

ハイアット・ペリカンヒル

The steeply sloping 12-hectare (30-acre) site overlooks the Pacific Ocean and Catalina Island. Although the region is rapidly urbanizing, the site itself is surrounded by open space: two golf courses (on the ocean side) and a steep slope covered with natural vegetation.

The SWA Group worked with architects from the Housden-Barnard Company to develop a site plan conforming to restrictions previously set by public agencies. The building height, for example, was limited so as to fall below the ridge line of the hill above the resort. SWA also completed the landscape design, including 56,000 m² (14 acres) of specialized gardens near the hotel.

Approaching the resort from below, one enters what appears to be a private world as the road slips under a bridge and rises between two revegetated slopes. The hotel's driveway is aligned perpendicular to the ocean, so that one may look out across a golf course to the vast Pacific and, on a clear day, catch a glimpse of Catalina Island. This driveway leads to the flat, open 2,000 m² (1/2-acre) Arrival Piazza of decomposed granite, with the crescent-shaped lobby and grill restaurant along the ocean side. Parking is located out of sight, in a grove of trees.

The resort has been conceived as a Mediterranean hillside village, with ten structures housing 450 guest rooms, a spa, conference rooms, restaurants, and Camp Hyatt (for children). The hotel's lobby looks out along the main axis, a 180-meter (600-foot) sight line toward the ocean, above the first tee of the golf course. Two elliptical spaces carved out of the heavily forested slopes terminate the second axis (a 120-meter sight line). Throughout the gardens are water features, used in bold, exuberant, and more subtle ways. Beyond the gardens lie the fairways, lawns, and the magnificent borrowed scenery of ocean, island and sky.

"We found inspiration for the gardens in the countryside of Tuscany and some of the finest gardens of Italy, including Isola Bella, the Villa D'Este and the Sacro Bosco of Bomarzo. I thought it would be fun to experiment with some of the lessons learned in these wonderful places — ideas such as confounding scale relationships, layering of plant material and creating water garden elements that amuse and entertain. I hope there will be some delightful surprises!"
– Susan Whitin

敷地はカリフォルニア州オレンジカウンティの太平洋とカタリナアイランドを見下ろす約12haの急な斜面に位置している。この周辺は急激に都市化の進んでいる地域であるが、敷地そのものは、海側は2つのゴルフコースに、そして、山側は自然植生に覆われた急峻な斜面とオープンスペースとに囲まれている。

SWAはヒュースデン／バーナード設計事務所の建築家と協働し、事前に公的機関によって設定された規制事項を遵守しながら、このリゾート地の敷地計画を作成した。たとえば建物の高さは、敷地の上方の丘の稜線より低くすることが決められていた。SWAは、配置計画と同時に、ホテルに隣接する56,000m²の特殊な庭園計画を含む、ランドスケープデザインも担当した。

下方の海岸通りから敷地に近づくと、両側の法面が再植栽されたアプローチ道路に入り、橋の下を潜り、まるで別世界へ入っていくようにして上っていく。ホテルのドライブウェイは、海に直交するように一直線に走っているため、ゴルフコース越しに広大な太平洋が眺められ、天気のいい日にはカタリナアイランドも見える。しばらく行くと道は花崗岩を敷きつめた約2,000m²の平坦な前庭に着く。そこには三日月型のロビーと、海側にグリルレストランがあり、駐車場は視界に入らない森の中にある。

全体は、地中海地方のヒルサイドビレッジ風にまとめられ、450室の客室、温泉、会議室、レストラン、子供用のキャンプ・ハイアットなど10棟の施設からなる。ホテルのロビーは、ゴルフコースの1番ティーの上で、真っ直ぐに海に向かって約180mのびる庭園の主軸に沿って、眺望を確保している。さらに庭園の第2の軸線が、密生する林の中を切り開いてつくった2つの楕円形の広場まで約120mの長さでのびている。庭園の中では水を大胆に、豊かに、またさりげなく使っている。庭の向こうには、ゴルフ場の芝生が広がり、さらには太平洋、カタリナアイランド、空といったすばらしい眺めを借景できる。

「私たちは、イタリアのトスカーナ地方の田舎やその他の、たとえばイソラベッラ、ヴィラ・デステ、ボマルツォのサクロボスコといった、すばらしい庭園を参考にした。そうしたすばらしい場所から学んだことを活かしながら庭園を計画することは楽しい経験であった。それは、さまざまなスケールを関係づけ、植栽の種目を層状に重ね、人々を楽しませる水の庭園をつくることなどである。ここが楽しい驚きと喜びの場になることを望む。」

スーザン・ホワイティン

Suginoi Hotel

Beppu City, Ooita, Japan
杉乃井ホテル

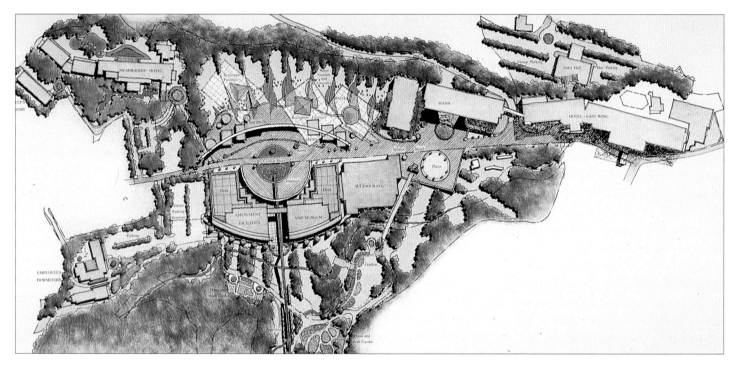

The Suginoi Hotel is a large historic resort located on a prominent ridge overlooking Beppu City on the Island of Kyushu, Japan. The owner and the Fujita Construction Company are in the process of renovating and rebuilding the entire facility to meet new requirements for the resort traveler in Japan.

The SWA Group in conjunction with Landscape International, Ltd. of Tokyo was retained to provide a Master Urban Design and Landscape Plan. The plan reorganizes the site to create a central plaza and new sense of arrival for the hotel guest. The plan accentuates the view side of the ridge overlooking the Bay by adding cascading water gardens and view terraces connected to new bath facilities.

The plan adds a new dimension — a stronger connection to a series of gardens on the mountain side of the resort. This more tranquil area is separated from the high excitement areas on the view side by a linear water element on a cross axis to the ridge.

By providing urban design ideas that use the site more effectively as a resort experience and that heighten the overall resort experience on the property, SWA contributes to a process of programming the overall redevelopment of the Suginoi resort. SWA will now continue to develop landscape concepts and plans in association with Landscape International to implement these ideas in conjunction with Fujita and the hotel management.

杉乃井ホテルは歴史のある大規模リゾートで，九州の別府市街を見下ろす丘陵地に建っている．オーナーとフジタは，目下この施設全体を，新しいリゾート客の要望に合わせて刷新し，建て替えることを進めている．

SWAは，東京のランドスケープ・インターナショナル社と協働して，マスタープランとランドスケーププランの作成に当たった．計画の中心は，敷地中央に，ホテルの客がここに着いたことを実感できるような広場を設置するように，配置を考え直すことであった．湾に向かって見下ろす景観にアクセントを添えるように，滝の流れる水庭と，新しく増設される温泉施設へ連絡する展望テラスを設置する．

さらに計画は，山側に向けて庭園をしっかりと連続させていく，という新たな側面ももっている．このより静かなエリアは，湾への眺望が開けた活発な部分とは，直交する軸線沿いに配された線状の水面によって区画されている．

敷地をリゾートの体験の場としてより有効に使い，結果としてリゾート体験を質的に高めるという，このアーバンデザインの考え方を取り入れることで，SWAは杉乃井リゾートの全体計画に貢献している．今後，このアイデアに基づいて，フジタやホテル側と一体となって，引き続きランドスケープのコンセプトづくりや計画を進めていく予定である．

Thoroughbred Park

Lexington, Kentucky, U.S.A.
サラブレッドパーク

This park is a gateway monument honoring the city as a worldwide center for thoroughbred horse breeding and racing. The design brings the imagery of the bluegrass countryside directly into downtown Lexington. It is a contemplative space surrounded by flowering trees, the centerpiece of which is a half-size bronze statue of the champion horse Lexington, sculpted by local artist Gwen Reardon.

"Industry, history and love in one novel: this is different from Williams Square, where wild horses were a metaphor for mankind's innate desire to be free. Thoroughbred Park speaks to humans and their love of the animal itself, as well as its training, breeding and lineage. Most important, the park speaks to memories and dreams of horses ridden and races won, of horses unborn and races yet to run. On a quick visit, you feel a part of the race we all run; and that, whether we cross the line first or last, we are all winners."
— **Jim Reeves**

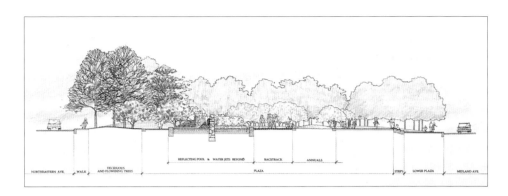

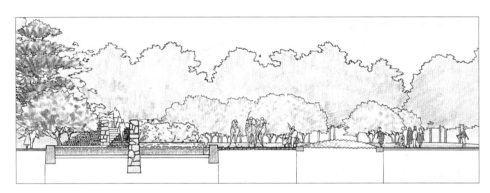

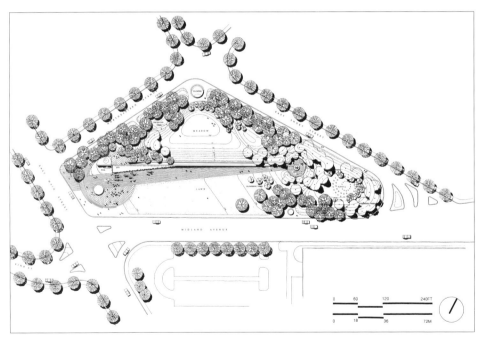

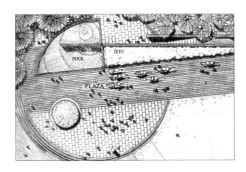

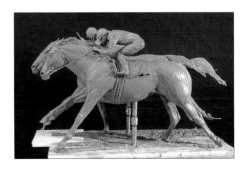

この公園は，世界的にサラブレッドの飼育と競争レースで名高いケンタッキー州レキシントン市の入口のモニュメントとして計画されている．レキシントンのダウンタウンに，牧草が茂るカントリーサイドの景観をそのまま持ち込んでいる．ここは，花木に囲まれた瞑想空間であり，その中心には，地元のアーチストのグエン・リアドン作のレキシントンのチャンピオン馬たちの1/2のブロンズ像が置かれる．

「ここでは産業，歴史，そして愛が1つになっている．野生馬が，人類の自由への願望のメタファーであったウィリアムズスクエアとは異なっている．サラブレッドパークは人類に語りかけ，動物の訓練，飼育，血統といったことと同様に，生き物のやさしさを表わしている．なかでも重要なことは，レースに勝った馬たち，そしてまだ生まれていない，あるいはレースに走っていない馬たちの思い出や夢をも表わしていることである．つかの間の訪問も，私たちすべてが走り続けているレースの一端を垣間見ることができる．ゴールラインを最初に越えようと最後に越えようと，最善を尽くした者たちはすべて勝者である．」

ジェームズ・リーブス

Alabang Centre

Metro Manila, Philippines

アラバンセンター

Alabang Centre was in a national competition sponsored by the Philippine government. Located about 18 km (11 miles) southeast of Manila, and just 10 km (6 miles) from Ninoy Aquino International Airport, the site lies in the province of Rizal in Muntinlupa, close to Laguna de Bay.

Alabang Centre represents a comprehensive collaborative planning effort between The SWA Group and Filinvest Development Corporation. SWA's land planning and urban design efforts included data inventory and analysis, formulation of the land use program, development of criteria for the infrastructure, and the resulting Master Development Plan and Urban Design.

When the competition was announced, a development program was not defined. The government looked to the imagination and creativity of the competing development teams. The problem statement invoked the best use of the land, taking into account the site's natural and cultural characteristics and the maximum pos-sible economic return for the government. Being the last large contiguous area in metropolitan Manila, SWA's challenge was to attempt a delicate balance between the development density alternatives and the natural resources of the site and its environs.

The plan also balances proposed development with the site's natural amenities of rivers, groves of mature acacia and mango trees; and the gently sloping topography punctuated by small hills.

The rivers and lakes running through the site will be self-contained and will provide recreational opportunities and meet utilitarian needs. As a recreational amenity, the rivers and lakes will function as a linear park. These waterways will be available to boaters to leisurely transport people to restaurants, shops and hotels located along the banks in a similar fashion to the San Antonio River Walk in Texas.

As a utilitarian element, this man-made basin will serve as a storm detention basin, water res-ervoir, source for irrigation and fire prevention, and as a buffer between land uses. The existing river at the southwestern edge will be rechanneled to rejoin its natural course at the northwestern edge of the site.

Responding to the site's sloping topography, high-rise offices gradually step down to form an amphitheatre that focuses views to Laguna de Bay — a large body of fresh water. Low-density office buildings will be sensitively sited among the existing mature trees. At the heart of the design is the social community of Alabang Centre (performing arts, museum, civic center, convention center), where the most diverse and exciting activities occur.

"Our challenge was to create a livable, attractive, self-sustaining new city centre, in order to help alleviate the overpopulation of metropolitan Manila."
– Justiniano Mendoza Jr.

アラバンセンターはフィリピン政府による国内コンペの入選案である。マニラの南東約18kmの、ニノイ・アキノ国際空港からちょうど10kmのところに位置している。敷地はラグーナ・デ・ベイ近くでムンティンルーパのリザール郡に属している。

アラバンセンター計画はSWAと地元のフィリンベスト開発会社との総合的な協同作業の成果である。SWAの役割は敷地の調査・分析、計画の基準づくり、インフラストラクチュア整備計画、それらの結果としてのマスタープランやアーバンデザインまでを含んでいた。

コンペ時には、まだ開発プログラムは明らかでなかった。政府はコンペ案にイメージや創造性を求めたのである。さらに政府は、敷地の自然、文化的な特性を生かし、できるだけ大きな経済効果が上がる、最良の土地利用を必要としていた。首都マニラ周辺に最後に残された広大な土地であるため、SWAは、開発地域の密度設定を敷地やその周辺の自然環境に微妙にバランスさせることを目指した。

計画はまた、提案した開発と敷地の中にある川、成長したアカシアやマンゴ林、小さな丘の連なりからなるゆるやかな傾斜地という自然のアメニティとをバランスさせている。

敷地内を流れる川や湖は、レクリエーションの場であり、さまざまな用途に役立つ。レクリエーション的なアメニティとして、川や湖は線状の公園としての機能を果たす。これらの水路により、テキサス州サンアントニオのリバーウォークのように、ボートに乗って川沿いのレストランや店舗、ホテルなどを楽しく行き来することができる。

便益的な用途としては、この人造湖は雨水調整池となり、貯水池となり、灌漑用水や消火用水として使われ、さらにそれぞれの土地利用の暖衝地となる。敷地南西部に端を発する水路は、敷地の北西部の境界にて再び自然の水路へと合流する。

敷地のゆるやかな傾斜に合わせ、高層のオフィス群は、ちょうど円形劇場のように、水をたたえたラグーナ・デ・ベイに向かって順にステップダウンする。低密度のオフィス群は既存の林の中に注意深く配置される。計画の中心は、ホールや美術館、市民センター、会議場といった社会的な施設群からなるアラバンセンターである。ここには最も多様で刺激的な活動が展開される。

「私たちは、首都マニラの超過密な状態を少しでも軽減するために、生き生きとした魅力的な自立する新しいシティセンターをつくり出すことを目指した。」　**ジュスティニアーノ・メンドーサJr.**

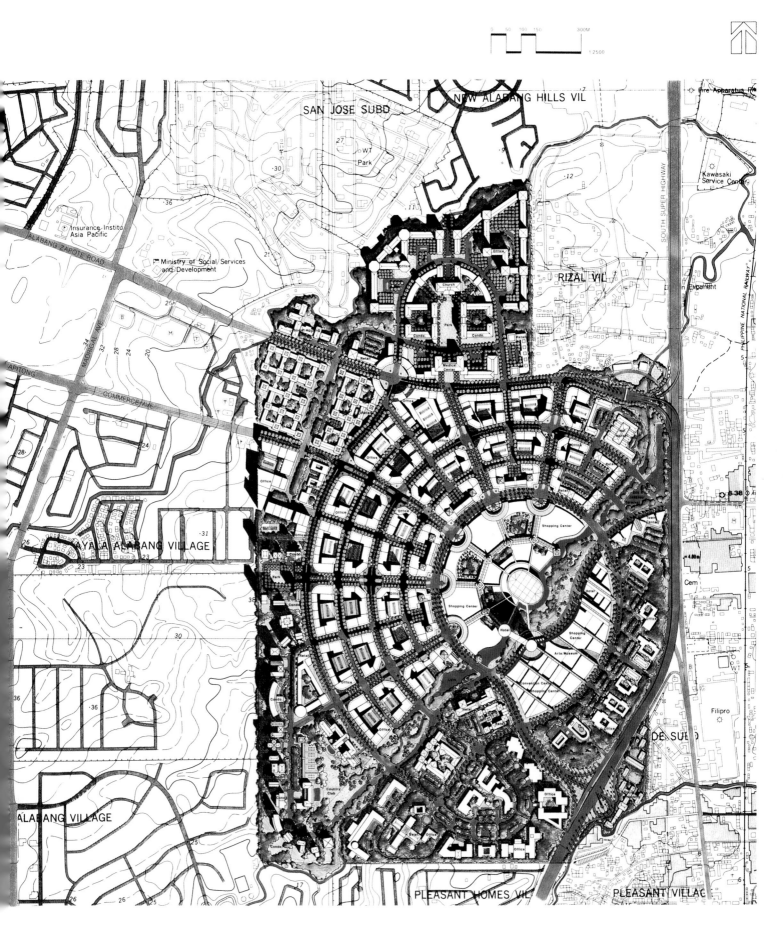

Nasu Highlands Park and Related Developments

Nasu, Tochigi, Japan

那須ハイランドパーク＋周辺開発計画

For the past four years, The SWA Group has been working with architects ED2 International on several planning and design projects for Towa Real Estate Development Company in Nasu, 150 kilometers northeast of Tokyo. These projects include theme park redevelopment and expansion, resort hotels, residential villas, vacation homes, private golf clubhouses, sports and recreational facilities, conference facilities, and master planning for a destination resort. Our work has involved all phases of design, from programmatic and conceptual design through site planning, schematic design, design development, review of construction documents and construction observation. By working within the different ecological, cultural and business environments in Japan, we have had to adapt to novel conditions and also expand the role of the landscape architect.

At Nasu Highlands Park, our challenge was to develop an idea for transforming a theme park (for one-day visits) into a destination resort, where guests stay longer, make repeat visits, and enjoy the secluded, unique environment.

At Fantasy Pointe, we transformed an existing small-scale amusement park into a major family-oriented entertainment center that contrasts with, but also melds into, the natural environment of forested mountains. First phase includes the Rock & Roll Plaza, with its 1950s Main Street; second phase is the Carousel Park, with a 38-meter high, ornately latticed carousel, landscaped with whimsical topiaries in a French parterre garden; and the third phase, The House of Cards with a special coaster ride and a new town center. A total of twelve major theme attractions will complete the development.

Akebien Membership Hotel is a destination resort type accommodation, featuring Japanese gardens with a Western design motif. Materials and the design of the Central Stone Garden evoke mysticism, history and romance. The Central Court and East and West Back Gardens evoke solitude and serenity, Man and Nature.

Nasu Highlands Country Club is an exclusive, Western-style membership club on a golf course designed by Robert Trent Jones II, International. Here gardens are refined, ranging from the stone-walled Arrival Court and the Great Lawn Terrace to small viewing gardens that extend into the forest setting.

"First and foremost, whatever we do, we want to retain the existing character of the region — that of a forest at the base of the mountains. That means we retain the existing vegetation wherever possible and reforest the areas that have been disturbed by previous development."
— *John Wong*

"We have evolved a very efficient system of building landscape projects at Nasu Highlands. The client, Fujita Construction Company and associated architects maintain clearly defined responsibilities, and we communicate often."
— *John Loomis*

Photo: Nasu Highlands Park

過去4年間, SWAは建築設計事務所ED2インターナショナルと協働して, 東京から約150km北東の那須において藤和不動産によるいくつかの計画およびデザインプロジェクトに携わった. プロジェクトは, テーマパークの再生および拡張計画, リゾートホテル, レジデンシャルビラ, 別荘群, プライベート・ゴルフクラブハウス, スポーツ・レクリエーション施設, 会議施設, 滞在型リゾートのためのマスタープランづくりなどを含んでいた. 私たちは, 初期の基本構想, 概念設計から配置計画, 基本設計, 実施設計, さらに現場監理にいたるまですべての段階に係わった. 自然生態も文化も業務の背景も異なる日本で仕事をするためには, 新しい状況に適応し, ランドスケープデザイナーの役割を大きく拡張することが必要であった.

那須ハイランドパークでは, 日帰りで楽しむテーマパークを, 人々がもっと長く滞在し, 繰り返し訪れ, ここだけで味わえる独特の環境そのものを楽しむという, 滞在型リゾートへと再生することを目指した.

ファンタジーポイントでは, 既存の小規模な遊園地を, 周辺の緑豊かな山々の自然に対比させると同時に融合するような環境とし, 家族揃って楽しめるような場所へ変身させることを試みた. 第1期は1950年代風のメインストリートとロックンロール広場, 第2期は, 38m高さの格子状に飾られた回転木馬の公園で, 奇抜なトピアリーのあるフランス風庭園に囲まれている. 第3期はニュータウンセンターと特殊なジェットコースター, そしてトランプの家である. 全体で12の主なテーマアトラクションにより, テーマパークが完成する予定である.

会員制のアケビアンホテルは, 滞在型リゾートホテルであり, 西洋風のデザインモチーフを用いた日本庭園としてデザインされた. 中央の石庭の素材やデザインは, 神秘, 歴史, ロマンスを表現している. セントラルコートと東西のバックコートは孤独と落着き, 人と自然を表現している.

那須ハイランドカントリークラブは, ロバート・トレント・ジョーンズ・Jr.デザインの西洋式高級会員制ゴルフクラブである. ここでは, 庭園は洗練されたスペースであり, 石垣で囲まれたアプローチの前庭および広大な芝生のテラスから, 小さな眺めのよい庭にまで至り, 周辺の森へとつながってゆく.

「第一に, ここではできるかぎり山裾の林の中に位置するという地域の特性を生かしたいと考えた. そこで, 既存の植生を可能なかぎり尊重し, それまでに造成などで裸にされたところは, 再植林するように努力した.」　　　　　ジョン・ウォン
「私たちは那須ハイランドでたいへん効果的にランドスケープ・プロジェクトを推進するシステムを開発した. クライアントも施工のフジタも, 関係した建築家もすべてが, それぞれの責任を明確に果たした. 頻繁にコミュニケイトを行なった結果でもある.」　　　　　ジョン・ルーミス

COMPETITIONS
設計競技応募作品集

Pershing Square

Los Angeles, California, U.S.A.
パーシングスクエア

Pershing Square is an historic urban park in downtown Los Angeles. This redesign of the Square attempts to recapture the total area defined by the surrounding buildings and returns the space to the pedestrian.

The square is organized around a central botanical garden that pays homage to the cultural heritage of Spanish/Mexican gardens of the last century. The rich palette used in the display gardens shows the evolution of native plant materials, from plants used by the Indians to horticultural and agricultural plants found in Mission gardens.

The design of the square encourages pedestrians to promenade along the perimeter and to walk from one activity to another. The changing scene can best be viewed from the gently sloping amphitheatre and palm grove pergola. Views of the gardens and fountains, combined with live performances and the passing people, offer a unique and glorious form of urban entertainment.

"With the great variety of activities, day and night, and the enhanced quality of the Square, I like to think that all the citizens of Los Angeles would be given a grand public space, re-establishing Pershing Square as the central historic park of the city."
— *John Wong*

パーシングスクエアはロサンゼルスのダウンタウンの由緒ある都市公園である．周囲を高い建物に囲まれた公園の用地を復活し，再度歩行者用の空間にすることが目的であった．

スクエアは，19世紀のスペイン／メキシコ式庭園の文化遺産に敬意を表して，中央の植物庭園を取り巻くように構成している．ディスプレイガーデンの色とりどりの花壇には，インディアンが使う植物から，ミッションガーデンに見られる園芸品種や農作物まで含めた，さまざまな自然の植物が植えられて，その進化発展を見せている．

歩行者が周囲をぶらぶらと散策し，活動的な空間からより静かな空間を歩きたくなるようにデザインされた．ゆるく傾斜した円形劇場やヤシの木のパーゴラから眺める景観の変化はすばらしい．ライブ・パフォーマンスや行き交う人々も一体となって，この庭園と噴水の景観は，都市の中にユニークで輝かしい楽しみの場をつくり出す．

「昼夜を通してのさまざまな活動，スクエアそのものの魅力によって，ロサンゼルス市民のすべてが享受できる，広々としたすばらしい公共空間を，市の中心にある歴史的な公園であるパーシングスクエアを再構築することで，手に入れることができる．」
ジョン・ウォン

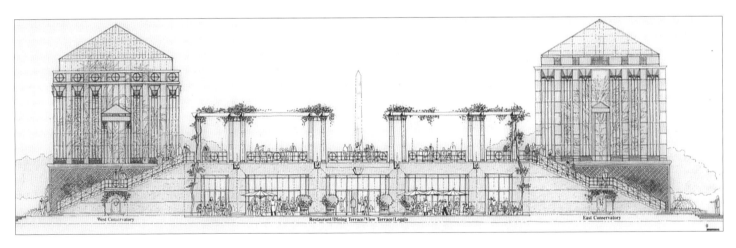

West Conservatory   Restaurant/Dining Terrace/View Terrace/Loggia   East Conservatory

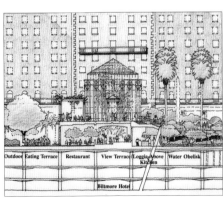

Outdoor Eating Terrace | Restaurant | View Terrace/Loggia Above Kitchen | Water Obelisk

Biltmore Hotel

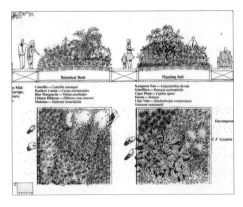

Botanical Beds   Planting Soil

Camellia—Camellia sasanqua
Feathery Cassia—Cassia artemisioides
Blue Marguerite—Felicia amelloides
Chinese Hibiscus—Hibiscus rosa sinensis
Mahonia—Mahonia lomariifolia

Kangaroo Paw—Anigozanthus flavida
Schefflera—Brassia actinophylla
Cigar Plant—Cuphea ignea
Fescue—Festuca
Lilac Vine—Hardenbergia comptoniana
Solanum rantonnetii

Decompose

3' Granite

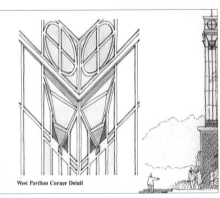

West Pavilion Corner Detail

125

Freeway Competition "Interchangeable Parts" and
Congress Avenue Lighting Competition
Houston & Austin, Texas, U.S.A.
フリーウェイコンペ&コングレスアベニュー・ライティングコンペ

The intent of this competition is to explore the elements of the urban freeway: more specifically, the freeway interchange as an urban art form.

The freeway is a necessary and integral component for urban living. Freeway culture exists and is defined through behavior, technology and aesthetics. This layering of human and technological cultures gives new dimension to urban civilization. The freedom and opportunity to redefine our culture's significant artifacts represent continual challenge for American art and society.

The artist and landscape architect worked closely to select a suitable image for this redefinition. These lawn spikes define a rhythm which reiterates existing vocabulary of vertical elements: Freeway structural columns and light poles. The rhythm sets up a predictability emphasizing the geometry of the interchange while amplifying the third spatial dimension. Injected molded black ABS cones in contrast to refractive prismatic acrylic cones provide continual interplay between light/dark and mass/void. During daylight changing climatic conditions lend interest while at night fiber optics illuminate the prismatic cones along the pole. Interchange geometry is reinforced and clarified. The light masts are dazzling. At the ground plane, plantings of oleander and cedar complement the lawn spikes with color and texture.

これはテキサス州ヒューストンのフリーウェイコンペ案である．このコンペの目的は，都市部のフリーウェイの，特にインターチェンジを都市のアートフォームとして変換していくために，フリーウェイの構成要素を開発することであった．

フリーウェイは都市生活にとって不可欠なものである．フリーウェイ文化は実在し，その行為，技術，美学によって定義づけられる．人類と技術的な文化の積層は，都市文明に新たな断面を付加した．こうした意義深いフリーウェイのさまざまな要素を再定義する自由と機会がいま与えられ，それはすなわち，アメリカンアートとアメリカ社会への絶え間ないチャレンジを意味する．

アーチストとランドスケープアーキテクトが一体となって，この再定義のためにふさわしいイメージを選び出す作業に取り組んだ．

ここでは芝生上のスパイクが，フリーウェイの構造的な柱や照明ポールといった，既存の垂直のエレメントにもう１つの垂直のリズムを加える．このリズムは，３次元空間を拡大しながら，インターチェンジの幾何学を強調することを予知させる．光を屈折するプリズム状のアクリルのコーンと，それとは対照的な鋳造の黒いABSのコーンが，絶え間ない光と影，無と有の交錯を表現している．昼は刻々と変わる自然の光を受け，夜は光ファイバーの光学的なイルミネーションがポール脇のプリズム状のコーンを照らし出す．インターチェンジの幾何学が強調され明瞭に浮かび上がる．照明柱はきらきらと輝く．地上では，キョウチクトウやシーダの植栽が，色やテクスチュアで芝生上のスパイクを補完してる．

The Congress Avenue area of Austin possesses extraordinary scenic beauty. The integration of the built environment with the natural is critical to reinforce these scenic qualities.

The SWA Group's design reflects both Austin's past and future by utilizing materials which recall the city's historic vernacular (cast iron), as well as innovative technological solutions (fiber optics). Metaphorically, then, the bridge would constitute a link between the city's past and its future.

The auroral buttons twinkle with varying intensity along the spans of the underside arches. At ground level the railing and metal hardware of the rods utilize cast iron materials. The mid-section of the rods has a translucent prismatic coating. During daylight hours the prisms would provide playful spectral reflections of sunlight while at night would be nearly transparent. After dark varying portions of the rods would glow with varying hues of fiber optic color. Sensors receptive to wind, motion of traffic and light would trigger waves of continuously changing colors.

"Streets and Freeways are among America's great public spaces . . . and totally untapped in their potential for artistic expression."
— *Kevin Shanley*

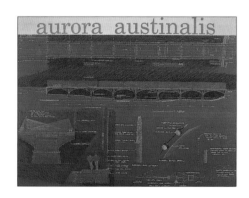

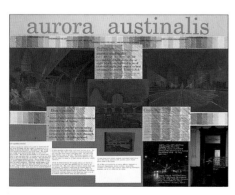

テキサス州オースチンのコングレスアベニューは特別すばらしい眺望を有している．人工の構築物と自然の統合が，このすばらしい環境の本質である．

SWAは，市の歴史を物語る素材である鋳鉄と同時に，光ファイバーといった先端技術の材料も併わせて使うことで，オースチンの過去と未来を反映したデザインを考えた．また，橋は比喩的に市の過去と未来を結ぶものとしてとらえられた．

橋の下のアーチには，曙光のような小さな光が，いろいろな密度に散りばめられている．橋の上では，手すりや柵に鋳鉄が使われた．柵の中心部は，透明なプリズム状のコーティングになっている．昼間は，プリズムが日光を反射してさまざまな表情を見せる．夜間はほとんど透明になる．そして夜の闇の中で，柵のあちこちで光ファイバーの色とりどりの饗宴が始まる．センサーが風，交通量，光などを感知して，絶え間なく変化する色の波をコントロールする．

「一般道路もフリーウェイもアメリカの偉大な公共空間の中にある．にもかかわらず，全体としては本質的にまだまだ芸術的な表現がなされていないところでもある．」　　ケビン・シャンレー

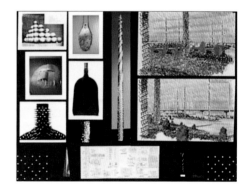

Fort Mason

San Francisco, California, U.S.A.

フォートメイソン

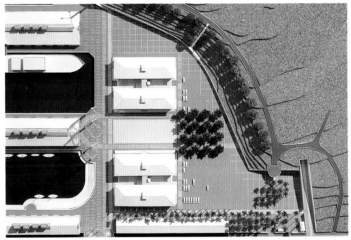

Fort Mason was an embarkation port during both World Wars and later, in the 1970s, it was incorporated into the Golden Gate National Recreation Area. It now houses non-profit cultural and education activities.

The administration and residents were invited to a competition held on the site. Because the site has historical importance, the approach of the competition was a minimalist one.

A 6,7-meter (22-foot) grid was to be painted on the paved staging area to accommodate an array of activities from parking to outdoor festivals. At each nexus was a tenon, accepting bollards or lights, and power sources. A "parade ground" was created in the center of the space. Palms which are traditionally found on California military bases, were used to structure spaces.

フォートメイソンは，2つの世界大戦のとき，そして1970年代にも，兵士が乗船し出ていく港であったが，その後ゴールデンゲート・ナショナル・レクリエーションエリアに編入された．現在は，非営利的な文化および教育活動が行なわれている．

このコンペには行政官や地域住民も参加が求められた．敷地は歴史的に重要な場所であったため，コンペにはミニマリストのアプローチを用いた．

駐車場あるいは屋外フェスティバルのための区画を示すために，6.6mのグリッドが舗装面に描かれ，それぞれの交点には，車止めや照明，電力源などを設置できるようにした．「パレードグラウンド」は空間の中央に設定され，カリフォルニアの軍事基地に伝統的に見られるヤシの木が，環境を形づくるために植えられた．

Kit Carson, A Sculpture Competition

Escondido, California, U.S.A.

キットカーソン公園彫刻コンペ

The SWA Group and artist Joyce Shaw collaborated to create a design for this open sculpture competition. The project site was set in a mature grove of Eucalyptus trees located within the 120-hectare (300-acre) Kit Carson Park.

The choice of culture, geography and history as the subject matter reflects a deconstructivist orientation. This sculpture challenges the idea of "pure" object making as relevant. Its subject is that meaning is always dependent on context and in fact that there is no meaning without context. Further, the subject is the many layers of information and meaning in this place, the richness, heterogeneity and complexity of culture, history and geography.

The piece explores the many local historic cultures. Cultural artifacts, languages and associations are also explored. The park is a "crossroads of cultures" of the people who inhabited the valley: the Native American Indians, the Franciscan Padres of the California Missions, the Mexican Californios, the United States Armies of the West, and pioneer settlers. The sculpture represents a journey through these histories.

Geography is another subject of the sculpture. The piece sets up a geometric relationship between the mountain, the valley and the plain. It is an earthwork, in that it establishes a geographic relationship with two off-site historic monuments of the Mexican-American War

which became the place maker and the idea giver.

The Eucalyptus grove is located at the geographic crosspoint of these two historic sites which lie beyond the park. On-site sculpture incorporates three elements in a triangular relationship: the Story Circle, the Memory Marker and the chimney of a historic ranch.

"The rich history, the surprising relationships of land forms and their complex interplay are not the subject of one sculpture, they are the sculpture. Each individual builds a sculpture of place and cultures in their mind."

– *Susan Whitin*

SWAは，この公開の彫刻コンペのためのデザインをアーチストのジョイス・ショウと協同で制作した．敷地は，カリフォルニア州エスコンディドに位置する120haからなるキットカーソン公園のユーカリ林の中に設定された．

デコン（脱構築）の考えの下で，文化，地形，歴史を主たる要素として選択している．この彫刻は，今日的に「ピュア」なものの表現を目指している．意味は常にコンテクストに従い，コンテクストのないところには意味がないということをテーマとしている．さらに，豊かさ，文化や歴史，地形の異種混成や複層といった，この場所のもつ情報や意味の多くの集積がテーマでもあった．

結果は地域独自のいろいろな文化を表現したものとなった．また，文化的な工芸品，言語，つながりといったものが表現された．公園は，アメリカの原住民であるインディアンやカリフォルニアの伝導師としてのフランシスコ派の神父，メキシコ系の人たち，西部に駐在する米軍，パイオニアたちといった，この谷間に住んださまざまな人々の文化の交流点である．彫刻は，こうした歴史の流れを表現している．

地形は，彫刻のもう1つのテーマである．作品は，周辺の山や谷や平原の間にあって，相互に関係して存在する．彫刻はアースワークである．この公園の由来でもあり，アイデアの源でもある，

敷地外にある2つの歴史的なメキシコーアメリカ戦争のモニュメントと地理的な関係を形成している．

ユーカリの林は，公園の向こうに位置する歴史的な2つのモニュメントが交差するところに位置する．敷地内の彫刻は，三角形に配置されたストーリーサークル，メモリーマーカー，伝統的な牧場の煙突の3つの要素を結合している．

「豊かな歴史，土地形態とそれに呼応した相互作用の驚くべき関係は，彫刻のテーマというだけでなく，それ自身が彫刻作品でもある．だれもが心の中にそれぞれの場所の文化や彫刻を形づくる．」

スーザン・ホワイティン

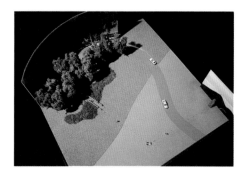

PROFESSIONAL
專門活動

Photography
写真

The visual experience is a key element at SWA. In 1967, Gerry Campbell, a painter and member of the southern California art movement, joined The SWA Group as a photographer. Since then, photography has become a highly defined and implemented process within SWA. Gerry set a high standard of excellence by which we not only judge our image making capabilities, but also the quality of the projects. Photographers Dixi Carrillo, Tom Fox, Tom Lamb, and Tim Harvey are now part of the SWA process of image and design. All the photographs (except where noted) in this issue are by the SWA photographers.

As image makers the responsibility rests in the continued pursuit of not only the highest quality of image, but also, through those images, a clarification and expansion of the experience we all share visually. Our goal is to aid and direct clients and others toward a clear understanding of the designs and plans produced by The SWA Group.

The visual experience begins the moment we begin to focus on a project. This process includes early site photography. Topography, vegetation and ecosystems, traffic patterns, neighborhood fabric, and other vital data are assembled. The images may be in slide form, video, or done by larger format and newer panorama cameras. Image boards and books are produced, aiding and defining designers' and planners' ideas and concepts. Historic relationships, character images, details, activities and events are all ingredients in the final plan. Photography helps communicate these plans.

Photographs also serve a more pragmatic function for us in the documentation of the design process by the recording of the drawn information, recording of the construction process and finally the built project. These images, combined with the character images, have formed a valuable visual library of well over a million images. This image bank contains the history of the development and environmental consciousness over the years. The beauty and implied truth of the photographic image allows for the combination of visual elements in a believable and meaningful relationship.

The art of photography, much like the art of design, is constantly in flux. The juxtaposition of new directions and concepts with old methods and ideas refines and clarifies the visual dialogue. The visual language aids in our continuing emphasis on the passing on information, drawing on past experiences and preparing for new challenges. Presentations and exhibitions of these visual ideas are presented to our clients, published in the leading design journals and shown in museums and galleries.

視覚的な体験は、SWAにおけるたいへん重要な要素となっている。1967年に画家でサザンカリフォルニアの美術運動のメンバーであったゲリー・キャンベルが、写真家としてSWAグループに参画した。それ以来、写真はSWAの中で、アイデアの明確化と計画の遂行に欠かせないプロセスになった。私たちが写真から、創造力を引き出せるだけではなく、プロジェクトの質そのものも含めて判断できるまでに、ゲリーは写真の水準を高めた。現在は、ディキシー・カリロ、トム・フォックス、トム・ラム、ティム・ハービーといった写真家が加わり、SWAのイメージやデザインプロセスの重要な担い手になっている。この特集号に掲載した写真は、特記してある以外すべてSWAの写真家によるものである。

イメージをつくり出すものとして、私たちの仕事の責任は、イメージの最高の質を追求するだけでなく、同時に、それらのイメージを通して、私たちがビジュアルに共有している体験の解釈や意味の拡大を追求し続けることでもある。最終的な目標は、クライアントやその他の人々が、SWAがつくり出すデザインや計画をはっきりと理解できるように手助けし、導くことである。

視覚的な体験は、プロジェクトに着手したときから始まる。このプロセスは初期の敷地の写真撮影から始まり、地形、植栽、生態系、交通パターン、近隣の都市構造、その他のさまざまなビジュアルデータが集められる。イメージはスライドやビデオになり、ときにはもっと大掛かりな、新しいパノラマカメラを駆使したイメージとしてまとめられる。これらのイメージを整理したパネルや冊子がつくられ、デザイナーやプランナーは、それをもとにアイデアやコンセプトを生み出し、築き上げていく。歴史との関連、それぞれ個別のイメージ、ディテール、さまざまな活動やイベントなどがすべて最終的なプランに盛り込まれる。写真はこれらのプランが相互にコミュニケイトするのを助けている。

写真にはまたもっと合理的な役割もある。すなわち、図面化された情報を記録し、また建設の過程や完成した姿を記録することで、デザインプロセスのドキュメンテーションを作成する。こうしたイメージは、個別のイメージと一体となって、無数のイメージにも匹敵する、視覚的な価値あるライブラリーを形成する。このイメージバンクは、長年にわたる開発や環境的な認識の変遷をも包含する。写真が表わす美やそれが暗示する真実は、プロジェクトの記録を鮮明にするだけでなく、デザイナーの思想を浮き彫りにしていく。

写真芸術は、デザインと同様、絶えず流動している。新しい方向や概念と、古い手法や考えが同時に存在することで、ビジュアルな言語が改良され、明らかになっていく。視覚的な言語は、私たちが常に強調している情報の往来の促進、過去の体験の想起、新たな挑戦への準備に役立つ。私たちは、こうした視覚的なアイデアのプレゼンテーションをクライアントに対して行ない、主要なデザイン雑誌に発表し、また美術館やギャラリーに展示している。

From left to right: Tim Harvey, Gerry Campbell, Tom Fox, Dixi Carrillo, Tom Lamb

Geographic Information Systems
地理情報システム

On large, complex land planning projects, The SWA Group utilizes GIS technology, an area of expertise in which one of its consulting principals, Dr. Douglas Way, has been a pioneer. Dr. Way was trained in landscape architecture, civil engineering, and geography. When he began his career, teaching at the Harvard Graduate School of Design, he became involved in early research projects, applying techniques of remote sensing and GIS to issues of landscape architecture and land planning. Later, he brought his strong commitment to "the land" to The SWA Group.

"I am very much concerned that landscape architects begin their design development with a thorough understanding of the site, how it evolved, its present conditions, and the processes acting upon it," says Dr. Way. "Only within this context can designers take full advantage of opportunities and be fully responsible to the site constraints and character."

Many changes have taken place since Dr. Way first came to landscape architecture. "At that time," he explains, "'analysis paralysis' was widely practiced. Walls full of colored maps (analysis overkill) were not very cost-effective in providing relevant information and conceptual direction for the designers." Now environmental regulations require detailed scientific study. Procedures for approving plans are more responsive to physical site conditions and require developers to provide sufficient justification. As a result, the demand for computerized GIS technology has greatly increased, within both private and public sectors.

"GIS today provides an incredibly powerful analytical tool," notes Dr. Way. "Complex layers of data can be sieved and examined in ways impractical by hand techniques to help justify a development program and design concept. It is analysis with a focus and direction — and with the analytical power of the computer for implementation."

In 1984, The SWA Group first used GIS — at Walt Disney World Resort. For the first time, then, Disney Development was able to get a comprehensive view of terrain conditions, both within and adjacent to the Disney properties. Proceeding from simplistic to more sophisticated analyses with this technology, The SWA Group has aided several clients, including the MacArthur Foundation, the Ministry of Defense and Aviation in Saudi Arabia, the Ministry of Fisheries and Agriculture of the Sultanate of Oman, and many private and municipal clients in the United States. In addition, Dr. Way assists several governmental agencies, including the Defense Mapping Agency, training in the area of terrain analysis and GIS applications.

大規模な複合の土地利用計画では、SWAは地理情報システム(GIS)を駆使している。この分野のパイオニアであり、SWAのシニア・プリンシパルであるダグラス・ウェイ博士の専門である。ウェイ博士は、ランドスケープアーキテクチュア、土木工学、そして地理学を修めている。彼がハーバード・デザインスクールの大学院で教鞭をとり始めた時、ランドスケープアーキテクチュアと土地利用計画に関してリモート・センシングとGISを応用して、私たちの初期の調査プロジェクトに参加した。その後、引き続きSWAの土地解析を助けてくれている。

「ランドスケープアーキテクトは、敷地がどのようになっているか、現状を正確に認識し、計画によってどのように変わるかということを充分に理解してからデザインに着手すべきだと考える」とウェイ博士は言っている。「このコンテクストの上に、初めてデザイナーは充分にその力を発揮することができ、また敷地の制約や特質に充分な責任をもつことになる。」

ウェイ博士がランドスケープアーキテクチュアの分野に参加して以来、多くの変革があった。「当時は、どこでも分析中毒にかかっていた。壁に張り出された、分析の結果のいろんな色を塗った図表類は、デザイナーになにひとつ適切な情報や概念的な方向を示唆しなかった」とウェイ博士は述懐している。いまや、環境に関する法規はもっと詳細な科学的な調査研究を要求している。計画を承認する過程には、実際の敷地の状況の一層の対応と、ディベロッパーへの充分な正当性の確保が必要になっている。結果として、私的な開発でも公的なものでも、コンピューターを駆使したGISの技術の需要が急増することになった。

「GISは今日では信じられないほど強力な分析の手段となった」と博士はいう。「データの複雑な重なりは、人の手で非能率的に捌いたり、調べたりすることは、もはや開発のプログラムやデザインコンセプトにとって何の助けにもならない。私たちの道具としてのコンピューターの分析能力を駆使しての、中心と方向をもった分析が必要である。」

1984年に、SWAグループはウォルト・ディズニーワールド・リゾートで初めてGISを使った。そのとき、ディズニー社も初めて、自社の所有地やその周辺の土地の状況のわかりやすい絵を見ることができた。この技術を次第に単純なものから複雑な、洗練した分析へと展開することで、その後SWAは、マッカーサー財団やサウジアラビア国防・航空省、オマーン国漁業・農業省、その他アメリカの民間・公共のクライアントの多くにこの方法を使って大いに貢献している。ウェイ博士は、国防地理院などの政府のいくつかの組織や委員会に対して、土地分析の分野でGISの援用についてのトレーニングを実施してもいる。

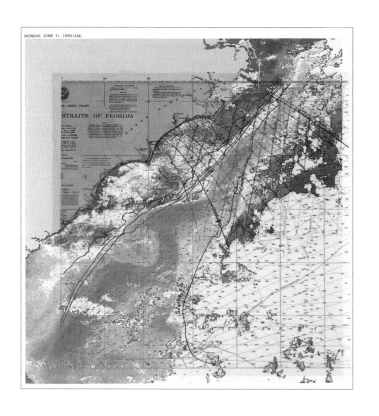

MONDAY, JUNE 11, 1990 (AM)

STRAITS OF FLORIDA

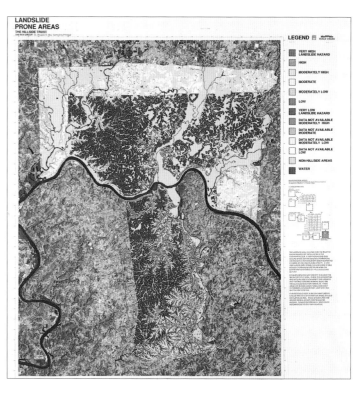

LANDSLIDE
PRONE AREAS
THE HILLSIDE TRUST

LEGEND

- VERY HIGH LANDSLIDE HAZARD
- HIGH
- MODERATELY HIGH
- MODERATE
- MODERATELY LOW
- LOW
- VERY LOW LANDSLIDE HAZARD
- DATA NOT AVAILABLE MODERATELY HIGH
- DATA NOT AVAILABLE MODERATE
- DATA NOT AVAILABLE MODERATELY LOW
- DATA NOT AVAILABLE LOW
- NON-HILLSIDE AREAS
- WATER

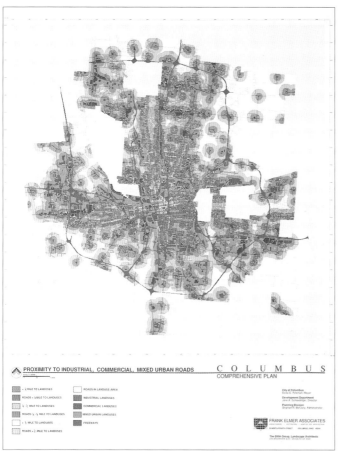

PROXIMITY TO INDUSTRIAL, COMMERCIAL, MIXED URBAN ROADS

C O L U M B U S
COMPREHENSIVE PLAN

FRANK ELMER ASSOCIATES

The SWA Group, Landscape Architects

SWA Professional Programs
SWAプロフェッショナルプログラム

The SWA Group Summer Program

In 1972 The SWA Group recognized the need for a program to rapidly increase the capabilities of recent landscape graduates. The landscape schools were suffering the impacts of 1960s turmoil, and it was difficult to find graduates who had even entry-level design skills. The program became successful and attracted students from around the country. The firm has kept the program active for almost 20 years, and it has been adopted by other firms, providing an enrichment to landscape education.

The original program was two months of intensive school problems in the SWA Sausalito office with field trips and critiques by the professional staff. As the schools changed, and when Peter Walker returned to Harvard to revitalize the landscape design program, the school shifted its emphasis to a true summer intern program for students working in all the SWA offices. Several SWA principals and other landscape architects of renown have come through this summer program.

SWA Group Teaching

SWA maintained its seminal connection with the Harvard Graduate School of Design, where its founders met and started the firm. Several principals of the firm taught on the faculty for a number of years and continue to teach or visit the school. Other principals expanded their involvement with MIT, Ohio State, Louisiana State University, Michigan, Cal Poly, UC Berkeley, UC Irvine, and other schools. SWA principal Dr. Douglas Way went on to become Chairman of the Ohio State University Landscape Architecture Program, and Gary Karner became a full-time professor at Cal Poly San Luis Obispo and wrote a definitive book on Landscape Architecture Contracts.

SWA Group Consulting Principals

To allow principals to retain their connection to The SWA Group and to teach and contribute to the profession by writing books, providing slide or video presentations or other activities, the SWA consulting principal group was created. The Consulting Principal status a concept of Mike Gilbert (himself a consulting principal for business management) allows continued close connection to the firm while giving freedom for other professional pursuits. Current consulting principals include Way, Karner and Gilbert, and Gerry Campbell, an artist and photographer who recently produced a video on Lawrence Halprin for the ASLA.

Information of Summer Program (1991)　1991年度サマープログラムの案内

The 1991 SWA Group Summer Internship

The SWA Group will be conducting its annual student summer internship program again this year. Since its creation in 1971 this special program has enabled students from all over the country to work in a leading landscape architectural design and planning firm. This year the program will be a twelve-week internship with one of the six participating SWA offices. This setup reflects the maturation of the SWA Group offices and their ability to each maintain a learning and work experience.

THE SWA SCOPE

The SWA Group is a professional firm specializing in land planning, site planning, urban design and landscape architecture. Since its formation over 30 years ago, we have consistently been committed to designing and building the finest projects in the profession. SWA serves a wide variety of public and private clients with services ranging from large scale environmental planning to sophisticated urban plazas in major cities. SWA has been recognized for its efforts through awards from the ASLA, AIA, and Urban Land Institute.

The SWA Group maintains eight full-service offices in Sausalito, Laguna Beach and Los Angeles, California; Houston and Dallas, Texas; Deerfield Beach, Florida; Boston, Massachusetts; and Alexandria, Virginia.

INTERNSHIP PROGRAM

A student must choose the participating office where they would most like to participate in the program. If selected, the student will work there and receive a salary for the twelve weeks. The emphasis of this program will be on the way a professional office functions: How design decisions are made, how work is programmed and completed on time and on budget, how we coordinate our work with other professionals, and how we actually produce our drawings and present them to our clients.

At our discretion, we will involve students in as many aspects of the day-to-day functioning of our office as possible. This may include meetings with clients, other consultants, in-house design and management meetings. Field trips may be scheduled with SWA principals and associates to round out the student's experience. A wide variety of opportunities are available during this session and we will do our best to work with individual students on their specific needs.

WHO SHOULD APPLY

The program is open to any student in Landscape Architecture, Urban Design, and Physical Planning with an intense primary interest in the built environment. Students who are preparing for their final year of graduate or undergraduate school are most likely to find the program useful to them though all applications will be reviewed.

WHEN TO APPLY

Applications will be accepted up to April 19, 1991 and a decision on the participants will be made by April 26, 1991.

WHAT TO SEND

Applications should include a portfolio of your work and statement of the reasons for your interest in the program, your academic record, job experience and any other comments or questions about the program. Examples of your work are the most important and are easiest for us to review and return to you if they are in an 8-1/2" x 11" format and held together in some kind of binder. All submissions should include your name, address and phone number, and a return envelope so that we can return your work to you. PLEASE DO NOT SEND ORIGINAL MATERIALS!!

WHERE TO SEND

Please choose The SWA Group office or offices where you would most like to participate in the Summer Internship Program (listed below). Send a complete set of materials to the office(s) of your choice to the attention of the Summer Program Coordinator.

The SWA Group
2200 Bridgeway Blvd.
Sausalito, CA 94965
(415) 332-5100

The SWA Group
811 W. 7th Street,
Suite 1230
Los Angeles, CA 90017
(213) 622-7242

The SWA Group
580 Broadway,
Suite 200
Laguna Beach, CA 92651
(714) 497-5471

The SWA Group
1245 W. 18th Street
Houston, TX 77008
(713) 868-1676

The SWA Group
2211 N. Lamar,
Suite 400
Dallas, TX 75202
(214) 954-0016

The SWA Group
401 Fairway Drive
Deerfield Beach,
FL 33441
(305) 427-0666

サマープログラム

1972年にSWAは最近のランドスケープの卒業生の早期養成・能力向上のための実習プログラムの必要性を痛感した．ランドスケープを教える学校は，1960年代のさまざまな騒動の影響で，卒業しても実戦に使えるレベルの学生を見つけることは困難な状況であった．このプログラムは成功し，全国の学生たちが集まってきた．実習プログラムはその後20年間にわたって継続され，他の事務所でも企画されて，結果としてランドスケープの教育水準を高めることにつながった．

オリジナルのプログラムは，SWAのサウサリート事務所を中心に，フィールド調査や専門のプロによる講評会を含む2か月間の集中講義という内容であった．学校の状況も次第に変化し，さらにピーター・ウォーカーがハーバード大学のランドスケープデザイン課程を活性化するために，SWAからハーバードに戻った時点から，このプログラムは純粋にSWAの各事務所で，学生が夏休みの期間実際の仕事を実習するということに主眼を置くように変わった．このサマープログラムには，SWAの何人かの役員や，その他の高名なランドスケープアーキテクトが参加する．

SWAメンバーの教職

SWAは，その創設者の関連以来，ハーバードの大学院とはずっと密接な関係を維持している．何人かの役員はそこで実際に繰り返し教壇に立って教えている．他にもMITやオハイオ州立大学，ルイジアナ州立大学，ミシガン，カリフォルニア工科大学，カリフォルニア大学バークレー校やアーバイン校，その他で教えている．特にダグラス・ウェイ

SWA Group International Programs

One of the summer students, Lilia Guzman de Ocampo, founded a Landscape Department at the University of Mexico which graduated the first Mexican Landscape Architect in 1990. Steve Calhoun, an associate of The SWA Group, went to Australia under a travel-work program and started the TRACT Consulting firm in Melbourne. Two former employees, Do Kim in Korea and Predapond Bandityonond in Thailand, maintain liaison with the firm for work in their areas. Hiroyasu Tanaka of Taisei Corporation is finishing his 16-month work-study program with The SWA Group, and the program is planned to continue with another Taisei associate from Japan.

SWA has begun a fruitful affiliation with Landscape International Ltd. of Tokyo to assist SWA on certain Japanese projects. In other Japanese projects SWA has affiliated with US or Japanese architects who have expertise in Japan. In Europe, SWA has begun a special relationship with Euro-Developpment to assist with work in the European Community.

In these ways The SWA Group participates in furthering the profession of Landscape Architecture in the US and other countries. It is our goal to increase awareness of the environment and the role landscape design and land planning can play in creating better living conditions, and to work with professionals in other countries for mutual education and practice.

The Employee Stock Ownership Program

Since 1973 The SWA Group has been an Employee Stock Ownership company. Ninety percent of the company is owned by a trust representing all employees. All employees have a stock account, and a contribution equal to ten percent of their total compensation in any year is made to their account by the firm. In a professional organization the quality and motivation of the employees are key ingredients. The ESOP allows each employee to benefit from ownership as well as salary and thereby provides motivation for quality and excellence as long-term investments in the firm.

博士は，オハイオ州立大学のランドスケープ学部長になっているし，ゲイリー・カーナーはカリフォルニア工科大学サンルイオビスポ校の専任教授であり，ランドスケープアーキテクチュアの業務についてのすばらしい本もまとめている．

SWAグループのコンサルティング・プリンシパル

役員がSWAとの関係を維持しつつ，教職についたり，本を書いたり，スライドやビデオや他の活動を自由に展開するために，SWAではコンサルティング・プリンシパルという役職を生み出した．これはマイケル・ギルバートがつくった役職で，彼自身も運営管理のコンサルティング・プリンシパルであるが，SWAと密接な関係を保ちながら，それ以外のプロとしての自由な活動も許容するというものである．最近ではダグラス・ウェイやゲイリー・カーナーやマイケル・ギルバート，そしてアーチストで写真家のゲリー・キャンベルなどがそうである．キャンベルは最近ASLAのためのローレンス・ハルプリンのビデオを作成している．

SWAの海外活動

サマープログラムの出身者の1人であるリリア・グスマン・デ・オカンポは，メキシコ大学にランドスケープ学部を創設し，1990年に初の卒業生を送り出している．SWAのアソシエイトの1人であるスティーブ・カルホーンは，調査旅行でオーストラリアへ行き，そのままメルボルンでTRACTコンサルティング事務所を設立した．2人の旧所員である韓国のドウ・キムやタイのプレダポンド・バンディチョノンドは，

それぞれの地域の仕事を通してSWAと密接に関係している．日本の田中弘靖氏は1年にわたるSWAの研修を終えようとしている．この研修プログラムは，他のメンバーに引き継がれて継続される予定である．

SWAは東京のランドスケープ・インターナショナル社と提携しているほか，日本の事情に精通したアメリカや日本の建築家を通じて，日本のプロジェクトに当たっている．また，ヨーロッパでは，SWAは新しいECの仕事でユーロ・ディベロップメント社と協働している．

このように，SWAはアメリカのみならず世界中でランドスケープアーキテクチュアのプロとして活躍の範囲を広げている．SWAの目標は，環境への認識を深めることであり，ランドスケープデザインや土地利用計画を通して，よりよい生活環境を形成していくことである．また，他のさまざまな国のプロと一緒に仕事をすることで相互のに教育し合い，活動することである．

社員持ち株制度

1973年以来，SWAは社員持ち株会社である．90％は全社員によって所有され社長はわずか10％を所有しているだけである．すべての社員が持ち株を有し，毎年その全収入の10％以内の配当金が配当される．プロフェッショナルな組織として，従業員すべての資質と意欲が基本的な要素である．このため，社員持ち株制度は，各人にサラリーと成功報酬を支払うだけでなく，組織を長く維持するための資質と優秀さを生み出す根本となる意欲をもつくり出している．

CHRONOLOGY

全作品リスト

*marked projects appear in this issue.
＊印は本文掲載作品

1

16

17

25

1959

1. Foothill College, Los Altos, California; Ernest J. Kump and Masten and Hurd, Architects

2. **Upjohn Corporation General Office Building**, Kalamazoo, Michigan; Skidmore, Owings & Merrill, Architects

1960

3. **Cabrillo College**, Santa Cruz County, California; Cabrillo Joint Union Junior College District; Ernest J. Kump and Masten, Hurd and Gwathmey, Architects

4. **Golden Gateway Redevelopment Project**, San Francisco, California; Wurster, Bernardi and Emmons, and Demars and Reay, Associated Architects

5. **Johnson County Community College**, Kansas City, Missouri; Marshall & Brown, Architects

6. **Los Gatos Civic Center**, Los Gatos, California; Stickney and Hull, Architects

1962

7. **Sequoias Congregate Housing**, Portola Valley, California; Skidmore, Owings & Merrill, Architects

8. **Stauffer Research Center**, Richmond, California; McCue, Boone, Tomsick, Architects

1964

9. **Alcoa Plaza**, Golden Gateway Redevelopment Area, San Francisco, California; Skidmore, Owings & Merrill and Wurster, Bernardi and Emmons, Architects

10. **Leverett House, Harvard University**, Cambridge, Massachusetts; Harvard University; Shepley, Bulfinch, Richardson and Abbott, Architects

11. **Pomeroy Green**, Santa Clara, California; Eichler Homes, Inc.; Claude Oakland, Architect

1965

12. **Crossroads Shopping Center**, Sacramento, California; Ernest J. Kump and Dean F. Unger Associates, Architects

13. **Sidney G. Walton Square**, San Francisco, California; Golden Gateway Center

1966

14. **Sacramento County Courthouse**, Sacramento, California; Starks, Jozen & Nacht, Architects; Aris Demetrios, Sculptor

15. **University Avenue Urban Design Study**, Berkeley, California; City of Berkeley; McCue, Boone, Tomsick, Architects

1967

16. Del Mesa Carmel, Carmel Valley, California; Alcan-Pacific Company

17. Harry S Truman Sports Complex, Kansas City, Missouri; Kivett & Myers, Architects

18. **The Villages**, San Jose, California; Guy F. Atkinson Company and Mackay Homes; Economic Research Associates

1968

19. **Cabot, Cabot & Forbes Industrial Park**, South San Francisco, California; Cabot, Cabot & Forbes

20. **Cosumnes River College**, Sacramento, California; Stark, Jozens, Nacht & Lewis and Cox-Liske Associates, Architects

21. **Fashion Island**, Newport Beach, California; The Irvine Company; Welton Becket Associates, Architects

22. **Kohala Coast Resort Region Master Plan**, Island of Hawaii; Dilrock-Eastern Company

23. **Newport Financial Center Area**, Newport Beach, California; The Irvine Company

24. **Sears Headquarters Building**, Alhambra, California; Albert C. Martin & Associates, Architects

25. Syntex Research Center, Palo Alto, California; McCue, Boone, Tomsick, Architects

＊26. **University Park**, Irvine, California; Stanley C. Swartz Company; Thomas and Richardson, Architects

27. **Western Addition Residential Redevelopment**, San Francisco, California; San Francisco Redevelopment Agency and Eichler Homes, Inc.; Claude Oakland and Jones and Emmons, Architects

1969

28. **Alza Research Corporation**, Palo Alto, California; McCue, Boone, Tomsick, Architects

29. **Atlantic Richfield Plaza**, Los Angeles, California; Albert C. Martin & Associates, Architects

30. **Berkeley Marina**, Berkeley, California; John A. Blume and Associates, Engineers; McCue, Boone, Tomsick, Architects

31. **Long Range Development Plan, University of California, Riverside**, Riverside, California; George Vernon Russell, FAIA, Architects

32. **Redwood Shores**, Redwood City, California; Leslie Properties, Inc.

37

38

48

59

61

69

71

76

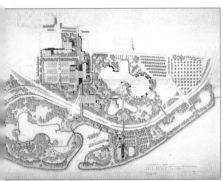

85

96

68. **Mammoth Lakes Environmental Study**, Mammoth Lakes, California; U.S. Forestry Service and Mono County Planning Department

69. Pescadero Creek Park Master Plan, San Mateo County, California

70. **Prototypical Site Development Programs for Maximizing Solar Energy Potentials**; U.S. Department of Housing and Urban Development, Bureau of Standards

71. Security Pacific National Bank World Headquarters Building, Los Angeles, California; Security Pacific National Bank; Albert C. Martin & Associates, Architects

72. **Segerstrom Properties**, Santa Ana and Costa Mesa, California; C.J. Segerstrom & Sons

73. **Squaw Valley Resort Master Plan**, Olympic Valley, California; Mainline Properties of America, Nevada; I.M. Pei and Partners, Architects

74. **Willows Shopping Center**, Concord, California; Eastman and Associates; Leason F. Pomeroy, Architects

1975

75. **Bank of America Data Center**, Los Angeles, California; Skidmore, Owings & Merrill, Architects

76. Concord Performing Arts Center, Concord, California; City of Concord; Frank O. Gehry & Associates, Architects

77. **Ethan's Glen**, Houston, Texas; GreenMark, Inc. and Gerald D. Hines Interests; Fisher-Friedman Associates, AIA, Architects

*78. **Golden Gate National Recreation Area Master Plan**, Marin County, California; United States Department of the Interior, National Park Service

79. **Knowland Zoo Master Plan**, Oakland, California; East Bay Zoological Society; Comarc Design Systems

80. **Mid-Continent International Airport**, Kansas City, Missouri; Kivett & Myers, Architects

*81. **San Diego Embarcadero Master Plan**, San Diego, California; San Diego Unified Port District; Deems and Lewis, Architects

82. **Weyerhaeuser Technology Center**, Tacoma, Washington; The Weyerhaeuser Company; Skidmore, Owings & Merrill, Architects

1976

83. **Columbus City Hall**, Columbus, Indiana; Skidmore, Owings & Merrill, Architects

84. **Griffith Park Master Plan**, Los Angeles, California; City of Los Angeles Recreation and Parks Commission

85. Long Beach Shoreline Plan, Long Beach, California; City of Long Beach

86. **Potters Walk**, Houston, Texas; Brownstone Builders

87. **Tuen Mun and Sha Tin New Towns Urban Design**, Hong Kong; Yuncken Freeman H.K. Architects; TRACT Consultants Pty., Ltd., Planners

1977

*88. **Green Meadows**, Des Moines, Iowa; Pioneer Hi-Bred International

89. **Life Insurance Company of California Headquarters**, San Diego, California; Urban Development Group, Development Management Services; Gruen Associates, Architects

90. **Merced Downtown Revitalization**, Merced, California; City of Merced

91. **George F. Moscone Convention Center**, San Francisco, California; City of San Francisco; Hellmuth, Obata & Kassabaum, Architects

92. **Shell Oil Woodcreek Exploration and Production Facility**, Houston, Texas; Shell Oil Corporation; Caudill, Rowlett, Scott, Architects

93. **Stanford University Library Fountain**, Stanford, California; Ernest J. Kump and Hellmuth, Obata & Kassabaum, Architects

1978

94. **California State University and Colleges Headquarters Building,** Long Beach, California; Headquarters Building Authority; Killingsworth, Brady & Associates and Bolling & Gill, Architects

95. **Crocker Plaza**, San Francisco, California; Universal Land Company; Welton Becket Associates, Architects

96. Fireman's Fund, Novato, California; American Express; Robinson, Mills & Williams, Architects

97. **Jubail Industrial City, District B**, Jubail, Saudi Arabia; Krueger/Monacelli Associates, Inc., Architects

98. **Moss Landing Marine Laboratory**, Moss Landing, California; San Jose State University; Marquis Associates, Architects

99. **Santa Rosa Subdivision Design Guide**, Santa Rosa, California; City of Santa Rosa

100. **South Coast Town Center**, Santa Ana, California; C.J. Segerstrom & Sons

101. **Village North Lagoon**, Salinas, California; Village North Incorporated, Developers; Backen, Arrigoni & Ross, Inc., Architects

1979

*102. **Refugio Valley Park**, Hercules, California; City of Hercules; John O'Brien & Associates, Architects

103. **Arvida Town Center**, Boca Raton, Florida; Arvida Corporation

104. **Carnegie Library/Quitman Park**, Houston, Texas; Ray B. Bailey, Architects

105. **Corpus Christi Waterfront Plan and Development Study**, Corpus Christi, Texas; City of Corpus Christi

*106. **Fort Mason Center**, San Francisco, California; Fort Mason Foundation; Robinson, Mills & Williams, Architects

107. **Four Leaf Towers**, Houston, Texas; Interfin Corporation; Cesar Pelli and Albert C. Martin, Architects

108. **Jesse H. Jones Fountain**, Houston, Texas; South Main Center Association

109. **North Carolina State University School of Veterinary Medicine**, Raleigh, North Carolina; Ferebee, Walters and Associates, Architects; Gerald M. McCue, Consulting Architect

110. **Port of Los Angeles Administration Building**, San Pedro, California; Los Angeles Harbor Department; John Carl Warnecke Associates, Architects

111. **Shoreline Regional Park**, Mountain View, California; City of Mountain View; Wilsey & Ham, Engineers; Robert Trent Jones, Jr., Golf Course Architect

*112. **Victoria Community Plan**, Rancho Cucamonga, California; The William Lyon Company

1980

113. **101 California Street**, San Francisco, California; Gerald D. Hines Interests; Johnson/Burgee, Architects

114. **400 South Hope Street**, Los Angeles, California; O'Melveny & Myers and Olympia and York; Welton Becket Associates, Architects

115. **Alameda Marina Village**, Alameda, California; Alameda Marina Village Associates; Fisher-Friedman Associates, AIA, Architects

*116. **Arvida Park of Commerce**, Boca Raton, Florida; Arvida Corporation

117. **Bixby Ranch Community Plan**, Long Beach, California; Bixby Ranch Company

118. **Charles Square**, Cambridge, Massachusetts; Charles Square Associates and Carpenter and Company, Developers; Cambridge Seven Associates, Architects

119. **Consulting Landscape Architects, San Jose State University**, San Jose, California; San Jose State University

*120. **Dallas West End Historic District**, Dallas, Texas; City of Dallas; Turner, Collie and Braden, Engineers

121. **Dallas West End Marketplace/Dallas Alley**, Dallas, Texas; Marketplace Developer Company

122. **First Colony**, Fort Bend County, Texas; Sugarland Properties, Inc.

123. **Harlequin Plaza**, Greenwood Village, Colorado; The John Madden Company; Gensler & Associates, Architects

124. **Hong Kong Ocean Park Master Plan**, Victoria Island, Hong Kong; EBC Hong Kong

125. **Lakewood Hills**, Windsor, California; Piombo Corporation

*126. **Lantern Bay Master Plan and Blufftop Parks**, Dana Point, California; Smyth Brothers, Inc. and Pacific Mutual Life Insurance Company

127. **Luis Pietri Garden**, Caracas, Venezuela; Alberto Chaves, Architect

128. **McCarran International Airport**, Las Vegas, Nevada; City of Las Vegas; The Richardson Associates, Architects

129. **New Seabury Master Plan**, New Seabury, Massachusetts; New Seabury Corporation

130. **North Fork Kern Wild and Scenic River Study**, Tulare and Kern Counties, California; United States Forestry Service

131. **Oakland City Center Renewal Plan**, Oakland, California; City of Oakland Redevelopment Agency; Robinson, Mills & Williams, Architects

132. **The Prudential Center Renewal Plan**, Boston, Massachusetts; The Prudential Insurance Company of America

133. **Riverway**, Houston, Texas; John Hansen Investment Builders

134. **Sheraton Grande Hotel**, Los Angeles, California; Sheraton Corporation; Maxwell Starkman Associates, Architects

135. **Tanajib**, Saudi Arabia; Aramco Services Company and Fluor Engineers

*136. **Williams Square**, Las Colinas, Texas; Las Colinas; Southland Investment Company; Skidmore, Owings & Merrill, Architects; Robert Glen, Sculptor

1981

137. **Antioch Park**, Houston, Texas; Antioch Baptist Church and Century Development Corporation

*138. **Boca Raton Hotel and Club, Boca Beach Club**, Boca Raton, Florida; Arvida Corporation; Killingsworth, Brady & Associates, Architects

139. **Corporate Woods**, Overland Park, Kansas; Jones & Company and Metropolitan Life Insurance Company; Marshall and Brown, Architects

114

115

123

133

139

140

159

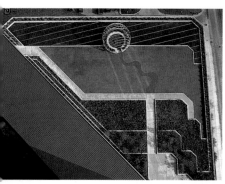

168

169

178

179

186

190

192

208

141

230

239

241

244

249

214. **GTE Data Services Technology Center**, Temple Terrace, Florida; GTE Data Services; Thompson, Ventulett, Stainback & Associates and Robbins, Bell & Kuehlem, Architects

∗215. **Hamptons Road,** Lexington, Kentucky; Boyd/Smith Developers; Robert A.M. Stern, Architects

∗216. **Hyatt Regency Scottsdale at Gainey Ranch**, Scottsdale, Arizona; Hyatt Development Corporation; Hornberger, Worstell & Associates, Architects

217. **Inn on the Park**, Houston, Texas; Morris Aubry, Architects

218. **Irvine Freeway Corridor**, Irvine, California; The Irvine Company

219. **Kezar Corner Master Plan**, Golden Gate Park, San Francisco, California; San Francisco Recreation and Parks Department; ED2 International, Architects

220. **Knott's Berry Farm Master Plan**, Buena Park, California; Knott's Berry Farm

221. **Laguna Canyon Village,** County of Orange, California; The Irvine Company

222. **Lombard Plaza**, San Francisco, California; Talden Architectural Group

223. **MacArthur Corridor**, Newport Beach, California; The Irvine Company

∗224. **Magee Ranch**, Danville, California; Diablo Ranch Development Company

225. **Main Street Improvements**, Allen, Texas; City of Allen

226. **Marin County YMCA**, San Rafael, California; ED2 International, Architects

227. **Meridian**, Raleigh-Durham, North Carolina; CMD Southeast, Inc.

228. **Methodist Hospital Redevelopment**, Houston, Texas; The Methodist Hospital; Morris Architects

229. **Miami Beach Convention Center Expansion**, Miami Beach, Florida; City of Miami Beach; Thompson, Ventulett, Stainback & Associates with Borrelli, Frankel, Blitstein, Architects

230. Old Main Restoration, Sam Houston State University, Huntsville, Texas; Ray B. Bailey Architects, Inc.

231. **Plano Downtown Development Plan**, Plano, Texas

232. **Plantation Park**, New Orleans, Louisiana; Joseph C. Canizaro Interests

233. **Silver Creek Resort**, West Virginia; Lowe Associates

234. **Tanner Fountain**, Cambridge, Massachusetts; Harvard University; Peter Walker, Associated Landscape Architect

235. **Tarpey Flats**, Monterey, California; Cypress Properties, Inc.

236. **University of California Santa Cruz Academic Core Master Plan and Natural Sciences Building III**, Santa Cruz, California; University of California, Santa Cruz; ED2 International, Architects

237. **University Center at Tulsa**, Tulsa, Oklahoma; University Center at Tulsa Foundation; HTB, Inc., Architects

238. **University of Washington Husky Stadium**, Seattle, Washington; University of Washington; TRA, Architects; Skillings, Ward, Magnusson, Barkshire, Inc., Structural Engineers

239. University of Washington Ranier Vista, Seattle, Washington; University of Washington; The Bumgardner Architects

240. **USAA Headquarters**, San Antonio, Texas; United Services Automobile Association

241. Volt Corporate Headquarters, Orange, California; Volt Information Services; The WZMH Group, Architects

242. **Wakefield**, Wake County, North Carolina; North Hills, Inc.

243. **Waterford Harbor Yacht Club**, League City, Texas; Emkay Development Company; Langwith, Wilson, King Architects

244. Weston Planned Community, Cary, North Carolina; North Hills, Inc.

245. **Wortham Theater Center**, Houston, Texas; Morris Aubry, Architects

246. **Wright Island**, Shreveport, Louisiana; U.L. Coleman; Fusch-Serold, Architects

1986

∗247. **The Andover Companies Corporate Headquarters**, Andover, Massachusetts; Shepley, Bulfinch, Richardson & Abbott, Architects

248. **Banning-Lewis Ranch**, Colorado Springs, Colorado; Aries Properties, Inc.; PRC Engineering

249. Boca Rio Golf Club, Boca Raton, Florida; Boca Rio Golf Club; Herbert Seigle and Donald Solow, Architects

250. **Campanile**, Atlanta, Georgia; Carter and Associates, Bell South; Thompson, Ventulett, Stainback & Associates, Architects

251. Capitol Commons, Indianapolis, Indiana; Lilly Endowment and Indianapolis Convention Center; Kennedy, Brown, & McQuiston, Architects; CMS Collaborative

252. **Cimarron Country Club**, Margarita, Venezuela; Edifica C.A., Architects; Joseph Lee, Golf Course Architect; Roberto Burle Marx, Associated Landsape Architect

253. **City of Tucson Main Library**, Tucson, Arizona; Anderson, DeBartolo, Pan, Architects

251

259

267

268

288

299

305

307

310

317

327. **Playas Espanolas**, Marbella, Spain; The Prime Group; DI Design and Kaufman/ Meeks, Architects

328. **Rabinowitz Residence**, Beverly Hills, California; Waldo Fernandez, Architect

329. **Ritz Carlton Resort Hotel**, Rancho Palos Verdes, California; Hon Development

330. The Ronald Reagan Presidential Library and Center for Public Affairs, Simi Valley, Ventura County, California; The Ronald Reagan Presidential Foundation; The Stubbins Associates, Inc., Architects; Phil Shipley, Consultant

331. **Ski Run Water Quality Improvement Project and Hotel**, South Lake Tahoe, California; City of South Lake Tahoe; K.B. Foster Engineering, Inc.

332. **Summerlin**, Las Vegas, Nevada; Howard Hughes Properties

333. The Water Garden, Santa Monica, California; J.H. Snyder Company; McLarand Vasquez & Partners, Architects

334. **Waterfront Centre**, Vancouver, British Columbia, Canada; Marathon Realty Company; Musson Cattell Mackey Partnership, Architects; Pavcleki & Associates, Associated Landscape Architects

335. **The Waterfront Hilton**, Huntington Beach, California; The Robert Mayer Corporation; Wimberly, Allison, Tong & Goo, Architects

336. **Western Digital Corporate Headquarters**, Irvine, California; Albert C. Martin Associates and Kohn, Pederson, Fox, Architects

1989

337. **550 South Hope Street**, Los Angeles, California; The Koll Company and Ohbayashi America Corporation; Kohn, Pederson, Fox and Langdon Wilson, Architects

＊338. **Akebien Membership Hotel**, Nasu, Japan; Towa Real Estate Development Company, Ltd., and Mitsubishi Corporation, Developers; ED2 International, Architects

339. **The Arboretum**, Santa Monica, California; Lowe Enterprises, Inc.

340. **AT&T Garden**, Irvine, California; The Irvine Company

341. **Ballston Station**, Arlington County, Virginia; London & Leeds Development Corporation; Dewberry & Davis and Gensler & Associates, Architects

342. **Boston Crossing**, Boston, Massachusetts; Campeau Massachusetts, Inc.; Skidmore, Owings & Merrill and RTKL Associates, Architects

343. **Consulting Landscape Architects, University of California, Irvine**, Irvine, California; University of California, Irvine

344. **Cornell University Special Collections Library**, Ithaca, New York; Shepley, Bulfinch, Richardson & Abbott, Architects

345. Dallas Downtown 2010, Dallas, Texas; Corgan Associates, Architects

346. **Fairway Terrace**, Waikoloa, Hawaii; TFK Development Company; Starnes, Stovall, Daniels, Architects

347. **Federal Reserve Bank of Dallas**, Dallas, Texas; Sikes, Jennings, Kelly & Brewer and Kohn, Pederson, Fox, Architects

＊348. **Freeway Competition, Interchangeable Parts**, Houston, Texas; Texas Highway Department and the National Endowment for the Arts

349. **Fresh Kills Landfill**, Staten Island, New York; City of New York, Department of Sanitation

350. **Hellenic College**, Brookline, Massachusetts; Linpro Development and GHM, Inc., Developers

＊351. **Hidiv Beldisi**, Istanbul, Turkey; HB Construction and Trading International

352. Hilton International Hotel, Antalya, Turkey; Hilton International

353. **Hilton International Hotel**, Mersin, Turkey; Hilton International; Mersin Enternasyonal Otelcilik, A.S.

354. Hobe Sound Plantation, Hobe Sound, Florida; Hobe Sound Partners, Ltd.; William Johnson, Associated Landsape Architect

355. **Hon Residence**, Monarch Bay, California; Mr. and Mrs. Barry G. Hon

356. **Huntley Meadows**, McHenry and Kane Counties, Illinois; The Prime Group, Developers

＊357. **Hyatt at Pelican Hill**, Newport Beach, California; Hyatt Development Corporation

358. **Intel Corporation Santa Clara Campus**, Santa Clara, California; Intel Corporation; HED Architects, Inc.

359. **Lancaster Business Park**, Lancaster, California; Lancaster Economic Development Corporation

360. **Liliuokalani Trust Property**, Kona, Hawaii; TFK Development Company

361. **Mission City**, San Diego, California; Mission Valley Associates; Skidmore, Owings & Merrill and The Nadel Partnership, Architects

362. **Montecito**, San Diego, California; MV Associates; ConAm, Developers

363. **Moody Gardens**, Galveston, Texas; Morris Architects

330

333

345

352

354

145

371

375

387

399

406

364. **Nasu Highlands Grand Hotel**, Nasu, Japan; Towa Nasu Resort Company, Ltd.; ED2 International, Architects

*365. **Nasu Highlands Golf Club**, Nasu, Japan; Towa Nasu Resort Company, Ltd.; ED2 International, Architects; Robert Trent Jones, II, International, Ltd., Golf Course Architects

*366. **Newport Coast**, Newport Beach, California; The Irvine Company; Richardson, Nagi, Martin Architects

367. **Pasadena Central Park**, Pasadena, California; City of Pasadena, Community Development Department

368. **Pelican Hill Road Landscape**, California; The Irvine Company

369. **Providence Convention Center**, Providence, Rhode Island; Providence Convention Center Authority; Canon and HNTB, Architects

370. **Rancho Santa Margarita Town Center**, Rancho Santa Margarita, California; Rancho Santa Margarita Company

371. NeXT, Inc. at Seaport Centre, Redwood City, California; NeXT, Inc..

*372. **Thoroughbred Park**, Lexington, Kentucky; The Triangle Foundation, Inc.; Mason-Hanger, Civil Engineers; Gwen Reardon, Artist

1990

373. **Anaheim Downtown Redevelopment Project**, Anaheim, California; Fredericks Development Company

374. **Anaheim Museum**, Anaheim, California; Anaheim Redevelopment Agency

375. Angel Kingdom, Ueno City, Japan; Taisei Construction; Miyashita Associates; Landscape International, Ltd., Affiliated Consultants

*376. **Bella Porta**, Santa Clarita, California; The Anden Group

377. **Cable Data**, El Dorado County, California; Cable Data

378. **Coast Guard Family Housing Master Plan**, Bayamon, Puerto Rico; U.S. Coast Guard; Arquitectonica International Corporation

379. **Columbia Pictures**, Hollywood, California; Columbia Pictures

380. **Cowell Ranch**, Contra Costa County, California; The Cowell Foundation

*381. **East Highlands Ranch**, San Bernardino, California; Mobil Oil

382. **Fujinomiya Springs Resort**, Mount Fuji, Japan; Nippon Gas Company; SSOE, Inc., Architects; Landscape International, Ltd., Affiliated Consultants

383. **Fujitsu Development**, Richardson, Texas; Fujitsu America; Omniplan, Architects

384. **Heritage Club**, Indian Wells, California; The Sunrise Company; Robert Altevers & Associates, Architects

385. **Hilton International Hotel**, Istanbul, Turkey; Hilton International

386. **Hilton International Hotel**, Izmir, Turkey; Hilton International; Enternaysonal Otelcilik, A.S.

387. Historic Torrance Downtown Redevelopment District, Torrance, California; City of Torrance Redevelopment Agency; Gascon Mar Ltd. and SLI, Developers; Bowlus, Edinger & Starck, Architects

388. **J.I. Case Corporate Headquarters Campus**, Racine, Wisconsin; Hoover & Furr and 3D International, Architects

389. **Jarvis Vineyards**, Napa, California; Mr. William Jarvis

390. **Karmina Palace Hotel**, Manzanillo, Mexico; Hornberger, Worstell Associates, Architects

391. **Kawauchi Heights Forest City New Town**, Tokyo, Japan; Environmental Systems Research Institute

*392. **Kit Carson, A Sculpture Competition**, Escondido, California; City of Escondido; Joyce Shaw, Artist

393. **Lagoon Valley Policy Plan**, Vacaville, California; City of Vacaville; McCuen Properties, Developers

394. **Long Beach Convention Center**, Long Beach, California; City of Long Beach; Thompson, Ventulett, Stainback & Associates, Architects

395. **Manzanita Housing at Stanford University**, Stanford, California; Stanford University; Fisher-Friedman Associates, AIA, Architects

396. **Marriott Hotel Acapulco Competition**, Acapulco, Mexico; Kohn Pederson Fox, Architects; Cementos Mexicanos, S.A.

397. **Nasu Highlands Garden Villas**, Nasu, Japan; Towa Nasu Resort Company, Ltd.; ED2 International, Architects

398. **Riverside Marketplace**, Riverside, California; Birtcher Development; DeRevere Partnership and 30th Street Architects

399. S'Agaro Park, S'Agaro, Spain; Kepro Costa Brava, S.A.

400. **Sangiacomo Residence**, Phoenix, Arizona; Trinity Properties

401. **Sky Valley**, Vallejo, California; Misawa Homes of America; Backen, Arrigoni & Ross, Inc., Architects; The Palmer Group, Golf Course Architects

402. **Sky Valley Specific Plan**, Benicia, California; City of Benicia

403. **Stanford University Medical Center Design I Guidelines**, Stanford, California; Stanford University

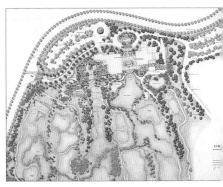

407

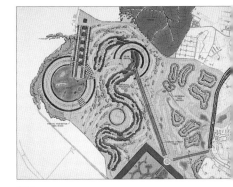

408

413

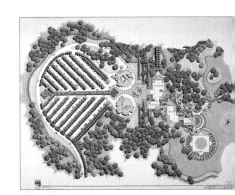

430

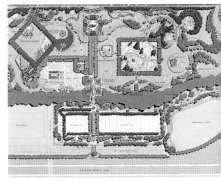

438

PROJECT DATA
掲載作品データ

Golden Gate National Recreation Area
Marin County, California
Client: U.S. Department of the Interior, National Park Service
Date: 1975
Size: 90,000 acres

Elkhorn at Sun Valley
Sun Valley, Idaho
Client: Johns-Manville/Idaho and The Sun Valley Company
Architects: Killingsworth, Brady & Associates, Architects
Golf Course Architect: Robert Trent Jones, Jr.
Date: 1971
Size: 2,500 acres

San Diego Embarcadero Master Plan
San Diego, California
Client: San Diego Unified Port District
Architects: Deems and Lewis
Date: 1975
Size: 3-1/2 linear miles

Florida Story - Arvida Corporation Projects

Boca West
Boca Raton, Florida
Client: Arvida Corporation
Date: 1974
Size: 1,400 acres

Boca Raton Hotel & Club
Boca Raton, Florida
Client: Arvida Corporation
Date: 1981
Size: 217 acres

Arvida Town Center
Boca Raton, Florida
Client: Arvida Corporation
Date: 1979
Size: 100 acres

Arvida Park of Commerce
Boca Raton, Florida
Client: Arvida Corporation
Date: 1980
Size: 720 acres

Arvida Villages at Boca Raton
Boca Raton, Florida
Client: Arvida Corporation
Date: 1972 - 1988
Size: 4,000 acres

Irvine Ranch Story

University Park
Irvine, California
Client: Stanley C. Swartz, Developers
Architects: Thomas & Richardson
Date: 1968
Size: 1,200 units

Baywood
Newport Beach, California
Client: The Irvine Company
Architects: Fisher-Friedman Associates, AIA, Architects
Date: 1974
Size: 28 acres

Promontory Point
Newport Beach, California
Client: The Irvine Company
Architects: Fisher-Friedman Associates, AIA, Architects
Date: 1970
Size: 30 acres, 520 units

Newport Coast
Newport Beach, California
Client: The Irvine Company
Architects: Richardson, Nagy, Martin
Date: 1989
Size: 10,000 acres

MacArthur Court
Newport Beach, California
Client: The Irvine Company
Architects: Skidmore, Owings & Merrill
Date: 1984
Size: 19 acres

Village of Woodbridge
Irvine, California
Client: The Irvine Company
Date: 1973
Size: 1,750 acres

Southern California Communities

Victoria Community Plan
Rancho Cucamonga, California
Client: The William Lyon Company
Date: 1979
Size: 2,200 acres

Heritage
Fontana, California
Client: City of Fontana and Joe Di Iorio
Date: 1984
Size: 110 acres

North Peak Specific Plan
Lake Elsinore, California
Client: TMC Development
Date: 1988
Size: 2,000 acres

Bella Porta
Santa Clarita, California
Client: The Anden Group
Date: 1990
Size: 960 acres

Regency
Omaha, Nebraska
Client: United Benefit Life Insurance Company
Architects: Robert Gladstone Associates
Date: 1969
Size: 500 acres, 400 residential lots, 600 townhouses, 60 acres retail and office, 25-acre lake

Green Meadows
Des Moines, Iowa
Client: Pioneer Hi-Bred International
Date: 1977
Size: 400 acres

Hampton Road
Lexington, Massachusetts
Client: Boyd/Smith Developers
Architects: Robert A.M. Stern
Date: 1985
Size: 10 acres

Magee Ranch
Danville, California
Client: Diablo Ranch Development Company
Date: 1985
Size: 600 acres, 257 homes

Liliore Green Rains Housing at Stanford University
Stanford, California
Client: Stanford University
Architects: Backen, Arrigoni & Ross, Inc.
Date: 1986
Size: 11.3 acres

The Andover Companies Corporate Headquarters
Andover, Massachusetts
Client: The Andover Companies
Architects: Shepley, Bulfinch, Richardson & Abbott
Engineers: Beals and Thomas
Date: 1986
Size: 27 acre, 110,000 SF building

IBM Almaden
San Jose, California
Client: IBM Corporation
Architects: MBT Associates
Date: 1982
Size: 580 acre, 500,000 SF laboratory

Meridian
Aurora, Illinois
Client: CMD Midwest, Inc.
Date: 1982
Size: 600 acres

Westwood Gateway
Los Angeles, California
Client: Bren Investment Properties
Architects: Skidmore, Owings & Merrill
Date: 1986
Size: 8 acres

Fountain Court at Curtis Center
Philadelphia, Pennsylvania
Client: The Kevin F. Donohoe Company
Architects: Oldham & Seltz
Fountain Consultants: CMS Collaborative
Fiberglass Urns Artist: Marla Weinhoff
Date: 1984
Size: 1,000,000 SF

International Jewelry Center
Los Angeles, California
Client: Cabot, Cabot & Forbes
Architects: Skidmore, Owings & Merrill
Date: 1981
Size: 6,500 SF

Worldwide Plaza
New York, New York
Client: New York Communication Center Associates
Architects: Skidmore, Owings & Merrill
Date: 1986
Size: One-acre site, 1.5 million SF office, 49 stories, 300 residential units

Arizona Center
Phoenix, Arizona
Client: Rouse-Phoenix; a Subsidiary of The Rouse Company
Architects: Howard, Needles, Tammen and Bergendoff (HNTB), Two Arizona Center; HKS, Inc., One Arizona Center; ELS/Elbassani-Logan, The Shops at Arizona Center
Date: 1988
Size: 18.5 acre, 5 acre phase one, 3.2 million SF mixed-use center

Fashion Island
Newport Beach, California
Client: The Irvine Company
Architects: The Jerde Partnership
Date: 1986
Size: 450 acres total site, 70,000 SF retail, 250,000 SF plaza areas

Hyatt Regency Scottsdale at Gainey Ranch
Scottsdale, Arizona
Client: Hyatt Development Corporation
Architects: Hornberger Worstell & Associates
Water Features Consultant: Howard Fields & Associates
Date: 1985
Size: 28 acres, 500 rooms

Williams Square
Las Colinas, Texas
Client: Southland Investment Company
Architects: Skidmore, Owings & Merrill
Sculptor: Robert Glen
Date: 1980
Size: 200' x 300' plaza, 10 mustangs, 1-1/2 x life size

Dallas West End/Dallas Alley
Dallas, Texas
Client: City of Dallas
Engineers: Turner, Collie & Braden
Date: 1980
Size: 55 acres

National Bank of Commerce Plaza
San Antonio, Texas
Client: Century Development Corporation
Architects: Cambridge Seven Associates, Inc.
Date: 1986
Size: 110,600 SF total site, 47,000 SF plaza

Greater Fort Lauderdale/Broward County Convention Center at Northport
Fort Lauderdale, Florida
Client: Northport Venture Associates Inc.; Broward Conty; Port Everglades Authority
Design/Build Client: Centex Rooney Construction
Design Architect: Thompson, Ventulett, Stainback & Associates, Inc.
Associated Architect: Cannon/Yan
Civil Engineer: Craven Thompson & Associates
Sculptor: Kent Ullberg
Fountain Consultant: The Fountain People
Date: 1991
Size: 33 acres for Northport site, 370,000 SF for Convention Center

Sparks Street Mall
Ottawa, Ontario, Canada
Client: City of Ottawa
Architects: Harvey Harman
Associated Landscape Architects: Cecilia Paine
Date: 1986
Size: 4 city blocks

Burnaby Civic Square and Library
Burnaby, British Columbia, Canada
Client: City of Burnaby
Architects: James K.M. Cheng
Associated Landscape Architect: Durante & Partners
Date: 1988
Size: 4.8 acres

Lantern Bay Blufftop Parks
Dana Point, California
Client: Smythe Brothers, Inc. and Pacific Mutual Life Insurance Company
Date: 1980
Size: 76 acres

Refugio Valley Community Park
Hercules, California
Client: City of Hercules
Architects: John O'Brien & Associates
Date: 1979
Size: 18 acres

Shethar Memorial Garden
Tacoma, Washington
Client: Weyerhaeuser Company
Date: 1983
Size: .75 acre

East Highlands Ranch
San Bernardino, California
Client: Mobil Oil
Date: 1990
Size: 200 acres

Mayaluum
Cancun, Mexico
Client: H. Caribbean Investments, S.A., Holding
Date: 1991
Size: 1,600 acres

Hidiv Beldisi
Kanlica, Istanbul, Turkey
Client: HB Construction Industry & Trading Company
Date: 1989
Size: 133,000 square meters

Hyatt at Pelican Hill
Newport Beach, California
Client: Hyatt Development Corporation
Date: 1989
Size: 30 acres, 450 rooms

Suginoi Hotel
Beppu City, Kyushu, Japan
Client: Fujita Construction Company
Affiliated Consultants: Landscape International, Ltd.
Date: 1990
Size: 30 acres, 500 rooms

Thoroughbred Park
Lexington, Kentucky
Client: The Triangle Foundation, Inc.
Artist: Gwen Reardon
Engineers: Mason-Hanger, Civil Engineers
Date: 1989
Size: 3.1 acres

Alabang Centre
Metro Manila, Philippines
Client: Filinvest Development Corporation
Traffic Engineers: LSA Associates, Inc.
Engineers: D.M. Consunji, Inc.
Date: 1991
Size: 244 hectares

Nasu Highlands Park and Related Developments

Fantasy Pointe, Nasu Highlands Park
Nasu, Japan
Client: Towa Nasu Resort Company, Ltd.
Architects: ED2 International
Date: 1988
Size: 142 acres

Akebien Membership Hotel
Nasu, Japan
Client: Towa Nasu Resort Company, Ltd.
Architects: ED2 International
Date: 1989
Size: 15 hectares, 300-room hotel

Nasu Highlands Golf Club
Nasu, Japan
Client: Towa Nasu Resort Company, Ltd.
Architects: ED2 International
Golf Course Architect: Robert Trent Jones, II, International
Date: 1989
Size: 60 hectares

Pershing Square
Los Angeles, California
Architects: Robert A.M. Stern
Date: 1986
Size: 5 acres

Freeway Competition, Interchangeable Parts
Houston, Texas
Sponsor: Texas Highway Department and the National Endowment for the Arts
Date: 1989
Size: 100 acres

Congress Avenue Bridge Lighting Competition
Austin, Texas
Date: 1988
Size: 500' linear feet

Fort Mason Center
San Francisco, California
Client: Fort Mason Foundation
Architects: Robinson, Mills & Williams
Date: 1979
Size: 13 acres

Kit Carson, A Sculpture Competition
Escondido, California
Sponsor: City of Escondido
Artist: Joyce Shaw
Date: 1990
Size: 300 acres

HONORS
受賞リスト

1991

ASLA Texas Chapter, Honor Award - Unbuilt Projects, Playas Espanolas, Marbella, Spain; The Prime Group; DI Design; Kaufman/Meeks, Architects

ASLA Texas Chapter, Merit Award, Dallas Downtown 2010 Study, Dallas, Texas; Corgan Associates, Architects

ASLA Texas Chapter, Merit Award, Tucson Library, Tucson, Arizona; Anderson, DeBartolo Pan, Architects

CC/ASLA Honor Award, Fashion Island, Newport Beach, California; The Irvine Company; The Jerde Partnership, Architects

CC/ASLA Merit Award, Shethar Memorial Garden, Tacoma, Washington; Weyerhaeuser Company

CC/ASLA Merit Award, Arizona Center, Phoenix, Arizona; Rouse-Phoenix Development Corporation, a subsidiary of The Rouse Company

CC/ASLA Merit Award, North Peak Specific Plan, Lake Elsinore, California; TMC Development

Pacific Coast Builders Gold Nugget Merit Award, Best Residential Project - Detached, Magee Ranch, Danville, California; Diablo Ranch Development Company

Pacific Coast Builders Gold Nugget Merit Award, Best Hotel or Resort, The Waterfront Hilton, Huntington Beach, California; Wimberly Allison Tong & Goo, Architects

1990

ASLA Merit Award, Liliore Green Rains Student Housing at Stanford University; Backen, Arrigoni & Ross, Inc., Architects

ASLA Texas Chapter, Award of Excellence, Christina Gateway Park, Wilmington, Delaware; The Linpro Company, Developers; WZMH Group, Architects

ASLA Texas Chapter, Honor Award, National Bank of Commerce Plaza, San Antonio, Texas; Century Development Corporation; Cambridge Seven Associates, Inc., Architects

ASLA Boston Society of Landscape Architects Merit Award, The Andover Companies Corporate Headquarters; The Andover Company; Shepley, Bulfinch, Richardson and Abbott, Architects

1989

ASLA Merit Award, Burnett Park, Fort Worth, Texas; Ann Burnett and Charles Tandy Foundation; The Office of Peter Walker and Martha Schwartz, Associated Landscape Architects

ASLA Merit Award, The Cullen Boulevard Entry, University of Houston, Houston, Texas; University of Houston

California Council of Landscape Architects Honor Award, Hyatt Regency at Gainey Ranch, Scottsdale, Arizona; Hyatt Development Corporation; Hornberger, Worstel & Associates, Architects

Canadian Society of Landscape Architects Merit Award, Sparks Street Mall Revitalization, Ottawa, Ontario, Canada; City of Ottawa; Cecilia Paine, Associated Landscape Architect; Harvey Harman, Architects

Landscape Architecture Foundation Honor Award, Westwood Gateway, Los Angeles, California; Bren Investment Properties; Skidmore, Owings & Merrill, Architects

1988

ASLA Merit Award, Two Harbors Community Plan, Santa Catalina Island, California; Santa Catalina Island Company

ASLA Merit Award, Lantern Bay Blufftop Parks, Dana Point, California; Smythe Brothers Inc., and Pacific Mutual Life Insurance Company

ASLA Southern California Chapter Award of Excellence, MacArthur Court, Newport Beach, California; The Irvine Company; Skidmore, Owings & Merrill, Architects

Landscape Architecture Foundation Honor Award, Newport Center, Newport Beach, California; The Irvine Company

1987

ASLA Honor Award, Fountain Court at Curtis Center, Philadelphia, Pennsylvania; The Kevin F. Donohoe Company; Oldham & Seltz, Architects

AIA Honor Award, Information and Computer Science/Engineering Research Facility, Irvine, California; University of California, Irvine; Frank O. Gehry & Associates, Architects

ASLA Merit Award, Sam Houston State University Old Main Restoration, Sam Houston University; Huntsville, Texas; Ray B. Bailey, Architects, Inc.

California Council of Landscape Architects Award of Excellence, Centennial Grove, Stanford, California; Stanford University; Robert Behrens, Sculptor

Landscape Architecture Foundation Honor Award, Plaza Alicante, Garden Grove, California; Beauchamp Enterprises; WZMH Group, Architects

Landscape Architecture Magazine Photography Competition, "Handicap Walk," Lantern Bay Blufftop Parks, Dana Point, California; "Williams Square," Irving, Texas; "Opening Celebration," Citicorp Plaza and Seventh Marketplace, Los Angeles, California; "Phoenix Tower Roof Deck," Houston, Texas; "Bridge in the Park," Refugio Valley Community Park, Hercules, California; "Poolscape," Inn on the Park Hotel, Phoenix Tower, Houston, Texas

National Endowment for the Arts, Design Arts Program, Finalist, "In the Spirit of Collaboration," Todos Santos Plaza Design Competition, Concord, California

Pacific Coast Builders Conference Gold Nugget Grand Award Winner, The Villages of Sweetwater, Sugar Land, Texas; The Greystone Group; House Reh Associates, Architects

1986

ASLA Honor Award, Refugio Valley Community Park, Hercules, California; City of Hercules

ASLA Merit Award, Antioch Park, Houston, Texas; Antioch Baptist Church/ Century Development Corporation

ASLA Florida Chapter Award of Excellence, Boca Beach Club, Boca Raton, Florida; Arvida Corporation; Killingsworth, Brady & Associates, Architects

ASLA Florida Chapter Award of Excellence, Les Jardins, Boca Raton, Florida; Amerifirst Development; Kenneth Hirsch Associates, Architects

ASLA Southern California Chapter Honor Award, Citicorp Plaza and Seventh Marketplace, Los Angeles, California; Oxford Properties, Inc.; Skidmore, Owings & Merrill, and The Jerde Partnership, Architects

ASLA Southern California Chapter Honor Award, Hyatt Regency Santa Barbara, Goleta, California; Hyatt Development Corporation

California Council of Landscape Architects Award of Excellence, Orange County Performing Arts Center, Costa Mesa, California; Caudill, Rowlett and Scott, Architects

California Council of Landscape Architects Award of Excellence, Irvine Coast Plan, Orange County, California; County of Orange

California Council of Landscape Architects Honor Award, Burke Gilman Park, Seattle, Washington; City of Seattle Parks Department; Mithun, Bowman, Emrich Group, Architects

California Council of Landscape Architects **Honor Award**, Victoria Community Plan, Rancho Cucamonga, California; The William Lyon Company

National Endowment for the Arts, Design Arts Program, Finalist, Pershing Square National Design Competition, Los Angeles, California

1985

ASLA Honor Award, Williams Square, Irving, Texas; Southland Investment Company; Skidmore, Owings & Merrill, Architects

ASLA Merit Award, International Jewelry Center Park, Los Angeles, California; Cabot, Cabot & Forbes; Skidmore, Owings & Merrill, Architects

ASLA Merit Award, Phoenix Tower Roof Deck, Houston, Texas; Albritton Development Corporation; Harwood Taylor/HKS, Architects

ASLA Merit Award, Shell Oil Woodcreek Exploration & Production Facility, Houston, Texas; Shell Oil Company; Caudill, Rowlett, Scott, Architects

ASLA Merit Award, 400 South Hope Street, Los Angeles, California; Olympia and York/O'Melveny and Myers; Welton Becket Associates, Architects

ASLA Merit Award, Village North Lagoon, Salinas, California; Village North Inc.; Backen, Arrigoni & Ross, Architects

ASLA New England Chapter (BSLA), Honor Award, Jefferson Park Housing, Cambridge, Massachusetts; Cambridge Housing Authority and Winn Development Company; Boston Architectural Team, Architects

ASLA Texas Chapter Honor Award, Dallas West End Historic District, Dallas, Texas; Turner, Collie and Braden, Engineers

American Association of School Administrators/ AIA Walter Taylor Award of Excellence, Mayer Campus, Tufts University, Medford, Massachusetts; Jung/Brannen Associates, Inc., Architects

Pacific Coast Builders Conference Gold Nugget Grand Award Winner, Lantern Bay Master Plan, Dana Point, California; Smythe Brothers, Inc., and Pacific Mutual Life Insurance Company

1984

ASLA Merit Award, Cambridge Center Garage Roof Garden, Cambridge, Massachusetts; Boston Properties; Moshe Safdie & Associates, Architects

ASLA Merit Award, Riverway, Houston, Texas; John Hansen Investment Builders

ASLA New England Chapter (BSLA), Honor Award, The Village at Loon Mountain, Lincoln, New Hampshire; Huygens and Tappe, Architects

ASLA Southern California Chapter Merit Award, Village of Woodbridge Master Plan, Irvine, California; The Irvine Company

ASLA Texas Chapter Award of Excellence, Allen Center, Houston, Texas; Century Development Corporation; Lloyd, Jones, Brewer & Associates, Architects

Bartlett Award, Cedar Square West, New Town/In Town, Minneapolis, Minnesota; Ralph Rapson and Associates., Inc., and Gingold-Pink Architecture, Inc., Architects

National Endowment for the Arts, Design Arts Program, Finalist, Copley Square National Design Competition, Boston, Massachusetts

Pacific Coast Builders Conference Gold Nugget Grand Award Winner, Lion's Head Apartments, Houston, Texas; The Greystone Group

1983

ASLA Northern California Chapter Merit Award, Elkhorn Valley Resort, Sun Valley, Idaho; Killingsworth, Brady & Associates, Architects

National Association of Home Builders Project of the Year, Fairway Bay, Longboat Key, Florida; Fisher-Friedman Associates, AIA, Architects

1980

National Association of Home Builders Grand Award, Victoria Community Plan, Rancho Cucamonga, California; The William Lyon Company

Pacific Coast Builders Conference Gold Nugget Merit Award, Surfside Village, Port Hueneme, California; The Howard T. Lane Company; Levitt-Turner, Inc., Architects

1979

AIA Houston Chapter and Houston Municipal Art Commission Award of Distinguished Achievement, Allen Center II, Houston, Texas; Lloyd, Jones, Brewer, Architects

Architectural Record Award of Excellence, The Village at Loon Mountain, Lincoln, New Hampshire; Huygens and Tappe, Architects

1978

AIA Honor Award, IBM West Coast Programming Center, Santa Teresa, California; MBT Associates, Architects

ASLA Merit Award, Landscape Planning for Energy Conservation

1977

AIA Honor Award, Concord Performing Arts Center, Concord, California; Frank O. Gehry & Associates, Architects

Pacific Coast Builders Conference Gold Nugget Merit Award, Village of Woodbridge, Irvine, California; The Irvine Company

1976

HUD Urban Design Concept Honor Award, Buchanan Street Mall, San Francisco, California; San Francisco Redevelopment Agency

1975

AIA Honor Award, Cedar Square West, New Town/ In Town, Minneapolis, Minnesota; Ralph Rapson and Associates, Inc., and Gingold-Pink Architecture, Inc., Architects

AIA Central States Region Award of Excellence, Johnson County Community College, Overland Park, Kansas; Marshall and Brown, Architects

AIA/House and Home First Honor Award, Ethan's Glen, Houston, Texas; Fisher-Friedman Associates, AIA, Architects

AIA/House and Home First Honor Award, Promontory Point, Newport Beach, California; Fisher-Friedman Associates, AIA, Architects

American Association of School Administrators Special Citation, Penn Valley Community College, Kansas City, Missouri; Marshall and Brown, Architects

AIP Certificate of Merit, The San Diego Unified Port District, The Embarcadero Development Plan, San Diego, California; San Diego Unified Port District

1974

HUD Urban Design Concept Honor Award, Works of Art/Golden Gateway; Wurster, Bernardi & Emmons, DeMars & Reay and Skidmore, Owings & Merrill, Architects

1973

AIA Collaborative Achievement Award, San Francisco Bay Area Rapid Transit, San Francisco, California; Bay Area Rapid Transit District

1972

AIA Honor Award, Weyerhaeuser Company Corporate Headquarters, Tacoma, Washington; Weyerhaeuser Company; Skidmore, Owings & Merrill, Architects

Architectural Record Award of Excellence, Cochiti, New Mexico (Housing Development); Antoine Predock, Architect

Bartlett Award, Weyerhaeuser Company Corporate Headquarters, Tacoma, Washington; Weyerhaeuser Company; Skidmore, Owings & Merrill, Architects

ASLA Merit Award, Crocker Plaza, San Francisco, California; Universal Land Company; Welton Becket Associates, Architects

ASLA Merit Award, Foothill College, Los Altos, California; Ernest J. Kump and Masten & Hurd, Architects

1971

ASLA Honor Award, Mariner Square, Newport Beach, California; Fisher-Friedman Associates, AIA, Architects

ASLA Merit Award, Upjohn Company Headquarters, Kalamazoo, Michigan; Skidmore, Owings & Merrill, Architects

ASLA Merit Award, Fashion Island Shopping Center, Newport Beach, California; The Irvine Company; Welton Becket Associates, Architects

1970

AIA Honor Award, Ruth Residence, Berkeley, California; Donald E. Olsen, Architect

Architectural Record Award of Excellence, Mariner Square, Newport Beach, California; Fisher-Friedman Associates, AIA, Architects

HUD Excellence Award, Diamond Heights Housing, San Francisco, California

1968

AIA Honor Award, Research Laboratory D, Chevron Research Company, Richmond, California; McCue Boone Tomsick, Architects

AIA Honor Award, Interim Facilities, Syntex Laboratories, Inc., Stanford Industrial Park, Palo Alto, California; Mackinlay/Winnacker & Associates, Architects

HUD Merit Award, Bay Area Rapid Transit District Linear Park and Station, Albany/El Cerrito, California; Bay Area Rapid Transit District

1967

AIA Honor Award, Los Gatos Civic Center, Los Gatos, California; Stickney and Hull, Architects

1964

FHA Honor Award, Carmel Valley Manor, Carmel, California; Skidmore, Owings & Merrill, Architects

FHA Honor Award, The Sequoias, Portola Valley, California; Skidmore, Owings & Merrill, Architects

1963

AIA First Honor Award, The Edward Clark Grosset Library at Bennington College, Bennington, Vermont; Pietro Belluschi and Carl Koch and Associates, Architects

1962

AIA First Honor Award, Foothill College, Los Altos, California; Ernest J. Kump and Masten & Hurd, Architects

Architectural League of New York Collaborative Medal of Honor, Thomas J. Watson Research Center; International Business Machines Corporation; Yorktown Heights, New York; Eero Saarinen and Associates, Architects

151

BIBLIOGRAPHY
著作リスト

Editor. "Williams Square." Architecture Magazine, December 1985.

Editor. "Centre Court." Architecture International, 1988. pp. 134-136.

Editor. "The Labors of Hercules." Architecture International, 1987. pp. 26-28.

Editor. "1985 ASLA Awards." Architectural Record Magazine, April 1990, pp. 98-101.

Pearson, Clifford A. "Fashion Update - Fashion Island." Architectural Record Magazine, April 1990, pp. 98 - 101.

Karner, Gary E. Chapter 10, "Legal Concerns." ASLA Handbook of Professional Practice.

Stockman, Leslie. "The New American Home '86." Builder Magazine, January 1986.

Editor. "The Fountain Court at The Curtis Center, The Village of Woodbridge, Cambridge Center Roof Garden, and Tanner Fountain." Contemporary Landscape Architecture: An International Perspective, September 1990, pp. 136-139.

Karner, Gary E. Contracting Design Services. Washington, D.C. American Society of Landscape Architects, 1989.

Editor. "New American Landscapes." Dialogue, April 1990, pp. 48-49.

Editor. "Amenities and the Arts: Matter of Urban Survival." Designers West Magazine, February 1985, pp. 92-102.

Editor. "Building the Urban Public Space." Designers West Magazine, November 1984, pp. 76-85.

Editor. Forest Notes Publication. Experimental and Demonstrative Forest Information.

Warren, Bill. "Feature Resorts, New Life for a Grand Old Dame," Florida Landscape Architecture, Volume 10-4, pp. 28-30.

Lowe, Clifton. "Quality of Change." Harvard Design Studio with Carl Steinetz. Published through funds from the National Endowment of the Arts for the Communities of Gunnison and Crested Butte, Colorado.

Gath, Jean Marie. "West End Historic District: Dallas, Texas." Institute for Urban Design - Project Monograph, September 1986.

Editor. "Outstanding Foreign Works." The Korean Landscape Architecture, November 1988, pp. 36-41.

Editor. "Desert Fantasies." Landscape Architecture Magazine, March 1989, pp. 66-69.

Editor. "Pasture of Plenty, Thirty Years of Corporate Villas in America." Landscape Architecture Magazine, March 1990, pp. 50-53.

Editor. "1989 ASLA Awards." Landscape Architecture Magazine, November 1989, pp. 77, 79.

Editor. "l987 ASLA Awards." Landscape Architecture Magazine, November 1987, pp. 44-47, 64-65, 82, 84.

Goldstein, Barbara. "Harlequin Plaza." Landscape Architecture Magazine, July 1983, pp. 56-59.

Kroloff, Reed. "A Phoenix Rises from the Dust." Landscape Architecture Magazine, April 1991, pp. 10-14.

Editor. "1985 ASLA Awards." Landscape Architecture Magazine, September, 1985.

Editor. "Hercules Plays on a Classical Identity" Landscape Architecture Magazine, September/October 1986, pp. 65-69.

Editor. "Antioch Park." Landscape Architecture Magazine, September/October 1986, pp. 71-72.

Editor. "Lantern Bay Blufftop Parks." Landscape Architecture Magazine, November 1988, pp. 40-41.

Editor. "Two Harbors Community Plan." Landscape Architecture Magazine, November 1988, pp. 80-81.

Berkson, David. "The Academy." Landscape Architecture Magazine, December 1988, pp. 93-95.

Karner, Gary E. "A Liability Checklist." Landscape Architecture Magazine, March 1988.

Taylor, John. "Fluid Illumination." Landscape Architecture Magazine, September 1991.

Berkson, David. "Fashion Island Renaissance." Landscape Architect and Specifier News, November 1991, p. 31.

Law, Richard K. "Plaza Alicante." Landscape Architect and Specifier News, November 1990, pp. 21, 23, 24, 25.

Shield, Lawrence. "1990 SCC/ASLA Awards." Landscape Architect and Specifier News, November 1990, pp. 62-65.

Gimmy, Lisa. "John Wayne Airport." Landscape Architect and Specifier News, November 1990, p. 36.

Law, Richard K. "Village of Woodbridge." Landscape Architect and Specifier News, May 1990, pp. 26-27.

Loomis, John S. "Hyatt Regency Scottsdale at Gainey Ranch." Landscape Architect and Specifier News, May 1991, pp. 24-25.

Loomis, John S. "Fluid Lighting - Designer Focuses on Fountains." Lighting Design and Application, May 1991, pp. 2, 3; 46, 47.

Editor. "Outstanding Foreign Works." "Interview with William Callaway, The SWA Group." Nikkei Resort, 1989, pp. 36-38.

Editor. "Lush Gardens, Special Touches." Professional Builder, June 1986.

Editor. "Citicorp Plaza, 1988 Professional Landscape of the Year." Professional Landscape Contractor Directory, 1988.

Editor. "Portfolio, Three Firms:" Interview with William Callaway, The SWA Group." Progressive Architecture Magazine, July 1989, pp. 78-79.

Fritzen, David W. "Frenchman's Reef Beach Resort." Resorts and Great Hotels, Spring 1988, pp. 18-25.

Temko, Allan. Articles featuring "Fort Mason Competition, Fireman's Fund, Crown Zellerbach." San Francisco Chronicle.

Editor. "The SWA Group: How a National Firm Responds to the Sunbelt Region." Southern Landscape Architecture Magazine, November/December 1989, pp. 29-36.

Way, Douglas S. Terrain Analysis, 2nd Edition, McGraw Hill, 1978; DWA 1986. Landforms, Chapter in The Manual of Aerial Photographic Interpretation (1990) ASPRS, Falls Church, Virginia.

Jacob, Robert. Town Planning Heritage Southern California. August 1991. TMC Group, Publisher. Printed by Warren's Waller Press, South San Francisco, California.

Bryson, Hope. "Ronald Reagan Library Lights Up." Landscape Architect and Specifier News, August 1991, p. 35.

Editor. "Nasu." Live, July 1991, Douway-Sya Corporation, pp. 34-43.

Editor. "Nasu." Live, March 1991, Douway-Sya Corporation, pp. 34-43.

SPECIAL THANKS

The SWA Group would like to thank the following people for their contribution to this issue of Process:

Allan Temko	Tim Harvey
Melanie Simo	Hiroyasu Tanaka
Barbara Casey	Donna Stolz
Anne Snyder	Dixi Carrillo
Sara Clark	Tom Lamb
Roxanne Brandt	Vicki Phillipy
Tom Adams	Nancy Hartwick
Theresa Clark	

All photography (except where noted) in this issue has been contributed by SWA photographers:

Gerald Campbell
Tom Fox
Tom Lamb
Dixi Carrillo

南欧の広場

著者　加藤晃規

ペーパーカバー　ジャケット付き
168ページ（オールカラー）
定価3,400円（本体3,301円）

本書は1980年7月初版発行のプロセスアーキテクチュアNo.16を一部改訂し，パリの航空写真を新たに加え，オールカラーの単行本として再編集したものである。古代ローマから中世，ルネッサンス，バロックにわたる代表的な美しい広場（イタリアの広場29，フランスの広場9）をとりあげ，成立の背景，形態の相異を検討する。ふんだんに掲載された航空写真が南ヨーロッパ都市の魅力をあますところなく表現している。

- ●書き下ろし論文／建築的な西洋広場
- ●論文／文化としてのイタリア広場
- ●事例／ポンペイ，ヴェローナ，ベルガモ，パルマ，フィレンツェ，シエナ，ピサ，サンジミニアーノ，アッシジ，ヴェネツィア，ローマ，ナポリ，パリ，他

アクアスケープ：水の造景

ハードカバー　ジャケット付
200ページ（カラー190ページ）
定価9,800円

【日本図書館協会選定図書】

かつては庭園や公園で脇役をつとめてきた水。最近では水に対する意識の高まりを受け，重要なスタンスを持つようになってきた。水がその場のコンセプトであったり，また水の遊び場であったり。このようなデザインされた水をアクアスケープと名づけ，水景の意味を見直す。この本では，最近の日本のアクアスケープを3章に分類し，100以上の好例を紹介する。

- ●論文／「水との直接性：その実体と空間的な働きの演出」鈴木信宏
- ●第1章 水のある建築／東京都葛西臨海水族園，水の教会，土門拳記念館，TIME'S
- ●第2章 水のあるランドスケープ／万博記念公園自然文化園，栃木県中央公園，他
- ●第3章 水の演出／モニュメント噴水，流れ・滝・壁泉，プール，イベント，音楽噴水，室内噴水，メッセージ噴水，フロート噴水

女性たちの庭　【日本図書館協会選定図書】

ペーパーカバー　ジャケット付き
200ページ（オールカラー）
定価5,600円

監修　杉尾邦江

女性の庭，それは珠玉のように育まれ，いつくしまれてできあがった美しい庭である。キッチンのまわり，バスルーム前，周囲の景色を借りた庭，廃品利用でつくった庭，生活の場としての手づくりの庭。美しい自然に満ちたニュージーランドの庭27，センシティブな日本の庭17を，美しい写真でめぐる。この本ではニュージーランドと日本というライフスタイルの全く対照的な2国の女性たちの庭を紹介する。

- ●ニュージーランド／詩情の庭，ロマンチックな隠れ庭，華麗なるフラワーガーデン，ベストガーデナーの庭，スロープの庭，森の庭，他
- ●日本／眺望の庭，東洋のイングリッシュガーデン，茶の湯の庭，奥嵯峨野風情の庭，和と洋が出会う庭，他

世界のランドスケープデザイン

ハードカバー ジャケット付
256ページ（オールカラー）
定価12,500円

【日本図書館協会選定図書】

本書では，世界の著名なランドスケープ・アーキテクトの仕事と作品を幅広く紹介する．世界18か国，97点の作品を収録し，庭園や都市計画を始め，自然環境や歴史的環境の保全・再生に至るまで多岐にわたっている．21世紀に向けて環境文化の創造と地球規模での環境保全が最も重要な社会的要請となっている今日，ランドスケープ・アーキテクトたちの活動は，そうした課題に取り組むための確かな手掛かりを与える．

- ●作品／ファウンテンプレイス，ウィリアムズ・スクエア，羽衣公園，チェスナット公園，ガス・ワーク・パーク，韓国記念ホール，エーゲ海アンドロス島近代美術館別館，修善寺町総合会館庭園，ストラウビング園芸博'89，水戸市植物公園，他

発行所／株式会社プロセスアーキテクチュア
〒151東京都渋谷区笹塚1-47-2-418
電話03-3468-0131　ファクシミリ03-3468-0133

近藤典生，もうひとつの世界

エコロジカル・パークの思想とその方法

A4変形ハードカバージャケット付き
120ページ（カラー 104ページ）
定価￥2,900（税込）
好評発売中

著者は育種学，遺伝学を専門とする研究者で，研究対象としての生きた動植物を確保する一方策として，動植物公園づくりに関わり始めた．動植物の生態を知りつくした著者によるこれらの公園では，動物も植物も，自然の中にあるがままの日常を営んでいる．
　本書では，作品と共に，地球儀温室計画案の壮大な構想を合わせて紹介する．公園づくりの考え方から環境問題，資源問題を論じ，その哲学に迫るとともに，動物達の魅力あふれる表情を伝える写真集となっている．
●対談／「自然思考の公園づくり」近藤典生＋進士五十八
　　　　「動植物の生態と公園づくりの手法」近藤典生＋朝倉繁春
●作品／伊豆シャボテン公園，地球儀温室，長崎鼻パーキングガーデン，鹿児島市平川動物公園，ボリビア共和国日本庭園，長崎バイオパーク，ひめはるの里のクリスタルグリーンハウス，名護自然動植物公園，地球儀温室計画案

都市環境のデザイン……空間創造の実践……

編・著　高橋志保彦

ペーパーカバー，ジャケット付き
196ページ（カラー179ページ）
定価￥3,900（税込）
4月発売予定

都市デザインは，単なる1つの分野でなく，様々な分野の関係で成り立つ「つなぎの文化」といえる（編・著 あとがきより）．本書はアーバンデザインの専門家，その他の関係機関など，その道の第一人者の叡智を結集してつくった都市を，様々な切り口からケーススタディを通して検証したものである．全国から16例を選出し，「アーバンオアシス」「みち空間」「都市のアメニティ」の3章に分け，そのプロセスを浮き彫りにする．
●主な事例・作品／1987年・新宿新都心，梅田センタービル・外部空間，大宮駅西口再開発構想，大阪ビジネスパーク，住友生命仙台中央ビル，イセザキモール，仙台東一番町商店街，アーケードシティ・高松，平塚市中心街・街づくり，ミュージアムステーション・阪急三番街，多摩センター，公園都市・呉市，全県公園化構想　山梨県・甲府，長崎・中島川界隈──JR長崎駅，他

SEKINE／Message from Environment Art Studio

編集　林 芳史

ペーパーカバー
112頁（カラー60頁）
定価￥3,000（税込）
5月発売予定

近代的な造形を超えて，総合的に環境を包含する環境美術の開拓を目指してきたパイオニア，関根伸夫の力強い空間演出を，その代表作のみを選りすぐって浮き彫りにする．常に人間の生の始原的感動に視線を注ぐ関根伸夫の世界に迫る．高級美術印刷による美的作品集である．
● 文／関根伸夫，林 芳史
●作品／東京都庁舎，江南女子短期大学，市町村アカデミー，筑波北部工業団地近隣公園，塩釜市総合体育館，奥久慈憩の森，世田谷美術館壁泉，グランドヒル市ヶ谷，新潟駅南口広場，箱根彫刻の森美術館彫刻，他

JAPAN LANDSCAPE

人・都市・自然のコミュニケーションマガジン 季刊［ジャパン・ランドスケープ］

定価2,580円
好評発売中

No.20 ●特集● 駅の景

序文

ステーションフロントの時代

計画および手法論

川崎駅東口広場／浜松駅前地区／川越駅東口広場／土気駅／丸亀駅／神戸総合運動公園駅／緑園都市駅

CREATIVE FORUM

プラットホーム

立松和平，神保憲二，麦屋弥生，丸田晴男

トピックス

駅にまつわる話いろいろ

民営化初の駅舎デザインコンペ，JRお茶の水駅／駅のエピソード／廃線駅を都市公園に，志免鉄道記念公園／地域振興の拠点づくり・道の駅づくりの実験が始まる／駅前の風情をまちぐるみで，JR豊後竹田駅

LANDSCAPE WORKS

山本紀久

人工都市にチャレンジする生きもの造園家

京都駅に提案する2つの駅

JR二条駅に新生京都のモニュメントを／北と南の緩衝帯として，丘状の駅を提案／新京都駅設計コンペにもの申す

連載

建築家の目に映った風景，都市風景塾，Keyword Playground，Keyword forum，テクニカルノート，BOOK REVIEW

座談会

駅のランドスケープ

東 孝光，多田道太郎，吉村元男，若林広幸

LANDSCAPE NEW WAVE

国営ひたち海浜公園，豊島区立目白公園，高知市中央公園，シーバンス，スノーアートとやま，山崎公園の水遊戯施設，地球縄ひろば，アメリカンプランニングのパラダイム，フォレスト・ヒルズ・ガーデン

発行／㈱プロセスアーキテクチュア 〒151東京都渋谷区笹塚1-47-2-418 ☎03(3468)0131・0131
編集／㈱マルモ・プランニング 〒150東京都渋谷区道玄坂1-16-6二葉ビル5A ☎03(3496)7046

PROCESS 96
: Architecture
海洋建築の構図

PROCESS Material appears in English and Japanese 96
: Architecture

Composition of Oceanic Architecture
海洋建築の構図
畔柳昭雄・渡辺富雄 編

水際から海域において見られる建築と海，河川とのかかわりから生み出されてくる建築的空間を海洋建築と総称し，計画的側面，デザイン的側面，技術的側面に焦点をあてる．
　ここでは集まった事例を施設の機能や構造形式によって分類するのではなく，水の利用形態と建築空間との対応関係から，「水を引く」「海に架ける」「海に浮く」「海を抱く」「海に潜る」の5つのキーワードで分類し，計画中のものも含めてその概要を紹介する．

●論文／「海洋空間を創造する海洋建築」畔柳昭雄
●作品／マリナシティ，カナダプレイス，長崎オランダ村，ブライトンピア，ピア39，バリアリーフ・フローティング・ホテル，浮かぶ劇場「世界劇場」，大阪海遊館，シアトル水族館，シドニー水族館，海中展望塔「足摺海底館」，他

責任編集者	畔柳昭雄，渡辺富雄
発　行　日	1991年6月
総　　　頁	160頁（カラー144頁）
文　　　章	日本語，英語
定　　　価	2,990円（本体2,903円）

PROCESS 97
: Architecture
デザインされた都市：ボストン

PROCESS Material appears in English and Japanese 97
: Architecture

Boston by Design A City in Development: 1960 to 1990
デザインされた都市：ボストン

Editors-in-Charge: Shun Kanda, Masami Kobayashi
責任編集者 神田 駿，小林正美

世界の海の玄関といわれるボストン．ウォーターフロントのみクローズアップされがちであるが，3世紀以上の歴史を持つボストンの魅力は建物，広場，街並みにあふれている．歴史と伝統を保存しながらの開発を模索する姿に，環境と開発のバランスのとれた都市のルーツを探ることができる．本書ではこうしたボストンの形成や現状，未来を分析し，都市計画から建築ガイドに至るまで，航空写真をふんだんに使って紹介する．

●論文／「ボストン都市散策」神田 駿
　　　　「ボストンは存在する」ジェーン・ホルツ・ケイ
　　　　「ボストンの生きてきた道」小林正美
●プロジェクト／サウスウェストコリドー，チャールズタウン・ネイビーヤード，セントラルアーテリー地下埋設計画，他

責任編集者	神田 駿，小林正美
発　行　日	1991年8月
総　　　頁	152頁（カラー127頁）
文　　　章	日本語，英語
定　　　価	2,990円（本体2,903円）

PROCESS 98
: Architecture
自然エネルギーと建築

PROCESS Material appears in English and Japanese 98
: Architecture

PASSIVE AND LOW ENERGY ARCHITECTURE
自然エネルギーと建築

PLEA

「環境志向型」建築は，太陽や風などのクリーンな自然エネルギーを活用することによって，非再生型エネルギーへの依存を減らし，かつ環境へ与える影響を和らげることができる．PLEA国際委員会は，世界各地の「環境志向型」建築の実践例の収集を計画し，この作業は日本建築学会パッシブデザイン研究グループによって進められてきた．本号はその成果を気候別に分類し，まとめたものである．

●論文／「地球的かつ地域固有の建築」ジェフリー・クック
　　　　「建築と技術：1990年代の環境を意識したデザイン」シモス・ヤナス
●作品／ネゲフ高地教育センター，大島の家，ガビオタス村熱帯病院，ソーラーハウスビレッジNo.3，世田谷区立宮坂地区会館，ニューカナーン自然センター園芸実験棟，苫小牧市立中央図書館，ウルム神経外科研究所，他

責任編集者	小玉祐一郎，ジェフリー・クック，シモス・ヤナス
発　行　日	1991年9月
総　　　頁	160頁（カラー144頁）
文　　　章	日本語，英語
定　　　価	2,990円（本体2,903円）

PROCESS 99
: Architecture
東京を開く：尾島俊雄の構想

PROCESS Material appears in English and Japanese 99
: Architecture

Imageable TOKYO:
Projects by Toshio Ojima

東京を開く
尾島俊雄の構想

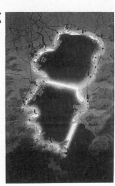

首都東京の都市環境を主眼に，都市のアメニティ，21世紀へ向けての再開発，ひいては首都大改造の具体的構想をイメージしてきた．絵に描いた餅といわれ続けてきたものだが今日のように豊かな時代に我々はすぐに食べられる餅をこれ以上つくる必要はない．尾島のイメージを中心に研究室が25年間繰り返し調査，研究してきた成果としての具体的構想を紹介する．

●構想／首都ランドマーク構想，銀座再開発構想，東京駅前地区再開発構想，新宿駅周辺再開発構想，池袋アーバンコンプレックス構想，下町マンハッタン構想，東京湾開放構想，首都圏臨界高層都市，アンダーグラウンドスペースネットワーク構想，ペントハウス構想，インダストリアル構想，エコロジカルハウス構想，レジデンシャルハウス構想，インテリジェントシティ構想，サテライトオフィス構想，アメリカンシティ構想

責任編集者	尾島俊雄，尾島俊雄研究室
発　行　日	1991年11月
総　　　頁	156頁（カラー142頁）
文　　　章	日本語，英語
定　　　価	2,990円（本体2,903円）

PROCESS :Architecture 100

好評発売中　特別定価4,600円

RENZO PIANO Building Workshop :
In search of a balance

レンゾ・ピアノ・ビルディング・ワークショップ　「バランス」を求めて

1991年5月23日，関西国際空港旅客ターミナルビル
の建設が始まった．ピアノはこの日を「夢がかたち
に変わる最初の時」と表現している．
　建設業の家に生まれたピアノの幼年期の経験は，
建築家になってからも彼に影響を与え続けた．
　この100号特別号では，彼の仕事を4つの時期に
分け，その発展のプロセスを探る．

●序文
「モノローグ」レンゾ・ピアノ
●作品
ポンピドーセンター，IRCAM音楽音響総合研究
所，シュルンベルグジェ社改築，パラッディオの
バシリカ修復計画，メニルコレクション美術館，
IBM移動巡回パビリオン，コロンブス大陸発見
500年記念国際博覧会，聖ニコラス・フットボール
競技場，ベルシー・ショッピングセンター，関西
国際空港旅客ターミナルビル，他

PROCESS :Architecture 101

好評発売中　定価2,990円

Jerde Partnership

Reinventing The Communal Experience ..... A Problem of Place

ジャーディ・パートナーシップ
共有社会的体験の再創出

アメリカの建築家ジョン・ジャーディは13年前に
事務所を創設，以来独自の建築言語「Mixed-use」
「Host place」「Placemaking」などを使って，空
間をディスプレイする街の脚本家である．代表作
にはファッションアイランドの増改築画，1984年
ロサンゼルスオリンピックのサインやゲートなど
装飾計画を演出．また，幕張タウンセンターなど
日本でのプロジェクトも進行中である．

主な作品
1984年ロサンゼルスオリンピック，ユニバーサル
シティ，ファッションアイランド，幕張タウンセ
ンター，ホートンプラザ，リバーフロント博多

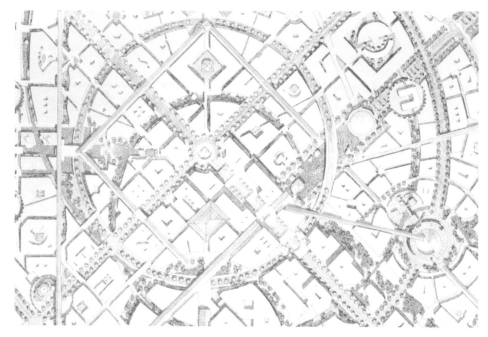

PROCESS
:Architecture 102

好評発売中　定価2,990円

The Structural Architecture of
CHICAGO

シカゴ：超高層建築の時代

ミース・ファン・デル・ローエによるレイクショアドライブの出現以来，シカゴのスカイラインは激変する．サリバンやバーナム＆ルートが活躍したシカゴ派の全盛期から半世紀後，シカゴは再び高層建築が競い合う建築の実験都市と化する．この時代をリードしたのはミースとその弟子たち．ミースの哲学が力強くシカゴの建築界をつらぬいていた．しかしそのシカゴにもポストモダンの波は押し寄せる．本書では，レイクショアドライブから，40年間の代表的ビル50例をあげて，設計思想の変遷をあとづける．

主な作品

レイクショアドライブ・アパート，インランドスチール，シカゴ・シヴィックセンター，マリナシティ，シアーズ・タワー，ジョーン・ハンコック・センター，イリノイ州政府センター，333ウエスト・ワッカー・ドライブ

PROCESS :Architecture 104

City Score : Up To Date

語りかける都市：そのテーマとメディア

本誌55号「街並みのスコア」(現在品切れ)に続く池沢寛氏の都市散策シリーズ。都市には人を魅きつけるものがある。本号ではこの魅力をいろいろな切り口でながめ、さまざまな言語で私たちに語りかける都市の表情を追う。

主要テーマ
風土とヴォキャブラリー、リゾートの環境、シティパーク、タウンスケープにおける街路樹、楽しさをもたらすもの、都市のなかのアトリウム、環境保存と開発調和と対比、他